The Impact of
Gender Quotas

THE IMPACT OF GENDER QUOTAS

Edited by

Susan Franceschet
University of Calgary

Mona Lena Krook
Washington University in St. Louis

Jennifer M. Piscopo
Salem College

OXFORD
UNIVERSITY PRESS

Oxford University Press

Oxford University Press, Inc., publishes works that further
Oxford University's objective of excellence
in research, scholarship, and education.

Oxford   New York
Auckland   Cape Town   Dar es Salaam   Hong Kong   Karachi
Kuala Lumpur   Madrid   Melbourne   Mexico City   Nairobi
New Delhi   Shanghai   Taipei   Toronto

With offices in
Argentina   Austria   Brazil   Chile   Czech Republic   France   Greece
Guatemala   Hungary   Italy   Japan   Poland   Portugal   Singapore
South Korea   Switzerland   Thailand   Turkey   Ukraine   Vietnam

Published by Oxford University Press, Inc.
198 Madison Avenue, New York, New York 10016

www.oup.com

Oxford is a registered trademark of Oxford University Press

Library of Congress Cataloging-in-Publication Data
The impact of gender quotas / Susan Franceschet, Mona Lena Krook, and Jennifer M. Piscopo, editors.
p.   cm.
Includes bibliographical references and index.
ISBN 978-0-19-983008-4 (pbk.)—ISBN 978-0-19-983009-1 (hardback) 1. Women—Political activity.
2. Women political candidates—Government policy. 3. Representative government and representation.
4. Women and democracy. 5. Women—Political activity—Cross-cultural studies.
6. Women political candidates—Government policy—Cross-cultural studies.
7. Representative government and representation—Cross-cultural studies.
8. Women and democracy—Cross-cultural studies. I. Franceschet, Susan, 1965– II. Krook,
Mona Lena. III. Piscopo, Jennifer M.
HQ1236.I465   2012
324.082—dc23   2011026323

Printed in the United States of America
on acid-free paper

Contents

Conclusion

Preface

Drude Dahlerup

Twenty years ago, no one would have imagined the rapid diffusion of electoral gender quotas that we have witnessed during the past decades. In all types of political systems and in all major regions of the world, gender quotas are now being adopted in order to rapidly change women's historical underrepresentation. Everywhere gender quotas stir important debates about why women are still underrepresented, since quotas touch upon so many important themes in feminist theory and in theories of democracy and representation.

Even if politics is still highly male-dominated—with 81 percent of the parliamentarians in the world in 2011 being men—and even if only a few quota systems aim as high as gender balance, the introduction of gender quotas in politics has no doubt increased women's representation worldwide. In some countries, such as Rwanda, Argentina, South Africa, and Costa Rica, gender quotas have even led to historical leaps in the presence of women in parliaments and in regional and local assemblies, leaps unheard of in the Scandinavian countries that were previously alone at the top of the world ranking of women's political representation.

As of spring 2011, fifty-two countries have introduced gender quotas in elections by law. In approximately forty other countries, at least some of the political parties have voluntarily introduced gender quotas for their own candidate lists (see www.quotaproject.org). More countries and individual parties are joining the quota family every year. Quotas represent a fast-track policy measure, in contrast to the well-known incremental-track model according to which gender equality will come in due time as a country develops.

In a way, gender quotas are a simple answer to a very complex problem, namely that of women's historical exclusion from political life. Perhaps quotas have become so popular and at the same time so controversial precisely because quota provisions set up an easily identifiable target by requiring a certain number of candidates of each sex (in the case of candidate quotas, whether they are legislated or voluntary) or a certain number of women being elected (in the case of reserved seats). It is easy to observe whether the prescribed aim is met. However, it is more complicated to evaluate the broader effects of electoral gender quotas, especially in a middle-range or long-range perspective.

This volume breaks new ground in quota research. In general, the rapid diffusion of electoral gender quotas has spurred research on gender quotas as a new field within gender and politics research. Quota research has targeted a number of issues, such as quota discourses, variations in quota design, the diffusion of quotas, and the implementation process. However, it is difficult to isolate the effects of gender quotas per se, which may be the reason for the lack of comparative studies on the effects of gender quotas in a broader perspective than just that of numbers. This volume represents a much-needed study based on just such a perspective.

There is no general agreement among quota researchers regarding the effects of electoral gender quotas. Different results may derive not only from different country cases but also from the use of disparate criteria for evaluation. This carefully edited volume brings together twelve in-depth case studies from four regions in the world. The book takes this field of research a large step forward by basing it on the development of common concepts, indicators, and criteria for evaluation. Which "effects" should be looked for, in both a short-term and a long-term perspective? What do we know about the effects of gender quotas? How should we evaluate the effects of various types of gender quota regimes on women's descriptive, substantive, and symbolic representation? The editors refer to this as a "theory-building exercise." And that is exactly what makes this book so exciting to read.

Acknowledgments

The introduction of electoral gender quotas in diverse contexts around the globe has attracted a great deal of scholarly and political interest. To date, research on these measures has focused primarily on their design, adoption, and effects on the numbers of women elected. While this remains a crucial focus, especially as additional countries implement quotas and revise existing policies to make them more effective, it is also important to recognize that quotas are not simply about changing the proportion of women in political office. Both supporters and opponents of quotas suggest, albeit from different perspectives, that positive action for women in candidate selection will influence the kinds of women elected, the policy-making process as it concerns women's issues, views of the general public toward women in public life, and the relationship between female citizens and the political process. Seeking to initiate a "second generation" of research on quotas, this volume represents a collective effort by its contributors to inspire a new literature focused on theorizing and studying their broader impact on politics and society.

The idea for this book emerged in 2008 during discussions among the three coeditors that later expanded to a broader group of scholars through a series of panels organized at the annual conferences of the American Political Science Association in 2008 and 2009, the Midwest Political Science Association in 2008 and 2009, and the European Consortium for Political Research in 2009. The editors would like to thank the contributors, first and foremost, for their willingness to write chapters for this volume and to participate in a broader discussion of the potential impact of quotas on a wide range of existing political dynamics. Their innovative work ranks among the most cutting-edge scholarship in this area to date. In addition, participants in the conference panels offered helpful feedback on many of the chapters, and, in particular, we would like to thank Lisa Baldez, Gretchen Bauer, Karen Bird, Richard Matland, Mark Jones, Leslie Schwindt-Bayer, Aili Mari Tripp, and Celia Valiente. Drude Dahlerup graciously agreed to write the preface to the volume and has provided generous support for the project as a whole. The enthusiastic encouragement of Angela Chnapko at Oxford University Press was also instrumental in helping to move from the initial idea to the book proposal to the final manuscript.

In addition to supporting travel to conferences, the editors' three institutions—the University of Calgary, Washington University in St. Louis, and the University of California, San Diego—provided funds and space for a face-to-face meeting of the editors in San Diego in November 2009. Further, Susan Franceschet would like to

x

acknowledge the support of the Social Sciences and Humanities Research Council of Canada. Mona Lena Krook acknowledges the fellowships at the Radcliffe Institute for Advanced Study and the Women and Public Policy Program at the Harvard Kennedy School. Jennifer M. Piscopo completed portions of this work while in residence as a visiting fellow at the Center for U.S.-Mexican Studies at the University of California, San Diego. A final round of meetings of the editors and many of the contributors in St. Louis in May 2011 was funded by a Faculty Early Career Development Award from the National Science Foundation. As a team, we hope the resulting product will lead to further comparative research on this topic to ensure that quotas achieve their stated goals of empowering women and promoting democracy.

The Impact of Gender Quotas

INTRODUCTION

1 Conceptualizing the Impact of Gender Quotas

Susan Franceschet, Mona Lena Krook, and Jennifer M. Piscopo

The past two decades have witnessed unprecedented gains in women's access to elected office. This trend has occurred across all major world regions, leading to dramatic increases in the percentage of women in national parliaments in countries as diverse as Rwanda, Sweden, Argentina, and Nepal. A major reason for these shifts has been the adoption of gender quotas aimed at increasing the proportion of female candidates for political office. While they take various forms, such measures now exist in more than one hundred countries, with the overwhelming majority appearing in just the last fifteen years. The recent and global nature of these developments has sparked both scholarly and popular interest in their design, origins, and mixed effects on women's political presence (Dahlerup 2006b; Krook 2009).

While such questions remain crucially important, the spread of quotas is not simply linked to efforts to increase the numbers of women in elected office. Advocates suggest that such measures will diversify the types of women elected, raise attention to women's issues in policy making, change the gendered nature of the public sphere, and inspire female voters to become more politically involved. At the same time, opponents say that quotas will facilitate access for "unqualified" women with little interest in promoting women's concerns, reinforce stereotypes about women's inferiority as political actors, and deter ordinary women's political participation. Such contrasting expectations indicate that quotas may have a host of positive and negative effects, above and beyond their impact on women's numerical representation. However, the empirical validity of these claims has not yet been systematically addressed (Dahlerup 2008; Franceschet and Piscopo 2008; Sacchet 2008; Zetterberg 2009).

This volume forges a new research agenda by presenting common concepts for analyzing quota impact, developed and illustrated through in-depth case studies from four regions of the world: Western Europe, Latin America, sub-Saharan Africa, and Asia and the Middle East. The book organizes quota effects in relation to three facets of political representation: *descriptive representation*, the basic attributes of those elected; *substantive representation*, attention to group interests in policy making; and *symbolic representation*, the cultural meanings and ramifications of the representative process (Pitkin 1967; Schwindt-Bayer and Mishler 2005). Closer examination of how quotas shape patterns of representation can reveal whether quotas achieve the ends anticipated by their advocates—or those feared by their opponents. It also provides an opportunity to link otherwise disparate literatures in political science by considering how electoral reforms affect trends in candidate recruitment and preparedness, policy-making processes, and public opinion and mass mobilization.

A large body of research analyzes gender and political representation. However, a key starting point in this book is that quotas may interfere with existing gendered dynamics. On the one hand, the public controversies surrounding quota adoption may shape expectations about who "quota women" are and what they will do once they reach political office. On the other hand, the varied design of quota policies and rates of quota implementation suggest that these measures are likely to have diverse effects on the composition of political elites. These patterns, in turn, may influence the capacities of quota women to pursue legislative change and may shape the broader meaning of quotas for democratic legitimacy and women's political empowerment. This volume therefore asks whether the *means* by which women enter politics influence *how*, *why*, and *to what extent* their presence affects different types of representative processes, exploring the conditions under which various scenarios are likely to occur.

To set out this collective theory-building enterprise, this chapter begins by briefly summarizing quota policies around the world and research on their introduction and numerical effects. The second section outlines major theories and findings regarding women's descriptive, substantive, and symbolic representation. The third section draws these two literatures together, reviewing the preliminary evidence on how quotas influence the attributes of the women elected, the policy actions of female legislators, and constituent responses to female newcomers. Building on this work and the case studies in this volume, the fourth section establishes definitions for theorizing and operationalizing quota impact with respect to these three facets of political representation. The section concludes with an overview of the following chapters, noting how the authors operationalize these questions and how they relate to one another. Taken together, the chapters suggest a rich and wide-ranging scholarly and political agenda, focused on ensuring that quotas combat, rather than perpetuate, existing patterns of domination and inequality.

GENDER QUOTAS: GLOBAL PATTERNS

The global diffusion of gender quotas to diverse contexts has met with intense interest among feminist scholars, who generally recognize three basic types: reserved seats, party quotas, and legislative quotas (Krook 2009). Some exclude reserved seats on the grounds that these provisions do not influence candidate nomination processes but make specific guarantees regarding who may accede to political office (Dahlerup 2006a). Others divide party quotas into two types: aspirant quotas, which affect pre-selection processes by establishing that only women may be considered, and candidate quotas, which require that parties select a particular proportion of women (Matland 2006). Still others draw distinctions among various kinds of legislative quotas, separating out those instituted through changes to electoral laws from those secured through constitutional reforms (Dahlerup 2006b; Dahlerup 2007). This book uses the term *quotas* to refer to all of these policies, which, irrespective of their mode of intervention or legal status, share the goal of increasing the number of women elected to political office.

Quota Policies

Quotas vary in terms of the countries in which they appear, the timing of their adoption, and the ways in which they attempt to alter candidate selection processes. *Reserved seats* exist in Africa, Asia, and the Middle East. They emerged in the 1930s and were the main type of quota adopted through the 1970s but, since 2000, have appeared increasingly in countries with low numbers of women in politics. Reserved seats mandate a minimum number of female legislators and are typically established through reforms to constitutions and electoral laws. *Party quotas* were initially adopted in the early 1970s by socialist and social democratic parties in western Europe. Over the course of the 1980s and 1990s, however, they began to appear in a diverse array of political parties in all regions of the world. They are adopted voluntarily by individual parties that commit to aim for a certain proportion of women among their candidates. *Legislative quotas*, finally, tend to be found in developing countries, especially in Latin America, and in postconflict societies, primarily in Africa, the Middle East, and southeastern Europe. They appeared first only in the 1990s, as women's representation became a priority of many international and non-governmental organizations (NGOs) (Krook 2006). Enacted through legal and some-times constitutional reforms, they constitute mandatory provisions applying to all parties.

Quota Adoption

Scholars offer four explanations for how quotas have reached the political agenda. The first is that women mobilize for quotas because they believe that equal representation is needed to promote justice and women's interests but will be achieved only through targeted actions to promote female candidates (Krook 2006). A second account is that elites adopt quotas for strategic reasons, both in competition with other parties and in efforts to maintain control over rivals inside the party (Baldez 2004; Chowdhury 2002; Meier 2004). A third is that quotas are adopted when they mesh with party- and country-specific norms. Left-wing parties are generally more open to quotas because these match their goals of equality (Opello 2006), while in some countries, gender quotas are viewed as similar to guarantees given to other groups based on linguistic, religious, racial, and other cleavages (Inhetveen 1999). A fourth story is that quotas are supported by international norms and spread through transnational sharing, primarily via declarations by international organizations recommending that member states aim for 30 percent women in all political bodies (Krook 2006). In practice, components of these four explanations tend to combine in individual cases of quota reform (Krook 2009). Yet how quotas reach the agenda may have important implications for their perceived legitimacy and their potential to alter dynamics of political representation.

Quota Implementation

Despite their stated goal to improve women's political presence, some countries have witnessed dramatic gains following quota adoption, while others have seen modest changes or even setbacks in the numbers of women elected. One reason for cross-national variations relates to the details of individual measures, for example their wording (Htun 2002), requirements (Meier 2004), sanctions (Murray 2004), and perceived legitimacy (Yoon 2001). A second concerns the fit between quotas and other political institutions. Quotas often have the greatest impact in countries with proportional-representation (PR) electoral systems, particularly when combined with closed party lists and high district magnitudes (Caul 1999; Htun and Jones 2002). Quotas also tend to improve women's representation in parties with left-wing ideologies (Kittilson 2006) and in countries where the political culture emphasizes sexual difference and group representation (Inhetveen 1999; Meier 2000). A third account points to the importance of political will. In a number of cases, elites take steps to mitigate quota impact, ranging from passive refusal to enforce quotas to more active measures, including electoral fraud, to subvert their effects (Costa Benavides 2003). However, other actors may also play a direct or indirect role in enforcing quota provisions, including women's organizations (Sainsbury 1993), courts (Jones 2004), and ordinary citizens (Baldez 2004). In most instances, these three components work together, shaping the implementation process. By the same token, the mechanisms by which quotas are translated into practice have ramifications for who gains election through quotas and thus the degree to which their presence may or may not transform politics as usual.

In sum, gender quotas differ in how they intervene in the electoral process. First, these mechanisms take various forms: reserved seats, party rules, or legislative mandates. Second, quotas restructure elections in numerous ways; for instance, they can require special slates of candidates or stipulate new nomination and oversight procedures. Third, they trigger multiple favorable and unfavorable reactions among political elites, civil society groups, and voters. These details must be accounted for as scholars explore quota impact—a point emphasized by this volume's case studies.

WOMEN AND REPRESENTATION: CONCEPTS AND TRENDS

Questions of political representation are a core focus of research on gender and politics. This literature explores why there are so few women elected to political office, whether women in politics represent women as a group, and how the presence or absence of women in politics affects voter perceptions and opinions. The first topic, which addresses women's descriptive representation, has received by far the most attention in comparative work, given that it is relatively straightforward to compare the percentages of women in legislatures across countries. The second, which analyzes substantive representation, has been the focus of some comparative analyses and a large body of single case studies, the latter because monitoring the effects of women's presence requires in-depth study of policy-making processes. Comparative studies of the third, in contrast, are much less common, as symbolic representation is often the least tangible outcome to study, creating difficulties with operationalization, measurement, and effects.

Descriptive Representation

Empirical studies of women's descriptive representation have primarily sought to account for cross-national variations in women's access to political office. Researchers have explored the impact of three categories of variables: institutional or "demand side" factors, such as electoral rules and candidate selection procedures; structural factors affecting the "supply" of female candidates, such as the proportion of women in the workforce and women's educational achievements; and cultural or ideational factors, such as beliefs about equality or the suitability of women for leadership roles. While mixed, the findings of large-n statistical analyses and small-n case studies signal the importance of dynamic relationships among these variables.

In terms of institutional factors, the percentage of women tends to be higher in countries with PR electoral systems than in those with majoritarian electoral arrangements (McAllister and Studlar 2002). In the latter, candidate selection can be viewed as a zero-sum game in which women and men compete for a single nomination. PR systems, in contrast, are organized around multimember districts. As district magnitude increases, parties can perceive advantages to placing at least some female names on the list. Opportunities for women to be elected are often enhanced when closed lists are used, as party leaders can place women in electable positions, in contrast with open lists where voters select individual names (Caul 1999). Nomination procedures also matter: they may be patronage-based or follow a bureaucratic logic (Norris 1997) and may involve decision making by party leaders or local constituency organizations (Caul 1999). In general, women tend to fare better in systems with clear and centralized rules (Lovenduski and Norris 1993).

Examining structural factors, many studies observe strong correlations between women's legislative presence and women's rates of education and labor force participation (McDonagh 2002) and levels of national development (Matland 1998). Scholars attribute these effects to modernization processes that help women move into higher social and economic roles, thus creating a greater "supply" of women to enter electoral politics. Finally, in terms of ideational variables, research uncovers close connections with cultural attitudes toward equality. The number of women in politics is typically higher in Protestant countries (Kaiser 2001) and in countries where citizens are more open to women in leadership positions (Inglehart and Norris 2003; Paxton and Kunovich 2003). These patterns suggest that changing ideas about gender roles are closely associated with women's increased access to elected office.

Others challenge these conclusions, however. Some emphasize women's strategies in interaction with features of the electoral system, noting that women's presence has increased in some cases without a change in the electoral system (Sainsbury 1993) or remained stable despite electoral reform (Beckwith 1992). Other studies confirm the relevance of women's social and economic status (Darcy, Welch, and Clark 1994) but dispute the importance of development, noting that many developed countries have low numbers of women, while some developing countries have seen dramatic increases in recent years (Goetz and Hassim 2003). Similarly, while egalitarian political cultures do appear to favor women's access (Bystydzienski 1995), women have assumed prominent positions in countries with strongly patriarchal religious and cultural norms, usually as a result of family connections or political patronage. These patterns suggest that context may mediate the impact of institutional, structural, and cultural factors to promote or undermine the election of women.

Substantive Representation

Research on women's substantive representation asks whether women seek and are able to promote women's issues once they are elected to political office. A key concern is to determine if women "make a difference," exploring whether women pursue alternative political objectives to those of men. Yet demonstrating these effects is not straightforward. While scholars often detect distinct policy priorities among male and female legislators (Thomas 1991), they also find that these differences do not always translate into policy gains for women as a group. The empirical literature has focused on three explanations: the proportion of women elected, such as the achievement of critical mass; individual factors that may affect the propensity of women to act for women, such as party membership and feminist attitudes; and institutional and contextual variables, such as party discipline, leftist parties in government, and civil society support.

Literature on the importance of proportions assumes that as the number of women approximates a critical mass, attention to women's policy concerns will grow (Childs and Krook 2008). The rationale is that as women become more numerous in legislative chambers, they will be increasingly able to form strategic coalitions and promote legislation related to women's interests (Thomas 1994). However, other scenarios are also possible: a rise in the number of women may influence men's behavior in a feminist direction (Bratton 2005); provoke a backlash among male legislators, who may obstruct women's policy initiatives (Hawkesworth 2003); reduce the effectiveness that female legislators experienced when their numbers were smaller and they were able to specialize in women's concerns without appearing to undermine male domination (Crowley 2004); and result in the election of a more diverse group that may or may not be interested in pursuing women's issues (Carroll 2001).

This diverse range of outcomes has led to calls to move beyond mere percentages to account for whether, how, and to what effect women act for women as a group (Beckwith 2007; Childs and Krook 2009). Some scholars point to individual-level variables such as party affiliation and feminist orientation, finding that legislators in left-wing parties and those with feminist attitudes are more likely to prioritize women-friendly policy initiatives (Htun and Power 2006; Tremblay and Pelletier 2000). While some argue that party matters more than sex, others note that women in conservative parties are often more progressive on gender issues than their male counterparts, even if they do not consciously self-identify as feminist (Carroll 2001). In countries with more weakly institutionalized parties, party ideology may be less coherent but party affiliation may remain important in light of its role in providing access to political patronage (Goetz and Hassim 2003).

A range of institutional and contextual factors likewise influence opportunities to act for women. Many point to the parliamentary rules and practices that compel women to conform to masculine legislative norms, undermining the integration of women's perspectives into policy making (Lovenduski 2005). Others investigate the impact of party discipline, women's seniority in the legislature, the presence of women's caucuses, and the influence of women's movements and public opinion on women's ability to develop and insert a gendered lens (Beckwith and Cowell-Meyers 2007; Dodson 2006; Reingold 2000). These factors are important, as research finds that female legislators tend to differ most from men when it comes to setting the legislative agenda and proposing bills that address issues of concern to women (Childs 2004), even though male legislators often later vote for these bills at similar rates (Tamerius 1995). In sum, this work acknowledges that achieving gains for women depends closely on individual priorities and features of the policy-making process (Dodson 2006; Franceschet 2011).

Symbolic Representation

Attempts to discern the shape and effects of women's symbolic representation consider how women's presence affects constituent perceptions and opinions in two main ways. One approach examines how women's presence affects the perceived legitimacy of elected bodies (Childs 2004; Schwindt-Bayer and Mishler 2005). Another explores how it alters voters' beliefs about the nature of politics as a male domain (High-Pippert and Comer 1998). Both sets of effects have been analyzed in terms of their impact on citizens as a whole and on women's attitudes and behavior more specifically. The findings thus far have been mixed, as research has sought to define and measure the more diffuse cultural meanings of political representation.

Addressing legitimacy, studies on citizens find that male and female respondents believe that government is more democratic when women are present (Schwindt-Bayer and Mishler 2005). In contrast, others focused on women report that women represented by women were more positive about their representatives but not about politics in general (Lawless 2004). In terms of politics as a male domain, several argue that women's increased presence sends signals to female citizens that lead them to become politically involved or feel more politically efficacious (Atkeson and Carrillo 2007; High-Pippert and Comer 1998). Others find, however, that the election of women has weak effects on trends in women's engagement (Karp and Banducci 2008). Some of these divergences result from distinct methods, which range from large-scale surveys comparing male and female attitudes and behaviors (Karp and Banducci 2008) to interviews with female legislators to gauge their views of the symbolic significance of their presence for constituents (Childs 2004).

QUOTAS AND REPRESENTATION: INITIAL EVIDENCE

These rich and varied literatures provide a starting point for exploring how quotas may affect women's political representation. We contend, however, that quotas do not simply generate more representation. Rather, controversies over quotas in many countries suggest that the insights about the causes and consequences of women's political representation—which are largely drawn from nonquota cases—cannot be uniformly applied to quota cases. For instance, quotas might improve women's descriptive representation, but these increases might transform candidate profiles and undermine "merit" in selection. Similarly, being elected through quotas may have contradictory effects on the promotion of women's policies: women elected under quotas may feel obliged to speak on behalf of women as a group or may seek to avoid the stigma of quotas by disavowing women's issues entirely. The introduction of quotas, finally, may signal inclusion by legitimizing women's presence, thereby challenging traditional stereotypes regarding women's roles. Alternatively, negative media attention may influence evaluations of performance and also dissuade other women from coming forward as candidates. While requiring empirical investigation, these possibilities indicate that quotas may alter the stakes of women's political presence.

Quotas and Descriptive Representation

The first wave of quota research offered insight into the effects of quotas on the numbers of women elected (Krook 2009; Tremblay 2007; Tripp and Kang 2008; Yoon 2004). This focus, however, does not exhaust the category of descriptive representation, which includes attributes other than sex. Analyzing the kinds of women elected via quotas can therefore help evaluate how effective quotas are in promoting diversity among elected women. A common objection is that quotas lead to the election of elite women (Dahlerup 2006a; Nanivadekar 2006) or those who serve as proxies and tokens and are therefore likely to reinforce the status quo by not taking feminist policy positions (Abou-Zeid 2006; Krook 2008). Despite this often-voiced concern, there has been little research on exactly what kinds of women benefit from quotas.

Existing studies suggest that quotas lead primarily to the recruitment of women with ties to powerful men (Bird 2003; Chowdhury 2002; Pupavac 2005; Rai et al. 2006), high levels of education (Sater 2007; Srivastava 2000), and close partisan loyalties (Cowley and Childs 2003; Tripp 2006). Others find that quotas promote women from marginalized groups (Mehta 2002), those with low levels of education (Schwartz 2004), those with lower-status occupations (Bird 2003), and those who are relatively young (Britton 2005; Burness 2000; Marx, Borner, and Caminotti 2007). Evidence also suggests that women who accede to office via quotas tend to have less political experience—and in some cases, different kinds of political experience—when compared with men and nonquota women (Kolinsky 1991).

These varied patterns may be partly caused by filling quotas in contexts where women had largely been absent from electoral politics. Without a large number of women in the pipeline, elites recruit women who were previously known to them—including their wives and daughters—and women with little professional formation or little of the political experience typically favored by party selectors. Whether these altered recruitment patterns mean that these women are less qualified, however, remains an open question. In particular, assessing female politicians' backgrounds and preparations according to norms established by men's longstanding participation risks ignoring or discounting the types of qualifications women do bring to politics, such as extensive backgrounds in grassroots or community organizing. In sum, quotas problematize the question of men's and women's preparedness for public office, prompting the question: Who are female (and male) legislators?

Quotas and Substantive Representation

A growing number of studies address the effects of quotas on women's substantive representation, seeking to establish whether quota introduction increases the number of policies proposed, debated, and passed on behalf of women as a group. Until recently, most of this scholarship framed its contribution in relation to the literature on substantive representation, treating the quota simply as a means by which more women achieve elected office (Chaney 2006; Childs 2004; Thomas 2004). Yet the introduction of quotas may change the very expectations about what female legislators should and can do.

In most countries, quota campaigners assert that politics will change as a result of women's increased inclusion, suggesting that women behave differently in terms of priorities and policy styles (Skjeie 1991), at the same time that their presence fosters democratic legitimacy and good governance (Phillips 1995). Such claims may create a mandate effect, leading citizens, as well as legislators, to anticipate that women elected through quotas will promote women's concerns, perhaps more vigorously than women elected before quotas. Mandates can be undermined, however, if concerns about quota women generate a label effect that stigmatizes these legislators (Franceschet and Piscopo 2008).

Initial work finds support for both effects. Women elected through quotas report feeling obligated to act for women as a group (Schwartz 2004; Skjeie 1991) and are inspired to bring new issues to the table (Kudva 2003; Thomas 2004). However, others have sought to disassociate themselves from the quota and women's issues to demonstrate that they are "serious" politicians (Childs 2004). At the same time, many have been accused of acting only as proxies for men (Nanivadekar 2006) and of being excessively loyal to party leaders (Cowley and Childs 2003; Tripp 2006). In part, this is because quotas are often not rooted in processes of constituency formation (Burnet 2008; Hassim 2008; Pupavac 2005), preventing quota women from gaining skills that would make them less vulnerable to manipulation (Chowdhury 2002; Cornwall and Goetz 2005). In other cases, the situation is more complex: quota women may support women's rights legislation but tread carefully in response to harassment, intimidation, or security concerns (Longman 2006; Tamale 2000; Wordsworth 2007).

Further, an unfortunate and somewhat perverse outcome of the mandate effect is that women elected under quotas who are seen to fail to undertake substantive representation may be criticized more harshly than female politicians who ignore women's issues but were not elected under quotas. These various possibilities lead some scholars to suggest that women might be more effective in nonquota environments (Archenti and Johnson 2006). Others view these dynamics, however, as problems faced by female members of parliament (MPs) more generally, not related to quota provisions (Zetterberg 2008). Disaggregating the policy process reveals a more nuanced picture: quotas have been associated with a sharp rise in the introduction of women-friendly policy proposals, even if they have rarely altered policy outcomes (Devlin and Elgie 2008; Franceschet and Piscopo 2008). In terms of substantive representation, then, quotas affect more than how many women-friendly policies are produced. Quotas transform expectations about policy outcomes and potentially affect the maneuverability and success of female legislators within the policy-making process.

Quotas and Symbolic Representation

Given the controversies over justice and fairness that surround quotas (Bacchi 2006; Krook, Lovenduski, and Squires 2009), analyzing symbolic representation is central to understanding their broader impact on public attitudes and women's political empowerment. On the one hand, quotas may alter traditional gendered views of politics, legitimizing women as political actors. On the other hand, the election of more women through quotas may signal greater inclusiveness, inspiring ordinary women to get more politically involved.

In terms of public attitudes, some scholars suggest that quotas pose a radical challenge to politics as usual because they involve fundamentally renegotiating the gendered nature of the public sphere (Sgier 2004). Some evidence supports this claim by showing that exposure to female leaders as a result of quotas can weaken gender stereotypes and also eliminate negative bias in how the performance of female leaders is perceived among male constituents (Beaman et al. 2008). Other work reveals, however, that outward acceptance of the legitimacy of quotas often masks continued resistance. This is especially true among male elites, many of whom attribute women's underrepresentation to choices made by individual women, rather than to structural patterns of discrimination (Meier 2008; and see Holli, Luhtakallio, and Raevaara 2006).

Turning to political engagement, various case studies indicate that quotas increase the rate at which female voters contact their political representatives (Childs 2004; Kudva 2003). Others find that the adoption of quotas encourages women to enter politics, acquire political skills, and develop sustained political ambitions (Bhavnani 2009; Geissel and Hust 2005). At the same time, quotas may build support for women's movement organizing (Sacchet 2008). In contrast, a number of others conclude that quotas have little or no effect on women's political activities (Zetterberg 2009) or their political ambition (Davidson-Schmich 2009). Even more troubling, some suggest that quotas may be associated with the decreased strength (Britton 2005) and increased repression of women's groups (Hassim 2009; Longman 2006). At a symbolic level, therefore, quotas generate a variety of short-, medium-, and long-term effects, which are not only diverse but may also be contradictory across sample populations.

Putting these elements together, it becomes clear that—based on current theories and evidence—quotas may have positive, mixed, and sometimes even perverse effects on women's political representation. To enable research on quota impact to develop in a more cumulative fashion, this section identifies indicators that might be employed to analyze quota effects. The goal is to assess how quotas influence (1) descriptive representation, delineated as the numbers and kinds of women elected; (2) substantive representation, conceptualized as the form and content of policy making; and (3) symbolic representation, theorized as public attitudes toward women in politics and trends in the political engagement of female constituents. Each discussion offers a theoretical conceptualization and reflections on methodological challenges, followed by an overview of the chapters in the book. To situate the emerging research agenda in comparative context from the outset, the case studies address the impact of quotas on each facet of representation in one of four regions: Western Europe, sub-Saharan Africa, Latin America, and Asia and the Middle East.

At the outset, it is worth signaling that research in all three areas faces a common methodological challenge: detecting effects that can be attributed to the presence of women generally versus the adoption of a quota specifically. The extent to which scholars resolve this problem of "observational equivalence" will depend on the design of quota policies and on data availability. Where reserved seats are used, analysts might compare the women who are elected to reserved versus open seats. In countries with party or legislative quotas, a contrast might be made between women elected before and after quotas are introduced. When party quotas are not employed by all parties, the analysis might focus on the characteristics and behaviors of female candidates put forward by parties with and without quota policies. Yet in some countries, these research strategies are simply not possible. Women may not win any nonquota seats, or, in countries where quota laws apply to all seats and districts, little information may exist about women elected before the quota.

A second set of methodological challenges relates to parsing out direct and indirect effects and effects over time. More specifically, the impact of quotas on political representation may change as successive generations of women enter parliaments and as citizens and elites adjust to these policies. In most countries, quotas have applied to only one or two electoral cycles, allowing scholars—including contributors to this volume—to study their direct and immediate effects, which may ultimately change with time. Attending to these issues from the beginning requires moderating conclusions somewhat by recognizing that the dynamics set in motion by quotas may evolve in different directions.

Studying Descriptive Representation

Studying the effects of quotas on descriptive representation has mainly focused on *how many* women are elected. However, asking *what kinds* of women benefit from quotas opens up questions about the diversity and qualifications of women elected under these measures. Expanding the concept of descriptive representation offers at least three advantages. First, it contributes to a better understanding of how quotas disrupt, or are undermined by, traditional practices of candidate selection. Second, a closer look at the attributes and pathways to office of quota women sheds light on questions of representation more generally. In particular, quotas may affect the overall diversity of legislatures, depending on how the profiles of quota women compare with their nonquota counterparts, both female and male, in terms of age, ethnicity, marital status, education, occupation, degree of political experience, and family connections, to list but a few possibilities. Third, examining how quotas shape descriptive representation offers new leverage for analyzing patterns of substantive and symbolic representation, whose effects may depend to a large degree on who representatives are in this fuller sense.

Chapters in Part I of this book point to a number of ways in which questions about qualifications and representativity might be addressed. Chapter 2 evaluates the common criticism that quotas violate the principle of merit. Comparing women elected after the passage of a legislative quota in France with their male counterparts and with women elected before the quota, Rainbow Murray separates quota women, nonquota women, and men. She examines indicators of political background, including age, profession, and levels of prior political experience, in addition to measures of legislative activity, including the number of bills, reports, and questions introduced. This dual focus produces intriguing insights: the distinct profiles of male and female MPs suggest that quotas may help women overcome barriers to a political career, while similar levels of legislative activity demonstrate that quota women are as competent as men once they are elected. These findings support the need for quotas to overcome barriers to women's access, at the same time that they negate charges that quotas produce second-rate parliamentarians.

Chapter 3 focuses in greater depth on legislators' backgrounds, also exploring whether legislative quotas in Argentina lead to the nomination of undeserving or unqualified female parliamentarians. Susan Franceschet and Jennifer M. Piscopo compare male and female legislators' demographic data, including age, marital status, and number of children; their education and professional backgrounds; and their extent and type of political experience before holding office. While all female legislators are quota women, the differences between men and women in the Argentine parliament show that quotas have not eliminated gendered political career patterns. Notably, as compared with men, the women are similar in age, are less likely to be married, and tend to have fewer children; they are equally highly educated but with distinct educational and professional backgrounds; and they are much less likely to have held executive-level office before their election. Yet, as in the French case, these differences do not reveal an innate inferiority of female politicians. Further, by applying to all women, legislative quotas may enhance the overall diversity among MPs, bringing different demographic, occupational, and political perspectives to the policy-making process.

Combining elements of these approaches, chapter 4 studies the personal and political characteristics of women elected to reserved seats in Uganda, assessing whether quotas promote inexperienced and unqualified female party loyalists. Using biographical sketches, Diana Z. O'Brien compares the profiles of quota women and their nonquota counterparts, both male and female. Although the earlier mode of selecting women to reserved seats via an electoral college did not contain checks on candidate quality and clearly promoted elitism and patronage, the direct election of candidates implemented in 2006 has altered these patterns in significant ways. The statistical data suggest that on the vast majority of measures, quota women do not differ significantly from other MPs. Indeed, on some indicators, they appear to be better prepared for office than nonquota legislators. The evidence demonstrates that, as in France and Argentina, quotas in Uganda have not advanced women who are less qualified or more elite than other MPs. Moreover, reforms over time, such as the 2006 switch to direct elections, may even facilitate access for qualified women who might not otherwise be elected.

Adopting a similar focus on demographic and political characteristics, although operationalizing these differently, chapter 5 addresses the impact of reserved seats in Morocco. Implemented thus far in two election cycles, in 2002 and 2007, these measures account for most of the women elected to parliament. To categorize the women benefiting from quotas, James N. Sater draws on two sets of data: an original questionnaire to reveal the educational and class backgrounds of female MPs and data from candidate nomination lists and news coverage to uncover their political status as party loyalists and their links to prominent male leaders. The evidence suggests that dynamics of political patronage play a major role in shaping who gains access to parliament, as illustrated by the elite backgrounds and political connections of quota women. Yet these dynamics also affect men's ascension to political office, signaling how quotas in Morocco—as in Argentina—may unfairly tarnish women as the sole beneficiaries of nepotism. Further, quota women's ties to elite networks may affect their willingness to identify with women as a group, shaping broader prospects for women's empowerment.

Studying Substantive Representation

Investigating the impact of quotas on substantive representation involves assessments of the contradictory expectations that arise in the course of quota debates. Differences across campaigns create different expectations of whether and how quota women will represent women as a group. Yet there may also be conflicts and tensions faced by individual quota women as they confront the opposing pull of mandate and label effects. Moreover, these dynamics play out within distinct political and institutional contexts that create their own incentives for, or obstacles to, the pursuit of women's interests. Finally, the salience of gender identity in defining constituencies, in addition to disagreement over the content of "women's interests," also influences legislator behavior. The range of anticipated outcomes is therefore diverse, complicating how scholars might design their research and evaluate their findings.

To ground substantive representation in these cultural, political, and institutional contexts, scholars must attend to both the *form* and the *content* of policy making. Activities at different stages of the policy process may count as substantive representation, including policy priorities, proposals, and behind-the-scenes mobilization, in addition to publicly debating, voting, and enacting legislation. In terms of form, researchers might compare the behavior of quota versus nonquota women at a single point of the policy-making process. They might also explore several interconnected moments, tracing whether the use of quotas has a clear impact on one aspect of legislative activity but not another. Finally, analysts might consider whether policy-making processes change as a result of women's entrance: as quotas apply to more electoral cycles, female newcomers might find themselves increasingly empowered or increasingly marginalized.

Determining whether the content of women's actions should count as substantive representation involves judgments and careful attention to context. Findings may depend on whether scholars opt for feminist or nonfeminist interpretations of "women's interests." Findings will also differ when the analysis focuses on individual parties, whose ideologies may inform content, or distinct countries, where salient issues may vary. Finally, the definition of women's interests may itself evolve, as more women contribute their voices to the debate and as different policy problems become more or less urgent.

The chapters in Part II illustrate why it is important to outline and justify the choices made when studying the form and content of substantive representation. Chapter 6 explores the effects of party quotas introduced in the early 1990s by the Labour Party in the United Kingdom. Because this policy took the form of all-women shortlists (AWSs) applied in some districts but not others, it permits a comparison between quota and nonquota women to assess whether the mode of candidate selection leads these two groups to assume distinct roles vis-à-vis women's substantive representation. Sarah Childs and Mona Lena Krook draw on three waves of interviews with Labour women first elected in 1997—thus controlling for party and cohort—to analyze how female MPs experience the mandate and label effects theorized by Franceschet and Piscopo (2008). They find that mandates are more common than labels among all MPs but that there are important differences in how quota and nonquota women approach policy making, with labels being more acute for women selected via AWS. The stigma of being a quota woman lessened over time, however, as legislators became more experienced and responded more to mandates to act on behalf of women.

Operationalizing the form of substantive representation differently, chapter 7 examines the actual behavior of female deputies elected under Brazil's legislative quota. Studying committee membership, bill introduction, and parliamentary discourses, Luis Felipe Miguel exposes how quotas exploit but also reinforce stereotypes linking women to social issues. This both informs and potentially devalues women's legislative work. On the one hand, the evidence shows that female MPs—all of whom are quota women—give greater priority to social and women's rights issues than their male counterparts do. On the other hand, Miguel finds that women remain absent from positions of political influence and that, according to some data, women are less successful in passing their legislative initiatives than men are. Quotas thus produce a double bind: female legislators' choices to focus on women's rights and social issues may undercut their ability to amass the political clout needed to legislate successfully. The Brazilian case further demonstrates how quotas create obstacles for women: while female legislators in the United Kingdom find themselves unfairly labeled, Brazilian legislators are associated with less prestigious policies and thus less power.

Chapter 8, in turn, explores the substantive effects of the party quota adopted by the leading party in South Africa, the African National Congress (ANC), and finds that women's presence alone does not necessarily lead to improved policy outcomes for women. Scrutinizing women's rights initiatives in the first two postapartheid parliaments, Denise Walsh discovers a disconnect between women's access and women's voice, noting that as the numbers of women in parliament have increased, the opportunities for pursuing women-friendly legislation have declined. The data suggest that these outcomes are directly related to the ANC's quota policy: in the second parliament, the quota allowed ANC leaders to handpick women who would toe the party line, allowing leaders to centralize their power while reinforcing the perception that the ANC was committed to women's equality. Consequently, the ability of female MPs to advance women's rights was undermined by an increasingly dominant executive who became emboldened to ignore women's rights while hiding behind the quota. This contradiction demonstrates the potentially paradoxical effects of gender quotas: while bringing more women into politics, the quota can serve as an alibi for ignoring and even suppressing the promotion of a robust women's rights agenda.

Developing the theme of barriers to substantive representation further, chapter 9 investigates the impact of reserved seats in Afghanistan. Despite the quota, parliament has produced little legislation promoting women's gendered interests. This outcome is not surprising given the relatively short life span of parliamentary government in Afghanistan, but it appears curious given systematic discrimination against women in recent and past history. Through original interviews with MPs, Anna Larson reveals three obstacles to substantive representation, stemming from a mix of political, institutional, and sociocultural factors in Afghanistan: (1) the enormous challenge of constructing a collective identity based on gender, rather than ethnicity or region; (2) a legislative environment full of informal rules that impede women's ability to promote women's rights; and (3) a rapidly deteriorating security environment, which means that advocating women's rights is both personally and politically risky. As with the South African case, this study reveals the challenges in promoting women's rights in countries struggling to build new democratic institutions. Similarly to the other chapters in this section, it also emphasizes that quotas guarantee neither that elected women will pursue women's rights nor that they will do so successfully. Nonetheless, the small changes achieved by quotas, especially in inchoate or struggling democracies, cannot be discounted.

Studying Symbolic Representation

Gauging the impact of quotas on symbolic representation is complicated, as these effects are often the least tangible. One set of outcomes relates to what quotas symbolize for *all citizens*, measured by trends and changes in the attitudes of mass publics. First, quotas may alter gendered ideas about the public sphere that traditionally associated men with the realm of politics and women with the realm of home and family. By electing more women, quotas may raise awareness of what women can achieve and legitimize women as political actors, unraveling previously accepted gender roles. Second, quotas may change how citizens feel about government more generally, leading them to judge democratic institutions as more fair and legitimate. Citizens may also view these institutions as qualitatively improved, stemming from beliefs that women will be less corrupt and more oriented toward the general welfare of society. Together, these arguments suggest that quotas may affect public attitudes by eroding resistance to women in politics and linking women's presence to "good governance."

A second set of effects concerns what quotas symbolize for *female citizens* more specifically, as observed through patterns of women's political engagement. Quotas may—in the course of undermining traditional gendered notions of the public sphere—encourage women to become more involved as voters, activists, and candidates. Moreover, the greater inclusion of women may lead female citizens to feel more connected to the political process. Quotas may have the opposite effect on male citizens: if men perceive that quotas give women preferential treatment, they may begin to view politics as unfair or biased. Likewise, male elites and aspiring officeholders may resist the quota and become resentful of women's participation. These possibilities indicate that quotas may have different meanings for women versus men. These attitudinal, behavioral, and cultural shifts may also vary over time, shifting in response to domestic political developments and evolving perceptions of women's success as officeholders.

Analyzing the ways in which quotas affect public opinion and mass mobilization is thus a complex task, obliging researchers to establish the type of symbolic impact being investigated, in addition to the expected audience for these effects. Further, researchers will find separating the effects of women's presence from the effects of the quota particularly difficult, as survey questions and survey respondents may not distinguish between quota and nonquota women. The chapters in Part III highlight various ways of operationalizing, measuring, and analyzing the impact of quotas on symbolic representation.

Chapter 10 focuses on the extent to which party and legislative quotas in Belgium have altered the beliefs and actions of political elites. Capitalizing on the opportunity to design her own survey, Petra Meier asks specific questions about whether quotas have caused party officials to rethink the importance of gender equality and to recognize a gender equal public space. She finds that whereas female politicians believe that the quota coincides with and deepens the democratic foundations of the Belgian state, male politicians believe precisely the opposite. Meier then analyzes party statutes, linking male politicians' disapproval of quotas to the failure to incorporate greater commitments to women's equality into party documents. The chapter highlights how men and women may think differently about underrepresentation and discrimination and illustrates how the introduction of a quota may actually aggravate such disagreements.

Shifting attention away from political elites, chapter 11 explores whether the legislative quota in Mexico has altered the attitudes and behaviors of ordinary citizens. Using mass survey data from the federal and state levels, Pär Zetterberg tests whether the quota has increased women's political engagement or enhanced citizens' positive valuation of or confidence in democratic institutions. The findings are inconclusive.

While the analysis reveals that the period during which the quota has been implemented coincided with a decrease in rates of men's and women's political participation, this relationship may be spurious. Numerous other factors, including allegations of electoral fraud and a deepening economic crisis, may also account for recent political disenchantment among Mexicans. The absence of more conclusive findings in this case draws attention to a key methodological challenge, namely using secondary surveys to establish a direct, causal link between quotas and trends in women's political engagement and public attitudes. Unlike Meier, who designed her own survey in Belgium, Zetterberg relies on public opinion surveys whose original authors did not pose questions about quotas.

Chapter 12 also addresses trends among ordinary people but suggests an alternative method for establishing causality between quotas and changes in citizens' beliefs. By conducting a series of interviews and focus groups in Rwanda, Jennie Burnet asks citizens about quotas directly. Burnet's fieldwork on reserved seats and legislative quotas indicates that quotas have encouraged women to participate more actively in community life, work outside the home, speak in public meetings, and demand greater equality in their intimate relationships. Yet these dramatic cultural shifts in women's roles have caused indignation among men, many of whom resist the quotas' ability to redefine gender roles, leading them to express resentment as women become more empowered. In highlighting the resistance of male citizens to the quota, the analysis echoes the findings for male elites in Belgium. Yet the chapter also echoes the Mexican case, as changed gender roles and attitudes in Rwanda are also attributed to broader patterns of political and social change. The larger context of democratization may dilute the specific impact of quotas over time. Burnet consequently demonstrates that quotas can be *part of* broad processes of cultural change and that men and women may experience these ideological transformations quite differently.

Taking yet another approach, chapter 13 employs surveys and field experiments to determine how reserved seats for women at the local level in India have altered citizens' views regarding women as leaders. Focusing on developments in the state of West Bengal, Lori Beaman, Rohini Pande, and Alexandra Cirone ask whether the increased presence of female village council leaders achieves the quota's goals of both ensuring female participation and reducing voter bias against women as policy makers. The data reveal that exposure to female leaders has caused constituents to update their implicit beliefs about women's ability to lead and has made villagers more willing to vote for women. However, exposure neither shifts stated attitudes toward women more generally nor leads to female empowerment specifically; the authors find that women remain unable to travel unless escorted by male relatives and that women continue to shoulder the burdens of domestic work. This latter finding also appeared in the Rwandan case, as men remained reluctant to undertake the domestic chores that elected women were leaving behind. The India case also highlights an important dimension of quotas' short- and long-term impact: symbolic effects are lagged, as they result from the substantive actions of female politicians. When women pursue different and more effective policies than men with tangible results, this may provoke a greater shift in the perception of politics as a male domain.

Conclusions and Directions for Future Research

The case studies in this book demonstrate the wide range of effects that quotas may have on women's political representation. The authors employ a variety of measures to theorize and analyze what quotas might imply for patterns and changes in the dynamics of political recruitment, legislative behavior, and public attitudes and political engagement. Viewed as a whole, the chapters do not provide a uniform answer but, instead, point to multiple possible meanings of descriptive, substantive, and symbolic representation that influence how these trends might be assessed.

To make sense of these variations, chapter 14 revisits the empirical findings of each chapter, seeking to discern common themes in what they say regarding each facet of representation. Susan Franceschet, Mona Lena Krook, and Jennifer M. Piscopo consider possible connections between methodology and conclusions. That is, how do authors' choices of operationalization and data collection affect their interpretation of the empirical findings about quotas' impact? How are normative conclusions linked to different ways of conceptualizing descriptive, substantive, and symbolic representation? The concluding chapter then delves further into these variations, comparing insights across sections to explore how features beyond the quota's presence may shape the effects observed, including (1) quota design, adoption, and implementation; (2) political institutions and context; and (3) learning over time. Putting these various elements together, the final part of the concluding chapter draws on the case study evidence to theorize and illustrate how patterns with regard to one facet of representation may shape those in relation to the others. Based on this collective theory-building exercise, the volume concludes with some thoughts on avenues for future research, emphasizing the importance of generating both cumulative and comparative frameworks for studying the impact of gender quota policies.

REFERENCES

Abou-Zeid, Gihan. 2006. The Arab Region: Women's Access to the Decision-Making Process across the Arab Nation. In Drude Dahlerup, ed., *Women, Quotas, and Politics*, 168–193. New York: Routledge.

Archenti, Nélida, and Niki Johnson. 2006. Engendering the Legislative Agenda with and without the Quota. *Sociología* 52: 133–153.

Atkeson, Lonna Rae, and Nancy Carrillo. 2007. More Is Better: The Influence of Collective Female Descriptive Representation on External Efficacy. *Politics & Gender* 3 (1): 79–101.

Bacchi, Carol Lee. 2006. *Arguing for and against Quotas*. In Drude Dahlerup, ed., *Women, Quotas and Politics*, 32–51. New York: Routledge.

Baldez, Lisa. 2004. Elected Bodies: The Gender Quota Law for Legislative Candidates in Mexico. *Legislative Studies Quarterly* 24 (2): 231–258.

Beaman, Lori, Raghabendra Chattopadhyay, Esther Duflo, Rohini Pande, and Petia Topalova. 2008. Powerful Women: Does Exposure Reduce Bias? Faculty Research Working Paper Series, Harvard Kennedy School, Cambridge, Mass.

Beckwith, Karen. 1992. Comparative Research and Electoral Systems: Lessons from France and Italy. *Women & Politics* 12 (2): 1–33.

———. 2007. Numbers and Newness: the Descriptive and Substantive Representation of Women. *Canadian Journal of Political Science* 40 (1): 27–49.

Beckwith, Karen, and Kimberly Cowell-Meyers. 2007. Sheer Numbers: Critical Representation Thresholds and Women's Political Representation. *Perspectives on Politics* 5 (3): 553–565.

Bhavnani, Rikhil. 2009. Do Electoral Quotas Work after They Are Withdrawn? Evidence from a Natural Experiment in India. *American Political Science Review* 103 (1): 23–35.

Bird, Karen. 2003. Who Are the Women? Where Are the Women? And What Difference Can They Make? Effects of Gender Parity in French Municipal Elections. *French Politics* 1 (1): 5–38.

Bratton, Kathleen A. 2005. Critical Mass Theory Revisited. *Politics & Gender* 1 (1): 97–125.

Britton, Hannah. 2005. *Women in the South African Parliament*. Boulder, Colo.: Lynne Rienner.

Burness, Catriona. 2000. Young Swedish Members of Parliament. *NORA* 8 (2): 93–106.

Burnet, Jennie E. 2008. Gender Balance and the Meanings of Women in Governance in Post-Genocide Rwanda. *African Affairs* 107 (248): 361–386.

Bystydzienski, Jill M. 1995. *Women in Electoral Politics: Lessons from Norway*. Westport, Conn.: Praeger.

Carroll, Susan J. 2001. *The Impact of Women in Public Office*. Indianapolis: Indiana University Press.

Caul, Miki. 1999. Women's Representation in Parliament: The Role of Political Parties. *Party Politics* 5 (1): 79–98.

Chaney, Paul. 2006. Critical Mass, Deliberation, and the Substantive Representation of Women: Evidence from the UK's Devolution Programme. *Political Studies* 54 (4): 691–714.

Childs, Sarah. 2004. *New Labour's Women MPs*. New York: Routledge.

Childs, Sarah, and Mona Lena Krook. 2009. Analysing Women's Substantive Representation: From Critical Mass to Critical Actors. *Government and Opposition* 44 (2): 125–145.

———. 2008. Critical Mass Theory and Women's Political Representation. *Political Studies* 56 (3): 725–736.

Chowdhury, Najma. 2002. The Implementation of Quotas: Bangladesh Experience. Paper presented at the IDEA Workshop, Jakarta, Indonesia, September 25.

Cornwall, Andrea, and Anne Marie Goetz. 2005. Democratizing Democracy: Feminist Perspectives. *Democratization* 12 (5): 783–800.

Costa Benavides, Jimena. 2003. Women's Political Participation in Bolivia: Progress and Obstacles. Paper presented at IDEA Workshop, Lima, February 23–24.

Cowley, Philip, and Sarah Childs. 2003. Too Spineless to Rebel? New Labour's Women MPs. *British Journal of Political Science* 33 (3): 345–365.

Crowley, Jocelyn Elise. 2004. When Tokens Matter. *Legislative Studies Quarterly* 29 (1): 109–136.

Dahlerup, Drude. 2006a. What Are the Effects of Electoral Gender Quotas? Paper presented at the International Political Science Association, Fukuoka, Japan, July 10–13.

———, ed. 2006b. *Women, Quotas, and Politics*. New York: Routledge.

———. 2007. Electoral Gender Quotas. *Representation* 43 (2): 73–92.

———. 2008. Gender Quotas—Controversial but Trendy. *International Feminist Journal of Politics* 10 (3): 322–328.

Darcy, Robert, Susan Welch, and Janet Clark. 1994. *Women, Elections, and Representation*, 2nd ed. Lincoln: University of Nebraska Press.

Davidson-Schmich, Louise K. 2009. Who Wants to Run for Office from Which Party? Paper presented at the Annual Meeting of the American Political Science Association, Toronto, September 3–6.

Devlin, Claire, and Robert Elgie. 2008. The Effect of Increased Representation in Parliament: The Case of Rwanda. *Parliamentary Affairs* 61 (2): 237–254.

Dodson, Debra L. 2006. *The Impact of Women in Congress*. New York: Oxford University Press.

Francheschet, Susan. 2011. Gendered Institutions and Women's Substantive Representation. In Mona Lena Krook and Fiona Mackay, eds., *Gender, Politics, and Institutions*, 58–78. London: Palgrave.

Francheschet, Susan, and Jennifer M. Piscopo. 2008. Gender Quotas and Women's Substantive Representation: Lessons from Argentina. *Politics & Gender* 4 (3): 393–425.

Geissel, Brigitte, and Evelin Hust. 2005. Democratic Mobilisation through Quotas: Experiences in India and Germany. *Commonwealth & Comparative Politics* 43 (2): 222–244.

Goetz, Anne Marie, and Shireen Hassim, eds. 2003. *No Shortcuts to Power: African Women in Politics and Policy Making*. New York: Zed.

Hassim, Shireen. 2008. Quotas and Interest Representation. In Naila Kabeer, Agneta Stark, and Edda Magnus, eds., *Global Perspectives on Gender Equality*, 159–182. New York: Routledge.

———. 2009. Perverse Consequences? The Impact of Quotas for Women on Democratisation in Africa. In Ian Shapiro, Susan C. Stokes, Elisabeth Jean Wood, and Alexander S. Kirshner, eds., *Political Representation*, 211–235. New York: Cambridge University Press.

Hawkesworth, Mary. 2003. Congressional Enactments of Race-Gender: Toward a Theory of Raced-Gendered Institutions. *American Political Science Review* 97 (4): 529–550.

High-Pippert, Angela, and John Comer. 1998. Female Empowerment: The Influence of Women Representing Women. *Women & Politics* 19 (4): 53–66.

Holli, Anne Maria, Eeva Luhtakallio, and Eeva Raevaara. 2006. Quota Trouble: Talking about Gender Quotas in Finnish Local Politics. *International Feminist Journal of Politics* 8 (2): 169–193.

Htun, Mala. 2002. Puzzles of Women's Rights in Brazil. *Social Research* 69 (3): 733–751.

Htun, Mala N., and Mark P. Jones. 2002. Engendering the Right to Participate in Decision-Making. In Nikki Craske and Maxine Molyneux, eds., *Gender and the Politics of Rights and Democracy in Latin America*, 32–56. New York: Palgrave.

Htun, Mala, and Timothy J. Power. 2006. Gender, Parties, and Support for Equal Rights in the Brazilian Congress. *Latin American Politics & Society* 48 (4): 83–104.

Inglehart, Ronald, and Pippa Norris. 2003. *Rising Tide: Gender Equality and Cultural Change around the World*. New York: Cambridge University Press.

Inhetveen, Katharina. 1999. Can Gender Equality Be Institutionalized? The Role of Launching Values in Institutional Innovation. *International Sociology* 14 (4): 403–422.

Jones, Mark P. 2004. Quota Legislation and the Election of Women: Learning from the Costa Rican Experience. *Journal of Politics* 66 (4): 1203–1223.

Kaiser, Pia. 2001. Strategic Predictors of Women's Parliamentary Participation. Ph.D. dissertation, University of California, Los Angeles.

Karp, Jeffrey A., and Susan A. Banducci. 2008. When Politics Is Not Just a Man's Game: Women's Representation and Political Engagement. *Electoral Studies* 27 (1): 105–115.

Kittilson, Miki Caul. 2006. *Challenging Parties, Changing Parliaments: Women and Elected Office in Contemporary Western Europe*. Columbus: Ohio State University Press.

Kolinsky, Eva. 1991. Political Participation and Parliamentary Careers: Women's Quotas in West Germany. *West European Politics* 14 (1): 56–72.

Krook, Mona Lena. 2006. Reforming Representation: The Diffusion of Candidate Gender Quotas Worldwide. *Politics & Gender* 2 (3): 303–327.

———. 2008. Quota Laws for Women in Politics. *Social Politics* 15 (3): 345–368.

———. 2009. *Quotas for Women in Politics*. New York: Oxford University Press.

Krook, Mona Lena, Joni Lovenduski, and Judith Squires. 2009. Gender Quotas and Models of Political Citizenship. *British Journal of Political Science* 39 (4): 781–803.

Kudva, Neema. 2003. Engineering Elections: The Experiences of Women in Panchayati Raj in Karnataka, India. *International Journal of Politics, Culture and Society* 16 (3): 445–463.

Lawless, Jennifer L. 2004. Politics of Presence? Congresswomen and Symbolic Representation. *Political Research Quarterly* 57 (1): 81–99.

Longman, Timothy. 2006. Rwanda: Achieving Equality or Serving an Authoritarian State? In Hannah Britton and Gretchen Bauer, eds., *Women in African Parliaments*, 133–150. Boulder, Colo.: Lynne Rienner.

Lovenduski, Joni, ed. 2005. *State Feminism and Political Representation*. New York: Cambridge University Press.

Lovenduski, Joni, and Pippa Norris, eds. 1993. *Gender and Party Politics*. Thousand Oaks, Calif.: Sage.

Marx, Jutta, Jutta Borner, and Mariana Caminotti. 2007. *Las Legisladoras: Cupos de Género y Política en Argentina y Brasil*. Buenos Aires: Siglo XXI Editora Iberoamericana.

Matland, Richard. 1998. Women's Representation in National Legislatures: Developed and Developing Countries. *Legislative Studies Quarterly* 23 (1): 109–125.

———. 2006. Electoral Quotas: Frequency and Effectiveness. In Drude Dahlerup, ed., *Women, Quotas, and Politics*, 275–292. New York: Routledge.

Mehta, G. S. 2002. *Participation of Women in the Panchayati Raj System*. New Delhi: Kanishka.

McAllister, Ian, and Donley T. Studlar. 2002. Electoral Systems and Women's Representation: A Long-Term Perspective. *Representation* 39 (1): 3–14.

McDonagh, Eileen. 2002. Political Citizenship and Democratization: The Gender Paradox. *American Political Science Review* 96 (3): 535–552.

Meier, Petra. 2000. The Evidence of Being Present. *Acta Politica* 35 (1): 64–85.

———. 2004. The Mutual Contagion Effect of Legal and Party Quotas: A Belgian Perspective. *Party Politics* 10 (5): 583–600.

———. 2008. A Gender Gap Not Closed by Quotas: The Renegotiation of the Public Sphere. *International Feminist Journal of Politics* 10 (3): 329–347.

Murray, Rainbow. 2004. Why Didn't Parity Work? *French Politics* 2 (4): 347–362.

Nanivadekar, Medha. 2006. Are Quotas a Good Idea? *Politics & Gender* 2 (1): 119–128.

Norris, Pippa, ed. 1997. *Passages to Power*, 1–14. New York: Cambridge University Press.

Opello, Katherine A. R. 2006. *Gender Quotas, Parity Reform and Political Parties in France*. New York: Lexington.

Paxton, Pamela, and Sheri Kunovich. 2003. Women's Political Representation: The Importance of Ideology. *Social Forces* 82 (1): 87–114.

Phillips, Anne. 1995. *The Politics of Presence*. New York: Oxford University Press.

Pitkin, Hanna Fenichel. 1967. *The Concept of Representation*. Berkeley: University of California Press.

Pupavac, Vanessa. 2005. Empowering Women? An Assessment of International Gender Policies in Bosnia. *International Peacekeeping* 12 (3): 391–405.

Rai, Shirin, Farzana Bari, Nazmunnessa Mahtab, and Bidyut Mohanty. 2006. South Asia: Gender Quotas and the Politics of Empowerment. In Drude Dahlerup, ed., *Women, Quotas, and Politics*, 222–245. New York: Routledge.

Reingold, Beth. 2000. *Representing Women*. Chapel Hill: University of North Carolina Press.

Sacchet, Teresa. 2008. Beyond Numbers: The Impact of Gender Quotas in Latin America. *International Feminist Journal of Politics* 10 (3): 369–386.

Sainsbury, Diane. 1993. The Politics of Increased Women's Representation: The Swedish Case. In Joni Lovenduski and Pippa Norris, eds., *Gender and Party Politics*, 263–290. Thousand Oaks, Calif.: Sage.

Sater, James N. 2007. Changing Politics from Below? Women Parliamentarians in Morocco. *Democratization* 14 (4): 723–742.

Schwartz, Helle. 2004. Women's Representation in the Rwandan Parliament. M.A. thesis, University of Gothenburg, Sweden.

Schwindt-Bayer, Leslie A., and William Mishler. 2005. An Integrated Model of Women's Representation. *Journal of Politics* 67 (2): 407–428.

Sgier, Lea. 2004. Discourses of Gender Quotas. *European Political Science* 3 (3): 67–72.

Skjeie, Hege. 1991. The Rhetoric of Difference: On Women's Inclusion into Political Elites. *Politics & Society* 19 (2): 233–263.

Srivastava, Rashmi. 2000. Empowerment of Women through Political Participation. In Niroj Sinha, ed., *Women in Indian Politics*, 195–217. New Delhi: Gyan.

Tamale, Sylvia. 2000. "Point of Order, Mr. Speaker": African Women Claiming Their Space in Parliament. *Gender and Development* 8 (3): 8–15.

Tamerius, Karin L. 1995. Sex, Gender, and Leadership in the Representation of Women. In Georgia Duerst-Lahti and Rita May Kelly, eds., *Gender, Power, Leadership, and Governance*, 93–112. Ann Arbor: University of Michigan Press.

Thomas, Aparna. 2004. Women's Participation in the Panchayati Raj. Ph.D. dissertation, Western Michigan University, Kalamazoo.

Thomas, Sue. 1991. The Impact of Women on State Legislative Policies. *Journal of Politics* 53 (4): 958–976.

———. 1994. *How Women Legislate*. New York: Oxford University Press.

Tremblay, Manon. 2007. Democracy, Representation, and Women. *Democratization* 14 (4): 533–553.

Tremblay, Manon, and Réjean Pelletier. 2000. More Feminists or More Women? Descriptive and Substantive Representations of Women in the 1997 Canadian Federal Elections. *International Political Science Review* 21 (4): 381–405.

Tripp, Aili Mari. 2006. Uganda: Agents of Change for Women's Advancement? In Gretchen Bauer and Hannah E. Britton, eds., *Women in African Parliaments*, 111–132. Boulder, Colo.: Lynne Rienner.

Tripp, Aili Mari, and Alice Kang. 2008. The Global Impact of Quotas. *Comparative Political Studies* 41 (3): 338–361.

Wordsworth, Anna. 2007. A Matter of Interests: Gender and the Politics of Presence in Afghanistan's Wolesi Jirga. AREU Issues Paper Series, Kabul.

Yoon, Mi Yung. 2001. Democratization and Women's Legislative Representation in Sub-Saharan Africa. *Democratization* 8 (2): 169–190.

———. 2004. Explaining Women's Legislative Representation in Sub-Saharan Africa. *Legislative Studies Quarterly* 29 (3): 447-468.

Zetterberg, Pär. 2008. The Downside of Gender Quotas? Institutional Constraints on Women in Mexican State Legislatures. *Parliamentary Affairs* 61 (3): 442–460.

———. 2009. Do Gender Quotas Foster Women's Political Engagement? Lessons from Latin America. *Political Research Quarterly* 62 (4): 715–730.

PART ONE
DESCRIPTIVE
REPRESENTATION

Descriptive representation, sometimes characterized as "mirror" representation, refers to the proportions of women and other minorities present in elected political bodies. A common approach is to count the numbers of group members, assuming that higher percentages indicate greater inclusiveness of the political system with respect to these social categories. Debates over gender quotas, however, highlight a range of features beyond sex that may affect how well quotas contribute to a better reflection of society. Supporters propose that by increasing the numbers of women, quotas will lead to the election of women from a diverse array of social, economic, political, and cultural backgrounds. Detractors, in contrast, suggest that quotas will reproduce the existing political elite or, worse, bring in "unqualified" women, thereby undercutting the potential for political renewal and decreasing the overall caliber of elected officials. Taken together, these discussions politicize questions of representativity and qualifications, raising important normative concerns about how best to evaluate indicators of change and continuity in the backgrounds, merit, and competence of quota women versus their nonquota counterparts.

Addressing these debates, the chapters in this section highlight important methodological challenges regarding how to evaluate quotas' impact on descriptive representation. First, they reveal that judgments about legislators' backgrounds and qualifications may be subjective, raising doubts about the possibility of defining objective criteria. A related challenge is how to interpret differences and similarities across the profiles of women and men. Gendered pathways to power may indicate variations in levels of education or past political experience, but they may also simply reflect the broader inequalities that shape access to electoral politics. These inequalities may cause elected women to have, for example, distinct age, marital, and professional profiles when compared with elected men—although such distinctions may not signal women's inherent lack of merit.

Second, researchers must distinguish among effects accounted for by sex, those attributable to quotas, and those stemming from interactions between the two. This analytical task may be facilitated or undermined by quota design and implementation, as some policies enable quota women to be identified more readily than others. At the same time, differential rates of numerical impact may influence findings by virtue of limiting the sample size.

Viewed as a group, the chapters also point to crucial tensions in efforts to gauge trends in descriptive representation. More specifically, the analyses reveal that there is often a disconnection between who quota women are and who they are perceived to be, stemming from lingering doubts about the suitability of women for politics and the legitimacy of quotas. In a slightly different vein, the chapters call attention to an important unanticipated consequence of reform, which is that quotas may cause attributes of legislators that were previously naturalized—for example, their status as elites, loyalists, and beneficiaries of nepotism and/or patronage—to be called into question. Such critiques may at first be directed at quota women but in some cases extend to legislators in general, allowing for a broader rethinking of the backgrounds and qualifications necessary to hold political office.

2 Parity and Legislative Competence in France

Rainbow Murray

France was the first country in the world to introduce a compulsory 50 percent gender quota, known as parity. Although the framers of parity ardently rejected the notion that it was a gender quota, perhaps influenced by the constitutional rejection of gender quotas in 1982, the principles are effectively the same. Parity requires all parties to field an equal number of men and women in most elections. Its first major impact was in 2007, when the proportion of women in parliament rose to 18.5 percent. As a result, 2007 is the watershed moment at which quota women entered the French National Assembly (NA).

In debates on descriptive representation, certain assumptions are made about the consequences of making parliaments more descriptively representative. Although a gender-balanced parliament may fail to be descriptive in other senses, such as race, the presence of more women in parliament may enhance the representation of other descriptive attributes. For example, there are fewer women than men with the elite occupational backgrounds that are frequently overrepresented within parliaments, so a gender quota might also lead to the representation of a wider variety of professions. At the same time, the notion of descriptive representation is also associated with the selection of less capable candidates. By prioritizing traits such as sex over more objective measures of ability, gender quotas might jeopardize the quality of parliamentarians. However, the stark overrepresentation of certain descriptive characteristics suggests that existing selection practices may not be meritocratic, and a quota might actually enhance the quality of representation by expanding the talent pool.

This chapter explores these different aspects of descriptive representation. It queries whether the increased representation of women makes parliament more descriptively representative of other traits, at the same time as it explores whether quota women perform their jobs to the same standards as men. After providing a background on gender quotas in France, this chapter explores debates about descriptive representation, with particular reference to competence and meritocracy. These hypotheses are then subjected to empirical analysis, outlined in the data section. Quota women are compared with other deputies in terms of their age, profession, and experience to determine whether they act as descriptive representatives of wider society or mirror male political elites. Their contributions to parliamentary life are then tested, using six measures of parliamentary activity. The findings indicate that women bring slightly different qualities and experiences to the NA but are no less likely than men to get on with the job effectively once elected.

PARITY AND THE POLITICAL CONTEXT IN FRANCE

France has long compared badly with its European neighbors in terms of women's political representation. In 1982, an attempt to introduce gender quotas was overruled by the Constitutional Council. In the early 1990s, a new movement demanding gender "parity" was launched, rejecting quotas in favor of equal representation of both sexes. The movement gained momentum throughout the 1990s, building public support and placing pressure on presidential candidates to support the idea (Bereni 2007). A constitutional revision to support parity in 1999[1] was followed by legislation in 2000 requiring parties to field equal numbers of men and women in legislative, European, and regional elections and also in larger districts for local and senatorial elections.[2]

Parity has been most effective in second-order elections using proportional representation and a placement mandate, although multiplications of lists in senatorial elections and bias toward men in the allocation of local executive positions have both limited the impact of the law (Bird 2003; Troupel 2006). For national elections, which use a two-round electoral system with single-member districts, parity is ineffective in two ways. There is no placement mandate, so women are often placed in unwinnable seats, and parties may field more than 50 percent men in exchange for sacrificing a small proportion of their state financing. As a result, parity had little effect in the 2002 elections to the NA, where the proportion of women rose from 10.9 percent to 12.3 percent. An improved effort by parties in 2007 generated a 50 percent rise in women to the current level of 18.5 percent. Thus, 2007 is the most appropriate turning point for measuring the impact of parity on descriptive representation in France.

France is a long-established democracy with a distinctive semipresidential system. The party system is fragmented and constantly evolving, but parties can be categorized broadly as belonging to the left, the right, and the far right. The president and parliament are elected separately. Presidential politics were instrumental in securing the passage of parity. In 1995, presidential hopefuls Jacques Chirac (of the right-wing Union for a Popular Movement, UMP) and Lionel Jospin (of the left-wing Socialist Party, PS) both expressed support for parity. In 1999, President Chirac was pressured by Prime Minister Jospin into enacting parity. Parity has enjoyed greater ideological support from parties on the left, which also have a stronger record in implementing the law. Although France currently has a right-wing majority, most women in parliament are from left-wing parties.

OPERATIONALIZATION, METHODS, AND DATA COLLECTION

One of the most contentious arguments about achieving descriptive representation through gender quotas is the claim that quotas may produce, or at least be seen to produce, second-class politicians (Bacchi 2006; Franceschet and Piscopo 2008; Karam 1999; Zetterberg 2008a). It is argued that if women cannot make it on their own merit without recourse to a quota, perhaps they should not be in politics at all. An emphasis on descriptive representation implies that candidates would be selected on the grounds of their sex rather than their ability to do the job. In the event that quota women are, in fact, inferior politicians, gender quotas will reduce the quality of representation for all and threaten the credibility of the institutions to which they are elected (Lovenduski 2005, 98).

The counterargument to women's lack of merit is that women's exclusion from politics is not an indication of their inferior ability but rather a result of institutional, structural, and/or psychological barriers. If women's talent is currently being overlooked, expanding the talent pool should actually raise standards in parliament. Advocates of parity in France also argued that women brought different and unique qualities to the political process, without which it could not be complete (Bataille and Gaspard 1999; Gaspard, Servan-Schreiber, and Le Gall 1992; Guigou 1997; Halimi 1994; Mossuz-Lavau 1998; Roudy 1995; Scott 2005). Opponents of parity argued that such claims essentialized women and that what mattered was not a candidate's sex but his or her ability to do the job (Lagrave 2000, 128). Emphasis on a so-called meritocracy was embedded in the French universalist model, where all were seen to be equal before the law and preferential treatment for any category was unthinkable.[3]

Both female politicians and the concept of descriptive representation were treated with suspicion. For example, Luc Ferry warns that parity "runs the risk of creating 'quota women,' elected women who could, rightly or wrongly, be suspected of owing their entry into politics more to legal obligations than to their personal merit" (Amar 1999, 124). Meanwhile, Catherine Tasca (Socialist deputy and minister in the Jospin government) declared that "there is a demand for proof of competence from women which is never required from men" (Halimi 1994, 241).

As a result, the question of competence is central to debates about parity. The effect of quotas on the quality of representation might be positive, if new perspectives are introduced into the representative process; neutral, if sex does not matter; or negative, if descriptive representation is prioritized over the competence of the candidates. It is assumed that there is a relationship between descriptive characteristics and legislative competence, especially if descriptive representation is achieved through quotas, yet there is little research to test this hypothesis.[4] Given the lack of objective information collected about male and female politicians, claims about quota women are liable to subjective interpretation, and it is difficult to confirm whether women have the confidence and capacity to perform legislative functions at the same rate as their male counterparts.

The sudden and dramatic influx of women into the NA in 2007 presents an ideal opportunity to test these claims and measure whether women are indeed more, equally, or less qualified and active compared with their male counterparts. The contrast between the composition of parliament on either side of the 2007 election facilitates comparison between those who came before and after parity. Male and female deputies before and after 2007 can be compared to see (1) whether they have different backgrounds and (2) whether there is any difference in their parliamentary activity. In this way, it can be determined whether quota women are any different from those elected without the help of a quota.

This chapter focuses on two central aspects of deputies: who they are, in terms of their descriptive background, and what they do, with regard to their parliamentary activity. These two measures enable us to determine whether gender quotas enhance the representation of other descriptive characteristics and whether descriptive representation comes at the expense of ability to do the job. Looking at deputies' backgrounds illustrates whether men and women have the same qualities and pathways to power. The areas of focus are deputies' age, profession, and prior political experience.

Looking at the parliamentary activity of deputies shows whether men and women are performing the same volume and kinds of tasks once elected. This provides an objective measure of whether there is a connection between deputies' sex and their job performance and whether this is affected by quotas. The 2002 and 2007 parliaments are compared, both to see whether there are any differences between men and women and to see whether anything changes following a greater influx of women. Alternative variables that may influence parliamentary activity, such as safety of seat, political party, and prior parliamentary experience, are also controlled for to isolate the effects of sex from other independent variables.

For both types of analysis, data are collected from the official NA Web site (National Assembly 2008). Data on deputies' backgrounds are taken from each deputy's NA home page, using information supplied by the deputy. Data on their activity are taken from the official parliamentary record. The research uses every available variable for both background and activity in order to offer as detailed a profile of candidates as possible. In this way, we can observe whether there are any noticeable differences in background and job performance between men and women and between women elected with and without a quota, both before and after election to the NA.

The data are mostly reliable, but there are two caveats. First, data on deputies' professions may be biased by deputies' attempts to present themselves in a favorable light. For example, Communist deputies may exaggerate their working-class roots, while some deputies may be classed as "other" to conceal an entire career based on professional political activity. Achin (2005, 135) also notes that deputies may have several different careers before entering parliament, and the one declared at their moment of election may not have been their principal career. As these caveats are not explicitly gendered, the data still give an indication of gender differences in deputies' professional backgrounds. Second, data for participation in plenary debates only date back to 2004, and data for participation in committees are only available for the current parliament.

31

Parity and Legislative Competence in France

COMPARING DEPUTIES' BACKGROUNDS BEFORE ELECTION

The first set of analyses focuses on the profile of deputies at the point of election to the NA. This research builds on earlier studies of the social attributes of France's male and female politicians, which have shown that France's female deputies have some significant differences from their male counterparts but on the whole are more similar to male politicians than they are to the average French woman (Costa and Kerrouche 2007; Murray 2004; Sineau and Tiberj 2007). The ages of deputies upon election reveal whether men and women start their parliamentary careers at similar life stages. Professional backgrounds are compared to see whether the wide gender differences in career paths present in broader French society are reflected in the composition of the NA. As also noted in later chapters in this volume (especially chapter 3), women are faced with an impossible double bind in this regard, as they are expected both to be more representative of French society, and especially of French women, and to meet the elite standards set by their (predominantly male) counterparts in parliament. Finally, the political experience gained by deputies is measured in terms of the number and level of offices they have previously held, to demonstrate whether women have similar political trajectories to those of men.

Age

Research has indicated that, because of domestic commitments, women are likely to enter the political arena later than men, for example, once the children have grown older (Pionchon and Derville 2004; Sineau 2001; Bird 2003 disputes this finding). I explore here whether this is still the case and whether age differences between male and female deputies can be explained in terms of gendered political careers.

The age of deputies at the point of election is reported in table 2.1. The mean age of women is 53.33, compared with 55.10 for men. In both cases, this represents a rise relative to 2002. This gender gap seems to be attributable not to women starting their political careers later than men but, rather, to women finishing earlier. Whereas in 2002 there was a noticeable trend for women to be concentrated in the 50-to-59 age bracket, the trend in 2007 was that women were evenly spread across all age groups except for the two oldest categories. One possible explanation for this is that a high proportion of women—nearly half—were new entrants, and new entrants to the NA are more likely to be concentrated in the lower age groups, whereas the oldest deputies tend to have served a number of terms already. This is confirmed by looking directly at the new entrants to the NA.

The new women entering the NA were, on average, younger than the existing women in the NA, and interestingly, they were also marginally younger on average than new male entrants. This suggests that the theory of women starting their political careers later in life than men is no longer valid. There is almost no difference between the age of new female entrants in 2007 and that of new female entrants in 2002. However, because

Table 2.1 Age of winning candidate at the point of election, 2002 and 2007

Age of deputy on election	2002		2007	
	Men (%)	Women (%)	Men (%)	Women (%)
Younger than 30	0.2	1.4	0.2	0.9
30–39	7.7	2.9	3.2	3.8
40–49	21.1	24.6	22.1	29.2
50–59	48.6	59.4	40.4	45.3
60–69	19.1	11.6	31.3	19.8
70–79	3.0	0	2.8	0.9
Older than 80	0.2	0	0	0
Total (n)	100 (507)	100 (69)	100 (470)	100 (106)

there were more new women this time (forty-five, compared with thirty-two in 2002), this may have pushed down the average age of female deputies, whereas a greater proportion of male deputies were old-timers: 42.5 percent of female deputies were serving their first term, compared with 21.5 percent of men, and the mean number of terms served by current male deputies was 2.02, compared with 0.90 for women. No woman had served more than five terms, whereas twenty-four men (5.1 percent) had served six or more terms, with one man currently serving his eleventh term in the NA.

Profession

Given that women within France are disproportionately concentrated in low-status, low-paid, and part-time work, they might also be victims of the class bias present in the NA, where members of the top professions have a disproportionate presence. At the same time, if women are following the same trajectory as men in order to get into politics, then they will be even further removed from the average woman than a male deputy is likely to be removed from the average man. This may hinder claims that female deputies would be capable of representing the substantive interests of women.

Table 2.2 reveals that overall, women are much less likely to be drawn from the male-dominated professional occupations, including managers and the liberal professions. However, the gap was reduced considerably in 2007, with no significant difference between new male and female entrants. In 2002, women were at least as likely as men to be drawn from the service sector, whereas a significant gender gap emerged in 2007, with men much more likely than women to come from the service sector. The areas in which women are disproportionately represented are in skilled nonmanual and "other" categories, including those with no career, suggesting that women do have slightly different career trajectories from men, even among the elite group of female politicians. Men are much more likely than women to have farming backgrounds; when farming is removed from the category of "manual and skilled nonmanual," the gender gap becomes even wider.

Profession	2007				2002			
	All deputies		New entrants		All deputies		New entrants	
	Men (%)	Women (%)	Men (%)	Women (%)	Men (%)	Women (%)	Men (%)	Women (%)
Professional occupations	51.7	35.8	36.7	36.6	52.5	31.7	61.9	31.4
Service sector	31.3	26.5	37.7	22.2	28.0	27.5	20.6	22.9
Manual and skilled nonmanual	5.8	13.2	6.0	13.3	7.5	17.3	7.1	14.3
Other	11.3	24.5	19.8	26.7	12.0	23.2	10.3	31.4
Total (n)	470	106	101	45	507	69	155	35

Women in 2007 were increasingly present in the higher socioeconomic categories, suggesting that they were better able to compete with men than before and challenging the argument that it is hard to find enough women with suitable qualifications. It is impossible for women to meet the double standard of being as highly qualified as men and at the same time sharing the descriptive characteristics of women more broadly in French society, where 61.3 percent of women are concentrated in manual and skilled nonmanual professions and only 12.2 percent have professional occupations (L'INSEE 2008; this double standard is also noted in chapters 3 and 4 below). Nonetheless, the new female entrants appear to have struck a balance, being more present in the highest socioeconomic categories than their female predecessors while still being less elitist than men. In terms of profession, at least, the findings suggest that women can make limited claims of political renewal while defending themselves against claims of being second-class politicians elected only through the parity quota.

Experience

The most common route into a political career at the national level is to build up a political career at the local level. However, despite the large increase to 47.5 percent women elected where the law applied in 2001, the presence of women stagnated in all areas where the law was not applicable (Bird 2003; Troupel 2002). In particular, women remained largely absent from two major sources of local power that serve as useful springboards to national office: local executives, especially the coveted position of mayor, and departmental councils (*conseils généraux*). As table 2.3 illustrates, current female deputies are less likely than men to have been a mayor, and only one woman deputy has ever presided over a *conseil general*, compared with twenty-eight men.

Table 2.3 Deputies and local executive office, 2007

		Not mayor in 2007[1]		Mayor: size of district (population)				President of Conseil Général	
		Formerly mayor	Never mayor	< 10,000	10,000–49,999	50,000–99,999	100,000+	Formerly	Currently
Male	n	68	162	103	102	28	7	7	21
	%	14.5	34.5	21.9	21.7	5.9	1.5	1.5	4.5
Female	n	5	75	10	12	2	2	0	1
	%	4.7	70.8	9.4	11.3	1.9	1.9	0	0.9
Total	n	73	237	113	114	30	9	7	22
	%	12.7	41.1	19.6	19.8	5.2	1.6	1.2	3.8

A x^2 test revealed the results to be significant to $p < 0.01$.

[1]Those who did not hold mayoral office in 2007 were divided into two categories: those who had previously been mayors and those who had never held mayoral office.

In addition to municipal and departmental executives, regional councils can also be a good entry point to national politics. In 2007, Ségolène Royal was the only woman in France who presided over a regional council, and she had announced that she would not defend her parliamentary seat in 2007 as a demonstration of confidence in her (unsuccessful) bid for the presidency. As a consequence, the opportunity to combine presidency of a regional council with the role of deputy was exclusively the preserve of men. In 2008, nine male deputies were also presidents of regional councils, with two more formerly having held such a position.

Table 2.4 illustrates that overall, men have served more terms in local office than women. These terms of office can include any position on a municipal, intercommunal,

Table 2.4 Number of terms of local office served for all and new deputies, 2007

		Experience in local politics, 2007 (terms of office)				
		0	Low (1–4)	Medium (5–8)	High (9+)	Total
Men	n	15	152	216	87	470
	%	3.2	32.3	46.1	18.5	100.0
Women	n	8	63	30	5	106
	%	7.5	59.5	28.3	4.7	100.0
Total (all)	n	23	215	246	92	576
	%	4.0	37.3	42.7	16.0	100.0
New men	n	9	56	28	8	101
	%	8.9	55.5	27.8	7.9	100.0
New women	n	5	33	6	1	45
	%	11.1	73.4	13.3	2.2	100.0
Total (new)	n	14	89	34	9	146
	%	9.6	61	23.2	6.2	100.0

A test revealed the results for all deputies to be significant to $p < 0.01$. The results for new deputies were not significant.

departmental, or regional council, with each period of election counting as one term. The mean number of terms served by a man was 5.39, compared with 3.63 for a woman. This trend carried through to new deputies, with new men having served an average of 3.69 terms, compared with 2.71 for new women. How one interprets these results can vary depending on the argument one wishes to pursue. The lower levels of women's presence in local politics are evident even at the national level. One could claim that less qualified women are being promoted unfairly, with inexperienced women getting selected for the NA more easily than men.

At the same time, it could be argued that the parity law, where applied, is compensating for inequalities where it does not apply. For example, the application of parity at the national level is helping to mitigate the absence of women in local executives, to which the law did not apply in 2001. It is also worth noting that although women overall have less experience than men, men are still being selected in higher numbers than women when they have no experience at all or very little. The proportions of women from this category may be higher, but the absolute numbers favor men. In other words, the majority of deputies with little or no prior experience in politics are male. This refutes the argument that parity is allowing underqualified women in through the back door, as the primary beneficiaries of fast-track promotions are men.

Summary

In terms of their overall background, the quota women newly elected in 2007 represent a mixture of change and continuity. They are younger and from higher professional backgrounds than the women who came before them, suggesting that women are increasingly competing on the same terms as men. This refutes claims that women who were selected as a result of the parity legislation were inferior candidates who could not have made it on their own terms. The increase in the quantity of women appears to converge with a corresponding increase in quality, if one judges women by the standards of the male norm. At the same time, female deputies remain slightly more representative of the social diversity of France. The gender gaps between men and female deputies are narrowing in some areas, such as age and profession, although gaps remain stark in certain areas.

Women remain underrepresented in certain powerful professions that are associated with political careers. Furthermore, women are heavily underrepresented in the areas of local politics most likely to serve as a springboard to national office, such as mayors, heads of departmental councils, and other local and regional executive positions, and women have less prior political experience overall. Women are also being given fewer opportunities than men, with men making up the majority of newcomers and also the majority of those new deputies with little or no prior political experience. This all suggests that the barriers to women's political representation remain, and without parity, women might find it even harder to get into parliament. The influx of quota women arguably has not compromised the quality of deputies in terms of background: these women appear to be located in the middle ground between imitating their male counterparts and representing the diversity of French women.

The second set of analyses considers the actions of deputies following their election. The data used are the actual number of times each deputy asked a question, authored a bill, cosigned a bill, wrote a report, participated in a plenary session in the NA, and contributed to a committee session. These six measures are based on publicly available information provided by the NA, and they are the most easily comparable activities performed by deputies. The data allow for comparison between men and women, and also between the 2002–2007 parliamentary session (known as the twelfth parliament), before the impact of parity was really felt, and the 2007–2008 session (the thirteenth parliament), following the significant rise of women in the NA. In order for the measure of their activity to be comparable, each deputy needs to have served an equal term. To ensure consistency, two precautions have therefore been taken. First, the data for the twelfth parliament were collected after all business had been concluded, and the data for 2007–2008 were collected over the space of a few days during the 2008 summer recess, in order to ensure equivalence among deputies. Second, any deputy who did not serve a full term was eliminated from the study. As a result, out of 577 deputies, the *n* for the twelfth parliament is 540, and the *n* for the thirteenth parliament is 567.

The first test of the data was to run cross-tabulations between each of the dependent variables and the sex of the deputies. For both the twelfth and thirteenth parliaments and across all dependent variables, chi-square tests revealed no significant relationship, indicating that there were no identifiable differences in the performances of men and women. Given the large range present in some variables—for example, the number of questions asked in the twelfth parliament ranged from zero to 4,049—it is very difficult to identify any meaningful patterns in a cross-tabulation. For this reason, the data were grouped into five categories based on percentile groups. The categories 1 through 5 represent, as closely as possible, the bottom 20 percent of deputies in terms of activity (1) through to the 20 percent most active deputies (5).[5] Once organized in this way, a couple of patterns emerged more clearly, although the statistical significance of the findings in table 2.5 (all of which were significant at $p < .05$) is to be interpreted with caution, being primarily for illustrative purposes. All variables other than those reported below continued to

Table 2.5 Patterns of activity, by sex

Approximate rankings of deputies	Contributions to plenary sessions, 2002–2007			Questions asked, 2007–2008			Contributions to committees, 2007–2008		
	Male	Female	Total	Male	Female	Total	Male	Female	Total
1	21.3%	6.2%	19.4%	21.3%	13.2%	19.8%	18.7%	12.3%	17.5%
2	19.6%	26.2%	20.4%	18.4%	25.5%	19.8%	23.2%	31.1%	24.7%
3	19.2%	26.2%	20.0%	19.5%	23.6%	20.3%	20.2%	17.9%	19.8%
4	19.6%	24.6%	20.2%	20.2%	21.7%	20.5%	16.1%	25.5%	17.8%
5	20.4%	16.9%	20.0%	20.6%	16.0%	19.8%	21.9%	13.2%	20.3%
Total (*n*)	475	65	540	461	106	567	461	106	567

show no relationship between sex and the dependent variable, with or without grouping.

As men remain numerically dominant in the NA, the division of deputies into percentile groups is predominantly influenced by male activity. It is unsurprising, therefore, that the distribution of men throughout these groups is fairly consistent. What is notable is that women do not follow the same pattern as men but, rather, tend to be bunched together in the middle categories, with relatively few women present in the categories of most and least active. Women are consistently least likely to be found in the bottom category of activity, suggesting that the least active—perhaps the most complacent or otherwise occupied—deputies tend to be men. Women are also less likely to be among the top performers, although men dominate positions of influence, such as president of the NA and executives of all parliamentary committees, which might explain why certain men are the most active members of parliament.

These results imply that there is no relationship between the sex of the deputy and the level of parliamentary activity. However, this finding may obscure the true relationship between sex and activity if there are other independent variables affecting the relationship, such as seniority, which itself is related to the number of terms a deputy has served. As women tend to serve fewer terms than men and are more likely to be newcomers, controlling for prior terms in the NA is important to help separate out the differences attributable solely to deputies' sex. Similarly, deputies in marginal constituencies might be more likely to prioritize activities within their constituency, for which no data are available, rather than focusing their efforts on work within the NA, so safety of seat was also brought in as a control variable.[6] Finally, the party to which a deputy belongs might have a big impact on levels of activity, depending on whether the party supports or opposes the government. Parties of the right have formed or supported the government since 2002, with parties of the left in opposition, so a dummy variable has been used to control for this.[7] The dependent variables were then tested again with ordinary least squares (OLS) regression analysis, using the four independent variables of sex, prior terms in the NA, safety of seat, and party (a left-right dummy).

Table 2.6 looks at different measures of agenda setting activity, controlling for other variables. The table reveals that all of the independent variables are significant at least once, except for sex. Prior experience in the NA is the only significant variable affecting the number of questions asked, and the negative sign suggests that those who have been in the NA longer are less likely to ask high numbers of questions. This may be because asking questions is a relatively simple task that does not require much seniority, while those with more experience may be more involved in demanding tasks, such as authoring reports and bills. In addition, Stevens (2003, 184) notes that "there is little evidence that questions are taken very seriously by the government and its officials. Many of the written questions put by members to ministers remain unanswered." As a result, more senior parliamentarians may not consider asking questions to be an effective use of their time, leaving this activity to those members who are conscientious in their role of scrutiny or who crave the dim limelight provided by the televised coverage of oral questions. This confirms Lazardeux's (2005) finding that questions are used by junior parliamentarians to obtain information about government policies. In any case, sex is insignificant both before and after 2007.

Conversely, safety of seat and party are significant when considering the number of bills authored. Right-wing MPs were more likely to author bills, perhaps with the tacit support of the government (Stevens 2003, 180). Those in safer seats were also more likely to author bills. As proposing bills is quite a time-consuming and also potentially controversial activity, those in marginal seats might prioritize spending time in their constituencies, leaving work on bills for those who can afford to focus their efforts on parliamentary activity. Neither sex nor prior experience is significant.

The R^2 for bills cosigned is higher than the other regressions, indicating that the model is better at explaining variance in the number of bills signed, with both prior experience and party being highly significant. Members of the governing party are much more likely to cosign bills, which is unsurprising given that most bills emanate from their party colleagues. More surprising is that deputies with higher levels of parliamentary experience are less likely to cosign bills than their more junior colleagues. Perhaps new deputies are keen to lend their names to everything going while more senior deputies are more discriminating. Again, sex is completely insignificant.

Writing reports is a relatively senior and time-consuming activity, and table 2.6 reveals that it is primarily the preserve of members of the governing party. While party is the key variable, experience is also significant at the $p < 0.1$ level, hinting that

Table 2.6 Agenda-setting activity

	Questions asked*		Private members' bills authored		Private members' bills cosigned		Reports written	
	2002–2007	2007–2008	2002–2007	2007–2008	2002–2007	2007–2008	2002–2007	2007–2008
Sex	.01	-.04	.05	-.21	-11.44	-1.70	-.45	-.19
	(.07)	(.06)	(.74)	(.27)	(12.10)	(2.39)	(.60)	(.18)
Terms in NA	-.05	-.04	.03	.04	-6.10	-1.37	.19	.07
	(.01)**	(.01)**	(.14)	(.06)	(2.25)**	(.52)**	(.11)	(.04)
Seat safety	.001	.002	.05	.03	.31	.11	.03	.004
	(.002)	(.002)	(.02)***	(.01)**	(.34)	(.13)	(.02)	(.005)
Party	0.05	.07	-1.13	-.64	-115.839	-16.52	-2.05	-.63
	(.05)	(.05)	(.54)***	(.21)**	(8.78)**	(1.87)**	(.43)**	(.14)**
R^2	0.002	0.013	0.021	0.039	0.296	0.142	0.059	0.049

Data are unstandardized coefficients; standard errors in parentheses.

* The data for this dependent variable were skewed, with a few deputies creating outliers at the top end of the range by asking very high numbers of questions. As the interest was in relative rather than absolute performance, this regression uses a logarithm of the dependent variable to reduce the distortion created by the outliers. An alternative method using a ranked dependent variable produced a similar outcome. This and all other regressions were tested for multicollinearity and heteroskedasticity and showed no evidence of either.

** = $p < 0.01$

*** = $p < 0.05$.

more experienced members are more likely to write reports. This is unsurprising and may also explain why more senior members focus on activities like this rather than less prestigious activities such as asking questions.

Table 2.7 illustrates deputies' debate participation. Contributions to plenary sessions appear first and foremost to be the preserve of the opposition, with a very strong relationship between the number of contributions and being in a left-wing party. Information on committee sessions is only available for the thirteenth parliament. Unlike plenaries, committee work appears to be a matter of experience rather than partisanship, with more experienced members being more likely to contribute to committee sessions. It should also be noted that all six parliamentary committees were presided over by men, and women occupied only five of the forty-seven executive positions on committees.[8]

It is reasonable to assume that the executive members of committees would contribute the most, so it is almost surprising that sex is not significant here. It may be that women are very active within their roles as ordinary members of committees. These findings all accord with Green's study of parliamentary committees, which concludes that the sexual division of labor within committees is a combination of seniority, with men more likely to have the level of seniority required to lead committees and be a member of the most prestigious committees such as finance; personal interest, with women orienting toward "useful" committees such as social affairs, rather than "prestigious" committees such as defense; and the structural problems associated with "a system [that] has evolved under male dominion" (2004, 157).

Considered collectively,[9] the measures of parliamentary activity indicate two important trends. First, the four independent variables used in this study all had a significant relationship with at least one form of parliamentary activity, with the notable exception of sex, which was never significant. Second, there were strong similarities in the data for the twelfth and thirteenth parliaments. Taken together, these trends suggest that the introduction of more women through the parity law has had no measurable impact on parliamentary activity. There is no significant relationship between sex and any kind of parliamentary activity observed here, and nothing changed following the 50 percent rise in women in 2007. These findings support the argument that the new female

Table 2.7 Debate participation

	Plenary contributions		Committee contributions
	2004–2007	2007–2008	2007–2008
Sex	-3.08 (6.08)	-1.30 (1.29)	-1.80 (1.50)
Terms in NA	.37 (1.13)	-.26 (.28)	.96 (.33)*
Safety of seat	.18 (.17)	.03 (.04)	.05 (.05)
Party	19.84 (4.41)*	4.43 (1.01)*	.44 (1.18)
R^2	0.033	0.028	0.019

Data are unstandardized coefficients; standard errors in parentheses.

* = $p < 0.01$.

deputies in the NA are performing at the same levels as men and as those who came before them.

CONCLUSION

This chapter has explored the impact of quotas on descriptive representation in two ways. It first looked at whether France's new quota women came from different backgrounds from those of the men and women around them. The findings suggest that newly elected women do have slightly different backgrounds from those of newly elected men, although the gap between men and women is closing. Thus, quota women are more like men than nonquota women, rather than the other way around. The gender differences that are present stem from inequalities in society, and quotas are helping women to overcome this barrier to entry. Even with these different backgrounds, as the second part of the chapter illustrated, there is no noticeable difference between men and women in terms of volume or type of parliamentary activity following election. Thus, gendered differences in prior qualifications do not appear to have an impact on activity. As O'Brien notes in chapter 4 below, perhaps we need to revisit our assumptions of what qualifications are actually necessary for holding elective office.

Two conclusions can be drawn from this study. First, an increase in the number of women made the French parliament more descriptively representative, both in terms of sex and in terms of age and profession. Thus, gender quotas may contribute both directly and indirectly toward making parliament more descriptively representative of society. Second, this study found no evidence that quota women were less effective in their role as parliamentarians than those elected without a quota. It was not possible to test every conceivable measure of quality or competence, but on the basis of participation in parliamentary life, the data do not support the widely held view that descriptive representation occurs at the expense of competence and meritocracy. On the contrary, gender quotas had the effect of drawing in talented women who had previously been excluded from the representative process. These findings support the contention that expanding the talent pool of parliamentary candidates may enhance, rather than threaten, the quality of political representation.

NOTES

1. To pacify opponents of parity, the word *parity* is absent from the revision.
2. For local elections, parity applies in towns of more than thirty-five hundred inhabitants. For senatorial elections, parity applies in districts with at least four seats.
3. A critique of the Republican universalist model is that it is based on a false universalism that has always favored men, resulting in sharp inequalities of fact disguised by a principle of equality in theory.
4. Zetterberg (2008b) notes that there is a surprising lack of research on what quota women do once they are elected to power.
5. It was not possible to split deputies into groups based on exact percentiles, as there were often multiple deputies sharing the same value. For example, the boundary for the bottom 20 percent of deputies asking questions in the twelfth legislature lay between forty-seven and forty-eight questions.

6. This was measured as the percentage lead of the winner over the runner-up in the relevant election.

7. A new party was formed in 2007, called MoDem, which represented a split from the UDF, a party of the center right whose remaining members continue to support the government. As MoDem does not support the government but cannot be considered a party of the left, its three seats have been excluded from this section of the study in the 2007–2008 data.

8. This has recently changed.

9. A test was also conducted of the total scores for all parliamentary activity combined, although some of the nuances of individual measures were lost when the scores were combined, producing a less reliable result. In this test, experience and party remained the dominant variables, while sex was insignificant.

REFERENCES

Achin, Catherine. 2005. Le Mystère de la Chambre Basse. *Comparaison des Processus d'Entrée des Femmes au Parlement France-Allemagne 1945–2000*. Paris: Dalloz.

Amar, Michelin, ed. 1999. *Le Piège de la Parité: Arguments pour un Débat*. Paris: Hachette.

Bacchi, Carol. 2006. Arguing for and against Quotas: Theoretical Issues. In Drude Dahlerup, ed., *Women, Quotas and Politics*, 32–52. London: Routledge.

Bataille, Phillipe, and Françoise Gaspard. 1999. *Comment les Femmes Changent la Politique et Pourquoi les Hommes Resistent*. Paris: La Découverte.

Bereni, Laure. 2007. French Feminists Renegotiate Republican Universalism: The Gender Parity Campaign. *French Politics* 5 (3): 191–209.

Bird, Karen. 2003. Who Are the Women? Where Are the Women? And What Difference Can They Make? Effects of Gender Parity in French Municipal Elections. *French Politics* 1 (1): 5–38.

Costa, Olivier, and Eric Kerrouche. 2007. *Qui Sont les Députés Français?* Paris: Presses de Sciences Po.

Franceschet, Susan, and Jennifer Piscopo. 2008. Gender Quotas and Women's Substantive Representation: Lessons from Argentina. *Politics & Gender* 4 (3): 393–426.

Gaspard, Françoise, Claude Servan-Schreiber, and Anne Le Gall. 1992. *Au Pouvoir Citoyennes! Liberté, Égalité, Parité*. Paris: Le Seuil.

Green, Amanda Dawn. 2004. Women and the National Assembly in France: An Analysis of Institutional Change and Substantive Representation, with Particular Reference to the 1997–2002 Legislature. Ph.D. dissertation, University of Stirling, Scotland.

Guigou, Elisabeth. 1997. *Etre Femme en Politique*. Paris: Plon.

Halimi, Gisèle, ed. 1994. *Femmes: Moitié de la Terre, Moitié du Pouvoir*. Paris: Editions Gallimard.

Karam, Azza. 1999. Beijing + 5: Women's Political Participation: Review of Strategies and Trends. Paper presented at the UNDP meeting on women and political participation, New Delhi.

Lagrave, Rose-Marie. 2000. Une Étrange Défaite: La Loi Constitutionelle sur la Parité. *Politix* 13 (51): 113–141.

Lazardeux, Sébastien. 2005. "Une Question Écrite, Pour Quoi Faire?" The Causes of the Production of Written Questions in the French Assemblée Nationale. *French Politics* 3 (3): 258–281.

L'INSEE. 2008. *Femmes et Hommes. Regards sur la Parité*. Paris: Statistique Publique.

Lovenduski, Joni. 2005. *Feminizing Politics*. Cambridge, U.K.: Polity Press.

Mossuz-Lavau, Janine. 1998. *Femmes/Hommes pour la Parité*. Paris: Presses de Sciences-Po.

Murray, Rainbow. 2004. Why Didn't Parity Work? A Closer Examination of the 2002 Election Results. *French Politics* 2 (3): 347–362.

National Assembly. 2008. www.assemblee-nationale.fr (accessed August 6–30, 2008).

Pionchon, Sylvie, and Grégory Derville. 2004. *Les Femmes et la Politique*. Grenoble: Presses Universitaires de Grenoble.

Roudy, Yvette. 1995. *Mais de Quoi Ont-Ils Peur? Un Vent de Misogynie Souffle sur la Politique*. Paris: A. Michel.

Scott, Joan Wallach. 2005. *Parité: Sexual Equality and the Crisis of French Universalism*. Chicago: University of Chicago Press.

Sineau, Mariette. 2001. *Profession: Femme Politique, Sexe et Pouvoir sous la Cinquième Republique*. Paris: Presses de Sciences Po.

Sineau, Mariette, and Vincent Tiberj. 2007. Candidats et Députés en 2002: Une Approche Sociale de la Représentation. *Revue Française de Science Politique* 57 (2): 163–185.

Stevens, Anne. 2003. *Government and Politics of France*, 3rd ed. Basingstoke, U.K., and New York: Palgrave.

Troupel, Aurélia. 2002. Pistes et Matériaux: Disparités dans la Parité. Les Stratégies de Contournement de la Parité dans le Département des Alpes-Maritimes. *Politix* 15 (60): 147–168.

———. 2006. Disparités dans la Parité: Les Effets de la Loi du 6 Juin 2000 sur la Féminisation du Personnel Politique Local et National. Ph.D. dissertation., Université de Nice-Sophia-Antipolis, France.

Zetterberg, Pär. 2008a. The Downside of Gender Quotas? Institutional Constraints on Women in Mexican State Legislatures. *Parliamentary Affairs* 61 (3): 442–460.

———. 2008b. The Impact of Candidate Selection on "Quota Women's" Legislative Behavior: Towards a Theoretical Framework. Paper presented at the Annual Meeting of the Midwest Political Science Association, Chicago.

3 Gender and Political Backgrounds in Argentina

Susan Franceschet and Jennifer M. Piscopo

Argentina was the first country in the world to adopt a national-level gender quota law, in 1991.[1] Over the past two decades, quota detractors have claimed that political parties are filling the quota with inexperienced women, elite women, and/or women who act as proxies for male party leaders. Following this volume's conceptualization of descriptive representation as not just *how many* women are elected but also the *attributes* of the women elected, we subject criticisms of quota women to empirical examination. We do so by focusing on legislators' biographical data: their personal characteristics (age, marital status, and number of children), educational backgrounds, and prior political experience. By comparing male and female legislators on these dimensions, we can evaluate the validity of charges that quota women are inexperienced. Moreover, debates on quotas raise questions about the representativity of officeholders, that is, about which characteristics and traits make officeholders representative of citizens. Our data further enable us to evaluate these claims by comparing the demographic data of female legislators with Argentine women in general.

Research conducted after the adoption of the Argentine quota revealed widespread public perceptions that party leaders were complying with the quota by replacing male candidates with the female relatives of male party elites (Waylen 2000; Piscopo 2006).[2] Significantly, these criticisms continued to be voiced by numerous legislators whom the authors interviewed between 2005 and 2009.[3] Although nepotism, particularly the practice of party leaders placing relatives on party lists, is widespread in Argentina, women are commonly perceived to be the main beneficiaries. Charges of nepotism and elitism imply that quota women are not adequately prepared to hold elected office, in addition to suggesting that such women cannot represent female voters in any meaningful way.

Through a comparison of men and women's educational backgrounds and prior political experience, our research tests these perceptions about female legislators. Since the Argentine quota regime applies universally, all female legislators are branded as quota women and thus tarnished by the negative beliefs associated with the label (Franceschet and Piscopo 2008). Unfortunately, we cannot assess allegations of nepotism directly; women in Argentina do not assume their husbands' last names, making family relationships difficult to identify. We can, however, test for sex-based differences in terms of legislators' educational levels and political backgrounds. These tests will not reveal whether the quota has changed female legislators' profiles in Argentina; what they show is whether detractors' claims about quota women have an empirical basis.

We find that while male and female legislators in Argentina do have distinct profiles, these differences do not support the conclusion that women are less qualified for office. The backgrounds of men and women in Congress differ as a result of gender role socialization but not preparedness for office. For instance, we find that female legislators are more likely to be educators, whereas male legislators are more likely to be engineers; yet both groups hold university degrees and thus have similar levels of education. Regarding political experience, we find that women are just as likely as men to have held other legislative and executive posts before their election.

These findings shed light on debates about quotas, tokenism, and representativity. The finding that both male and female legislators are educated, political insiders undermines claims that quota women are tokens. Yet this fact also renders quota women less representative of the general female population, who are not highly educated political insiders. Indeed, the debate about quotas, tokenism, and representativity illustrates the double bind that women elected through quotas face: if they do not possess similar levels of education and political experience to those of men, then they are deemed less deserving of their positions and treated as tokens. On the other hand, if female legislators are drawn from the political class, they are criticized for being too elite to represent female voters adequately. In this way, debates about gender quotas politicize issues of representation: before the adoption of the Argentine quota law, legislators' elite status or levels of qualification were not subject to widespread popular scrutiny. The fact that such traits became contentious after the quota law shows how female legislators are often held to standards not traditionally demanded of male elected officials.

THE LEY DE CUPOS AND ELECTORAL POLITICS IN ARGENTINA

Argentina's Ley de Cupos ("Quota Law") was passed by Congress in 1991 following a lengthy campaign led primarily by women in political parties and women's organizations in civil society. The quota campaign can be viewed as part of a wider struggle for women's rights and equality that emerged out of the country's transition to democracy in 1983. Women's organizing, in both human rights groups and feminist groups, played an important part in the countrywide protests against the 1976–1983 dictatorship. While the first postdictatorship government responded to a number of policy concerns raised by women, the number of women holding elected office remained small, and female activists felt that their demands remained unmet. In this context, women in the parties and in civil society began to view gender quotas as the most effective mechanism for increasing their access to and voice in politics.

A female senator from the Radical Civic Union (UCR) introduced a quota bill in 1989, and a group of female deputies from several different parties introduced a bill to the lower house shortly after. Over the next year, quota supporters lobbied male party leaders and legislators and also raised public awareness through media campaigns and street demonstrations. Feminists in the political parties created a "Network of Political Women," which included women from fifteen political parties, and organized information sessions with women in both provincial and national legislatures (Archenti and Johnson 2006; Lubertino 2003). Women's lobbying was successful, and eventually, the senate bill moved through various legislative hurdles and came to a vote in late 1990. Partly because senators did not expect their counterparts in the Chamber of Deputies to pass the bill, the senate bill was approved almost unanimously (Krook 2009, 169). This lent further momentum to women's mobilizing, and when the quota bill was debated in the lower house in 1991, women filled the observation galleries, cheering for legislators who supported the bill and booing those who opposed it. The legislative debate continued until the early hours of the morning, and opponents changed their position only after President Carlos Menem made his support for the bill known. In November 1991, the bill overcame its final hurdle and was passed with widespread support.

During this process, quota supporters appealed to norms of justice, arguing that basic fairness demanded that women have equal access to decision-making arenas. More important, quota supporters also argued that politics would change with women's presence. Advocates used the slogan "With few women in politics, it's the women who change. With many women in politics, politics changes" (Marx, Borner, and Caminotti 2007, 61). During the parliamentary debate, female proponents appealed to women's "difference," arguing that women would "contribute to the construction of a new discourse . . . attend to the daily realities of the people, and produce a renovation in leadership" (cited in Perceval 2001). Quota proponents thus advanced arguments not about *which women* quotas would elect but about *what women would do* once elected. Opponents, however, viewed—and continue to view—the quota as privileging sex over merit-based selection criteria; one observer claimed that the quota was "simply a prize for being female."[4] Yet opponents did not explicitly state worries that women elected under quotas would be tokens, spouses, or unqualified individuals. These allegations emerged only after the quota was implemented.

Argentina's quota law produced decisive gains in the number of women elected for several reasons. First, the law mandated that women's names be placed in electable positions and prevented noncomplying parties from entering the election. Following the first election held under the new rules, in 1993, women's seat share increased from 5 to 14 percent. Argentina renews half of the chamber every two years, so the full effect of the quota was felt in 1995, when women's seat share rose to 27 percent.

By 2007, women held 38 percent of seats in the Chamber of Deputies. The quota was first applied to the Senate in 2001, following a reform of its electoral rules. In the 2001 elections, women's presence in the Senate jumped from 6 percent to 37 percent (Marx, Borner, and Caminotti 2007, 81–83). Second, the law—and particularly the placement mandate—fit with the country's closed-list proportional representation electoral system. Argentina is a federal system composed of twenty-three provinces and the autonomous federal district that encompasses the City of Buenos Aires. The federal Chamber of Deputies contains 256 members who serve four-year terms. Deputies are elected from provincial districts, with each province receiving a number of seats relative to its overall population. The Province of Buenos Aires and the City of Buenos Aires are overrepresented, receiving significantly more seats than the remainder of the provinces. The quota's placement mandate has been structured by executive decrees, which have favored a maximalist interpretation: women's names must appear in every third spot on the list or, when parties are only contesting two or fewer seats, every second spot.

In terms of who the quota women are, features of Argentine politics beyond the electoral system become relevant. These features include candidate recruitment procedures, federalism, and patron-client relations. First, Argentine politicians generally do not consider election to the federal legislature to be the capstone of their political career. Most national legislators "begin their career at the provincial level and return to careers in the provinces following their brief tenure in the national congress" (Jones 2008, 42). Because legislative careers are uncommon, Argentine legislators have been termed "amateur legislators" but "professional politicians" (Jones et al. 2002). Indeed, between 1989 and 2003, a mere 19 percent of federal deputies were reelected (Jones and Hwang 2005, 126). Similar findings are reported by María del Mar Martínez Rosón, who classifies the majority of Argentine members of Congress as "experienced politicians" rather than "experienced legislators" based on the number and type of past political offices held (2008, 243).

Second, recruitment to the national legislature is shaped by deeply entrenched patterns of clientelism in Argentine politics, raising the value of elected and appointed positions that receive and distribute federal moneys, contracts, and jobs. In Argentina, the posts of governor and mayor and certain ministerial posts in provincial and federal cabinets offer the most opportunities for clientelism, thereby increasing the value of these offices and the status of those who hold them. This structure gives provincial executives large amounts of authority. Since the federal Congress is elected via provincial-level party lists, provincial party bosses—either the governor or the opposition leader—control candidate recruitment. Individual legislators generally do not decide for themselves whether they will seek reelection, and at any rate, legislators typically prefer to leave the Congress for more prestigious posts in the executive branch.

These features account for why, following quota implementation, opponents began to accuse female legislators of lacking the necessary qualifications or of unfairly benefiting from nepotism. We contest, however, that these allegations apply equally to male and female legislators.

OPERATIONALIZING WOMEN'S DESCRIPTIVE REPRESENTATION, HYPOTHESES, AND METHODS

In Hanna Pitkin's classic study of political representation, descriptive representation refers to representatives who stand for their constituents in that they possess attributes that mirror the social group from which they are drawn. Thus, descriptive representation as a normative ideal implies a legislative body that mirrors the social makeup of society. Yet this concept of resemblance immediately raises questions about which attributes or characteristics ought to be represented. As Pitkin explains, "representation as 'standing for' . . . is always a question of which characteristics are politically relevant for reproduction" (1967, 87). The adoption of a quota law implies that sex is a relevant basis for representation. Critics of quotas, however, dispute the significance of sex, typically arguing that a representative's qualifications are the most relevant criteria for office.

Such arguments create a double bind for female politicians, wherein being more like men—and thus more qualified for office—may also mean being less like voters and thus unrepresentative of their constituents. This tension demonstrates how gender quotas problematize the question of who representatives are. This chapter advances new ways of thinking about the descriptive attributes of legislators. In addition to sex, we conceptualize descriptive representation as including attributes such as age and family status, level and type of education, and past political experience. This operationalization of descriptive representation allows us to assess empirically the extent to which quota women mirror Argentine women generally and whether they possess qualifications that are similar to or different from those of their male colleagues.

In light of the forces shaping political recruitment in Argentina—namely, clientelism and the predominance of male party bosses—we expect to find sex-based differences in some aspects of legislator backgrounds. Given that party leaders value executive positions, particularly executive positions with patronage opportunities, we expect significant differences in the type of past political experience held by male and female legislators. Specifically, we predict that fewer women will have served in high-profile executive branch positions. We do not, however, anticipate substantial differences in legislative experience; because gender quotas have been applied federally since 1993 and are now applied in all but two provinces, we expect that women are just as likely as men to have served previous terms in legislatures (either provincial or national).

We also expect to find sex-based differences in terms of basic demographic features and educational backgrounds. We anticipate that the demands of a political career mean that female legislators are more likely to be unmarried and have fewer children when compared with male legislators. Given Argentina's level of development—a middle-income country with relatively good social indicators—we expect most women in Congress, along with their male counterparts, to hold university degrees. We predict, however, that educational specialization will reflect traditional gender roles, with men studying law and medicine and women studying education. Yet university education correlates with membership in elite social sectors, which means that the more elected women resemble their male colleagues, the less they resemble their female counterparts in society.

To test these hypotheses, we use data from the *Directorio Legislativo*, published by an Argentine research NGO created in 1999. Each legislative term, the NGO staff surveys legislators and compiles a directory that reports on the demographic, socioeconomic, and political careers for each member of Congress. Our data set thus includes biographical data from all lower-house legislators serving in the Argentine Congress. We cover 531 legislators from four congressional terms: 1999–2001, 2001–2003, 2003–2005, and 2005–2007. In a few cases, our data set contains deputies who began but did not finish their terms or legislators who entered to replace a resigning deputy. Including those who resigned and their replacements does not bias our results, as our focus is on the attributes that legislators have when they enter office. Likewise, we count legislators for every term served; this multiple counting captures how legislators' pathway data change each time they assume office. For instance, if the legislator served first from 1999 to 2003 and again from 2003 to 2007, we count that legislator twice: the first time, he or she is coded as having no prior lawmaking experience, and the second time, he or she is coded as an incumbent with lawmaking experience. In instances where serving multiple terms would not change the pathway data, such as for degrees and for prior political service, we count the legislators only once.[5]

We arranged the data so that the unit of observation was the legislator and the attributes were the variables of interest. Each attribute received a code that reflected a category of meaning relevant to the attribute. Degrees, for example, were assigned codes based on their type (where 1 = professional, 2 = liberal arts, and 3 = graduate).[6] When the coding ambiguity could not be resolved with background knowledge of the Argentine case (i.e., understanding the different degree titles), we dropped the observation of that attribute from the data set. Additionally, when the entry in the *Directorio Legislativo* was either blank or said "no response," we dropped the observation of the attribute for that legislator. For that reason, the number of observations for each analysis is always less than 531; not all legislators filled in all fields in the *Directorio*'s survey, leading to some missing data.[7]

Data on legislators' traits are not available before 1999. Our data set thus begins with the women elected four years after the Ley de Cupos had its largest numerical effect (in 1995) and six years after the Ley de Cupos first applied in a national election (in 1993). For these reasons, we cannot test for differences in the qualifications between pre-quota and postquota women, and so we cannot determine whether the quota caused parties to change their preferences for certain types of women. We can, however, compare the types of women elected postquota to the types of men elected postquota. This comparison reveals who female legislators are as a group, compared with who men are as a group, and whether the data support claims about quota women's lack of merit.

DEMOGRAPHIC ATTRIBUTES OF LEGISLATORS

In general terms, our study supports the hypothesis that female legislators' family lives are structured by the demands of political careers. First, we analyzed the differences in the proportions of male and female legislators in various age categories. We found that most legislators serve their terms during their thirties, forties, and fifties, with no meaningful or statistically significant difference between the ages of the men and the ages of the women (Chi^2 = 6.282; Pr = .280). Second, we compared legislators' marital status, finding that 81.4 percent of male legislators were married or in common-law relationships, compared with 55.7 percent of women. The results on marital status are statistically significant below the 1 percent level (Chi^2 = 49.949; Pr = 0), confirming strong differences between male legislators' and female legislators' relationship types. Female legislators appear less confined by domestic partnerships. Further, when comparing female legislators with women in the general population, we find slightly lower marriage rates for female politicians: the 2001 Argentine census reports that nearly 65 percent of households consist of cohabiting or married couples, compared with 55 percent for the female politicians in our data set.

Third, differences in family size indicate the greater constraints that caretaking responsibilities pose for women in politics. In the data set, 97 percent of male legislators have children, compared with 84 percent of women. In terms of the number of children, moreover, women report smaller families than men. While the proportions of women and men with one or two children are relatively close (34.9 percent of women, 42.7 percent of men), the gap between the proportions grows as the number of children increases. Sixty-one percent of men have three or more children, compared with only 41.3 percent of women, and 11.6 percent of men have five or more children, compared with only 4.8 percent of women. The differences in proportion are statistically significant (Chi^2 = 33.726; Pr = 0). While the majority of Argentine women have three or more children, the majority of female legislators (58 percent) have two or fewer.[8] These findings suggest that family obligations may diminish women's opportunities to pursue political careers, as evidenced by the fact that female legislators are more likely to be single and have fewer children when compared with the national average.

EDUCATIONAL LEVEL AND SPECIALIZATION

Overall, Argentine legislators are highly educated, with nearly 82 percent holding a degree. When examining the differences between men and women, we find a statistically significant difference: 21 percent of men have no degree, compared with only 12 percent of women (Chi^2 = 4.9011; Pr = .027). Women in Argentina's Congress are thus likely to be more educated than both their male colleagues and women in the general population. From 1999 to 2002, Argentine women's enrollment in tertiary-level educational institutions rose from 37 percent to 43 percent.[9] Less than 50 percent of Argentine women hold undergraduate degrees, compared with 88 percent of their female representatives. These data suggest two trends: first, female parliamentarians are well educated, and second, their higher levels of education mean that they are drawn from an upper tier of women within their own country.

Statistically significant and substantively interesting differences between male and female legislators appear when we examine the levels and types of degrees held by legislators. We divided legislators' university degrees into three categories: professional, liberal arts, and graduate. Professional degrees are those in law, medicine, dentistry, engineering, architecture, and accounting; liberal arts degrees are those in the social or physical sciences, arts, and education; graduate degrees are those earned at the master's or doctoral level in either a professional or a liberal arts field. Table 3.1 reports legislators' educational level by degree type. The data show that professional degrees are the most common, held by nearly 55 percent of legislators reporting their education. Men are more concentrated in this category, while women are more concentrated in the liberal arts category. Consistent with our findings that female legislators are likely to have strong educational credentials, nearly 12 percent of women have graduate degrees, compared with just 6 percent of men.

We explored educational differences further by analyzing the subtypes of degrees held by men and women in both the professional fields and the liberal arts fields. In the professional fields, we examined whether legislators were trained in architecture, law, medicine, accounting, or engineering. The typical legislator, whether male or female, held a law degree, highlighting the importance of legal training for political careers. Female legislators also held medical degrees more frequently than male legislators, again suggesting that female politicians need strong educational credentials. Women held accounting and engineering degrees less frequently than male legislators, although none of these differences was statistically significant (Chi^2 = 6.565; Pr = .161). In the liberal arts category, 58 percent of women were trained as educators, compared with 22 percent of men. By contrast, male legislators held degrees in the social sciences (nearly 67 percent) and the physical sciences (about 11 percent). These statistically significant differences (Chi^2 = 14.850; Pr = .001) suggest that female legislators' specialization in the liberal arts mirrors the occupational segregation found within Argentina.

PAST POLITICAL EXPERIENCE

Overall, Argentine legislators are experienced politicians. Yet men and women differ in their types of prior political experience. This section reports our findings on sex-based differences in past experience in the legislative and executive branches.

We begin with a straightforward assessment of the legislators' prominence within their party: their position on the party's electoral list. In Argentina, the candidate receiving the top position on a party list—the "list header"—tends to be a prominent political figure. The list header serves as the public face of the party's campaign, enjoying the most publicity and visibility. Since electoral lists are organized by province, the list header is the number one person representing the party in the province and, consequentially, well positioned to receive a leadership role within the party's congressional delegation. Thus, the top spot on a party list is a highly coveted position. Our data

Table 3.1 Legislators' educational level by degree type

	No degree	Professional	Liberal arts	Graduate	Total
Men	21.0% (60)	61.8% (176)	11.2% (32)	6.0% (17)	100% (285)
Women	11.9% (15)	38.1% (48)	38.1% (48)	11.9% (15)	100% (126)
Total	18.2% (75)	54.5% (224)	19.5% (80	7.8% (32)	100% (411)

Statistical significance (< 1%): Chi2 (3) = 49.3414; Pr = 0.

Table 3.2 Legislators appearing in top two list positions

	1	2	Total
Men	186 (87%)	45 (36%)	231 (68%)
Women	28 (13%)	81 (64%)	109 (32%)
Total	214 (100%)	126 (100%)	340 (100%)

reveal a gender gap in terms of men's and women's ascension to the top of the list. As shown in table 3.2, of the 214 list headers in the data set, women occupy only 13 percent of these prized positions. Parties appear not to choose female candidates for the most prominent positions.

This conclusion becomes stronger when we consider how the quota's placement mandate also affects parties' decisions about where to place candidates on the electoral list. According to the placement mandate, parties must place a female name in every triad with no more than two male (or female) names appearing in succession. So, if the party names a woman as the list header, this choice also determines the subsequent spots in which women are placed on the list. In this scenario, female candidates will then receive the first spot in each remaining triad: women will appear first, fourth, seventh, and tenth (rather than second, fifth, and eighth or third, sixth, and ninth). Parties thus face costs to promoting women to the top spots, for they will then have to rank women highly throughout the list. Moreover, if the party is contesting fewer than three seats, the placement mandate demands the ranking of women in either the first or the second slot (a de facto 50 percent quota). Given that no parties competing in congressional elections contest fewer than two seats, our findings demonstrate that parties are overwhelmingly relegating women to the lowest positions available that nonetheless comply with the quota. Parties largely place women in the number two slot; only 20 percent of men occupy the number two positions, compared with 74 percent of women.

To examine candidate preparedness in addition to candidate prominence, table 3.3 examines legislators' past experience in the congressional or executive branches. The values reported in the table account for all three levels of government: municipal, provincial, and federal. In terms of legislative experience, we find that a sizable majority of legislators (nearly 76 percent) have held a previous legislative post. There are no differences between women and men, with 72.4 percent of women and 77.3

Table 3.3 Legislators' past political experience

	Legislative experience			Executive experience		
	No	Yes	Total	No	Yes	Total
Men	22.6%	77.3%	100%	46.4%	54.6%	100%
	(61)	(208)	(269)	(119)	(143)	(262)
Women	27.6%	72.4%	100%	74.4%	26.6%	100%
	(35)	(92)	(127)	(81)	(29)	(110)
Total	24.2%	75.8%	100%	53.8%	46.2%	100%
	(96)	(300)	(396)	(200)	(172)	(372)

percent of men possessing lawmaking experience. Much of this experience is closely divided between legislators whose highest position was in municipal or provincial lawmaking bodies (60 percent) and those who served in the federal Congress (40 percent). Slightly more women than men entered the federal Chamber of Deputies from a subnational legislature, perhaps because of provincial-level quotas that facilitate women's local participation. Finally, while federal incumbency is low in Argentina overall (reelection rates in our data set were at 20 percent), slightly more women than men (23.6 compared with 19.0 percent) held consecutive national-level legislative posts. This finding implies that female legislators are more likely to remain in the Congress, rather than exiting to the more desirable executive positions. While none of the differences between men's and women's past legislative experience was statistically significant, the trends are nonetheless meaningful: whether past provincial legislators or federal legislative incumbents, female deputies in Argentina have parliamentary experience.

In terms of executive experience, we find greater divergence between men and women. Our categorization of executive offices includes the following positions: past presidents and vice presidents, governors, vice governors, mayors, and cabinet secretaries and ministers at the federal and provincial levels. These offices, as explained earlier, provide politicians with greater access to resources and are thus highly valuable. A majority of men, nearly 55 percent, have previously served as either a cabinet minister or chief executive of the federal government, a province, or a municipality, compared with only 26.6 percent of women (Chi^2 = 28.3218; Pr = 0).[10] However, when we examined the trajectories of the 46.4 percent of men and the 74.4 percent of women with no past executive experience, we did find that many of the women had held positions in public administration and local bureaucracies. These findings confirm two patterns. First, the majority of male and female deputies have some form of political experience, especially with lawmaking; very few men and women report no experience. Second, female deputies appear to enter the Congress from those legislative levels and bureaucratic positions to which political parties accord less value.

Finally, in order to assess legislators' overall experience, we devised a coding scheme incorporating all of the credentials of Argentina's "professional politicians." We accounted for legislators' past service in the legislative and executive branches, public administration, local bureaucracies, and political parties. Using our knowledge of the Argentine case, we categorized legislators as possessing four types of overall experience: none, low, medium, or high. Legislators with low overall experience have no prior legislative experience but may have held bureaucratic office at the municipal level or may have held leadership positions in interest groups, trade unions, or political parties, or have served as policy advisers.

Legislators with medium overall experience have some legislative experience at either the provincial or the municipal level, held bureaucratic office at the provincial or federal level, or are serving their second term as either a deputy or a senator in the federal Congress. Legislators with high overall experience have held executive office at the provincial or federal level, have served three or more legislative terms at the provincial or municipal level, or are serving their second or more term as a deputy or senator in the federal Congress. In coding both medium and high, which capture legislators' past legislative experience, we counted service as a constitutional delegate as one term at the corresponding level. In cases where legislators reported multiple elected and nonelected offices, we always counted the highest office present; for instance, if a legislator was both a trade union leader (low) and a provincial legislator (medium), he or she was coded as medium.[11]

In table 3.4, we see a number of gender-based differences when comparing the male and female deputies on their overall political experience. The differences between the group of male legislators and the group of female legislators are statistically significant well below the 1 percent level; our results are therefore both empirically relevant and substantively meaningful. First, very few women and very few men lack any background in politics whatsoever. Second, when combining the number of female legislators with both medium and high experience, we note that 91.7 percent of women enter congress with political experience, as do 93.4 percent of men. However, female legislators tend to possess medium levels of experience, compared with men who largely have high levels of experience: more than half of the women are well qualified and more than half of the men are extremely qualified for their current jobs as lawmakers. Yet a substantial portion of women are highly qualified as well—about 37 percent. Thus, while women as a whole may present fewer credentials when compared with men as a whole, the charge that quotas facilitate the entrance of incapable or unqualified women to the Congress is clearly not supported by the evidence. Female legislators in Argentina may enter the legislature having held fewer prominent positions within their parties and in politics. Nonetheless, like their counterparts in France (chapter 2 in this volume) and Uganda (chapter 4), quota women have, on average, extensive political résumés.

CONCLUSION: PATHWAYS, REPRESENTATIVITY, AND QUOTAS

This study began by expanding the concept of descriptive representation to include other potentially relevant attributes beyond sex. Our comparison of men and women serving in Argentina's national Congress reveals differences in men's and women's demographic, educational, and political backgrounds when assuming legislative office. Most notably, family commitments structure women's political careers, as evidenced by the substantial gap we find between men and women in their marital status and number of children. Further, male and female politicians in Argentina are similar in their educational levels, yet they differ considerably in the types of degrees they hold, with women less likely to hold professional degrees and much more likely

Table 3.4 Legislators' overall experience

	None	Low	Medium	High	Total
Men	3.3% (10)	3.3% (10)	37.2% (114)	56.2% (172)	100% (306)
Women	3.7% (5)	5.2% (7)	57.0% (77)	34.1% (46)	100% (135)

Statistical significance (< 1%): Chi^2 (3) = 18.694; Pr = 0 to hold degrees in the liberal arts, particularly education. Likewise, while both male and female legislators enter the national Congress with some degree of past political experience, women are less likely than men to have held those posts most highly valued in Argentine politics, that is, executive-level positions in the federal or provincial governments. As Murray notes in her analysis of descriptive representation in France (chapter 2 in this volume), differences between male and female legislators frequently stem not from women's innate inferiority but from gender-based inequalities within society and the continued barriers to parliamentary recruitment.

These findings have implications for women's representation, shedding additional light on the types of women elected through quotas. Our data show that female legislators are just as likely as male legislators to be drawn from the elite; they had access to university education and political positions before entering the federal Congress. While these data negate claims that quota women are unprepared or unqualified, they also imply that quota beneficiaries do not necessarily resemble their constituents. Our data confirm that female legislators have fewer family responsibilities, more education, and more professional opportunities than do women in society more generally. In short, beyond their sex, female politicians appear unrepresentative of women in the population.

Quotas have contributed to problematizing this distinction between elite politicians and ordinary citizens. The implementation of quotas in Argentina and elsewhere has fueled allegations of women's unpreparedness for office. Quota critics have further sought to delegitimize women elected through quotas by charging them with receiving nominations based on their elite status and connections rather than their qualifications. Yet male politicians are also elites and beneficiaries of nepotism and privilege, but they are less likely to be subjected to charges of being unrepresentative. This finding appears beyond Argentina. As O'Brien (chapter 4 in this volume) notes, in Uganda, all politicians are elite, although women receive more stringent criticisms for this status. And Sater (chapter 5) argues that in Morocco, all politicians benefit from being members of families with considerable political and economic clout. Perhaps one normative outcome of quotas—which can be evaluated in future empirical studies—will be to turn the lens of representativity onto male politicians in addition to female ones.

Further, our findings provide some empirical support for the expectation that female legislators, even if they do not perfectly mirror their female constituents, might be more inclined to act for women. For instance, many female legislators come from feminized fields of study, such as education, and have experience holding less valuable political offices, such as administrative posts; they may thus be more aware of gender discrimination both in the workforce and in political parties. These gendered experiences, in turn, can produce differences in legislators' priorities and activities. In fact, an earlier study shows that female legislators in Argentina take more responsibility for introducing bills that address women's rights issues (Franceschet and Piscopo 2008). Examining other descriptive features of legislators beyond their sex, as we have done here, provides some way of accounting for the different behavior of male and female legislators.

Much more research on this topic remains to be done. For instance, a focused study of family connections in Argentine politics would be enormously useful to address the quota's impact on assumptions about nepotism and draw comparisons between the Argentine and Moroccan cases. Anecdotal evidence indicates that both men and women benefit from nepotism in Argentina.[12] However, the rhetoric in both politics and the media emphasizes the large number of female candidates with prominent family members in politics. A task for future research is to administer a survey, along the lines of the one conducted with local candidates in France by Karen Bird (2003), to see whether there are indeed gendered patterns to nepotism in Argentina. Further testing allegations of nepotism, in addition to correlating legislators' descriptive attributes with their representative activities, would further advance our nascent understanding of who female legislators actually are and how quotas have altered patterns and understandings of descriptive representation.

NOTES

1. The authors would like to acknowledge Brian Williams for writing software that facilitated the download of the *Directorio Legislativo* data in raw form. We also thank Juliana Ramirez for early assistance in coding the data. For help with the concepts and categories in this chapter, we thank Rainbow Murray, Karen Beckwith, Mariana Caminotti, Brenda O'Neill, and Christian Höy. Jennifer M. Piscopo carried out parts of this research while in residence at the Center for U.S.-Mexican Studies at the University of California, San Diego. Susan Franceschet acknowledges the financial support of Canada's Social Science and Humanities Research Council.
2. Argentines commonly refer to this phenomenon as the *mujeres de* ("women of").
3. Jennifer M. Piscopo conducted research in Argentina from August to September 2005, in August 2007, and from February to August 2009. Susan Franceschet carried out research from July to September 2006 and June to July 2008. Both authors conducted interviews with legislators, congressional staffers, legislative assistants, and other researchers and experts on Argentine politics.
4. Piscopo interview, August 2009, Buenos Aires.
5. We also ran all analyses both ways—that is, either including or excluding the reelected legislators. In general, the results did not change based on including or excluding these few observations.
6. To ensure intercoder reliability, we communicated at each stage in data analysis; we agreed on the relevant categories, cross-checked each other's coding, and flagged and discussed any indeterminate cases.
7. In general, we discerned no systematic pattern to the missing data. The question would be, did certain types of legislators consistently not fill out the survey? Say, for instance, the legislators without any qualifications left their surveys blank, and we dropped all of those observations. Our results would then be unfavorably skewed to a subpopulation of legislators *with* qualifications, since we would be simply dropping (ignoring) the legislators *without* qualifications. We did not, however, notice any patterns wherein certain *types* of legislators left entries blank; as many male legislators as female legislators had "no response" for many items in the *Directorio*. We believe that the reasons for these "no responses" are sufficiently randomly distributed among the population of legislators and that dropping the "no responses" does not bias the results.
8. From http://globalis.gvu.unu.edu/indicator_detail.cfm?IndicatorID=138&Country=AR (accessed April 1, 2010).
9. From http://stats.uis.unesco.org/unesco/TableViewer/document.aspx?ReportId=121&IF_Language=eng&BR_Country=320 (accessed April 1, 2009).

10. This finding is also consistent with a study of gender in the Argentine Congress by Jutta Borner et al. (2009).

11. Readers who are interested in examining the coding scheme in more detail may contact the authors for a copy of their code book.

12. Las Listas, Llenas de Familiares, *La Nación*, October 8, 2007.

REFERENCES

Archenti, Nélida, and Niki Johnson. 2006. Engendering the Legislative Agenda with and without the Quota. *Sociología, Problemas y Prácticas* 52: 133–153.

Bird, Karen. 2003. Who Are the Women? Where Are the Women? And What Difference Can They Make? Effects of Gender Parity in French Municipal Elections. *French Politics* 1 (1): 5–38.

Borner, Jutta, Mariana Caminotti, Jutta Marx, and Ana Laura Rodríguez Gustá. 2009. *Ideas, Presencia, y Jerarquías Políticas: Claroscuros de la Igualdad de Género en el Congreso Nacional de Argentina.* Buenos Aires: PNUD Argentina and Prometeo Libros.

Del Mar Martínez Rosón, María. 2008. Legislative Careers: Does Quality Matter? In Manuel Alcántara Sáez, ed., *Politicians and Politics in Latin America*, 235–264. Boulder, Colo.: Lynne Rienner.

Franceschet, Susan, and Jennifer M. Piscopo. 2008. Gender Quotas and Women's Substantive Representation: Lessons from Argentina. *Politics & Gender* 4 (3): 393–425.

Jones, Mark P. 2008. The Recruitment and Selection of Legislative Candidates in Argentina. In Peter M. Siavelis and Scott Morgenstern, eds., *Pathways to Power: Political Recruitment and Candidate Selection in Latin America*, 41–75. University Park: Pennsylvania State University Press.

Jones, Mark P., and Wonjae Hwang. 2005. Provincial Party Bosses: Keystone of the Argentine Congress. In Steven Levitsky and María Victoria Murillo, eds., *Argentine Democracy: The Politics of Institutional Weakness*, 115–128. University Park: Pennsylvania State University Press.

Jones, Mark P., Sebastian Saiegh, Pablo Spiller, and Mariano Tomassi. 2002. Amateur Legislators—Professional Politicians: The Consequences of Party-Centered Electoral Rules in a Federal System. *American Journal of Political Science* 46 (3): 656–669.

Krook, Mona Lena. 2009. *Quotas for Women in Politics: Gender and Candidate Selection Reform Worldwide.* New York: Oxford University Press.

Lubertino, María José. 2003. Pioneering Quotas: The Argentine Experience and Beyond. Paper presented at International IDEA Workshop on the Implementation of Quotas: Latin American Experiences. Lima, Peru, February 23–24.

Marx, Jutta, Jutta Borner, and Mariana Caminotti. 2007. *Las Legisladoras: Cupos de Género y Política en Argentina y Brasil.* Buenos Aires: Siglo XXI Editora Iberoamericana.

Perceval, María Cristina. 2001. Avis Rarae: Impacto de la Ley de Cupo en la Argentina (1991–1998). Buenos Aires: PROLEAD–BID.

Piscopo, Jennifer M. 2006. Engineering Quotas in Latin America. Center for Iberian and Latin American Studies, Working Paper 23.

Pitkin, Hanna Fenichel. 1967. *The Concept of Representation.* Berkeley: University of California Press.

Waylen, Georgina. 2000. Gender and Democratic Politics: A Comparative Analysis of Consolidation in Argentina and Chile. *Journal of Latin American Studies* 32 (3): 765–793.

4 Quotas and Qualifications in Uganda

Diana Z. O'Brien

Gender quotas remain a controversial strategy for increasing women's presence in elected office. Central to the debates surrounding quota policies is the assumption that they promote undeserving female candidates at the expense of more meritorious male politicians. Beyond this concern, scholars and activists also worry that quotas promote elitism and are a tool for bolstering the governing regime. Despite the prevalence of these assertions, there has been only limited research on the qualifications of quota women. This chapter addresses this lacuna in the literature by using data from the current parliament of Uganda to compare the attributes of female politicians elected through the reserved seats system with those of both male and female parliamentarians elected without the assistance of affirmative action. Moving beyond the question of how many women hold elected office, it examines who is promoted via gender quota policies. In doing so, it broadens the interpretation of descriptive representation in order to explore the contradictory definitions of qualifications and provide empirical tests of the common criticisms facing quota women.

Existing studies of women's descriptive representation focus primarily on the number of seats in the legislature held by female representatives, and Uganda compares favorably with other states when viewed along this dimension. Since quotas were first implemented in 1989, Uganda has continuously met its target for women's presence in the National Assembly. Female representatives currently hold nearly one-third of seats in the legislature, the fourth-highest percentage among sub-Saharan African countries. Despite its success in promoting women's presence in office, the Ugandan quota system has been subject to concerns about candidate quality, elitism, and cronyism. Doubts about the characteristics and qualifications of the quota women have called into question the quality of women's representation in Uganda.

This chapter expands the application of the concept of descriptive representation to address these criticisms. Rather than examining only how many women the Ugandan gender quota has brought into office, it asks both who is being promoted by the reserved seats policy and how the attributes of these women compare with those of both male and female nonquota representatives. After introducing the Ugandan case, it uses insights drawn from criticisms of quota women to define three competing metrics by which their qualifications are often judged: the possession of attributes that traditionally define a meritorious candidate, elite status, and loyalty to the governing regime. Data culled from the biographies of current National Assembly members are used to assess the qualifications of quota women along these three dimensions. The data analysis explores the similarities and differences between quota representatives and other politicians on both demographic characteristics, including occupation and education level, and political attributes, including party identification, incumbency rate, previous experience, and interest in gender issues. The extent to which Ugandan quota women can be considered qualified for office is reexamined in light of this new information.

Several insights emerge from the empirical assessment of the often unquestioned assumptions about the qualifications of quota women. In contrast with criticisms forwarded by opponents of quota policies, in the Ugandan case, quota women do not differ significantly from other parliamentarians on the vast majority of indicators, and on some measures, they are even better prepared for office than nonquota legislators. Although many different measures of merit are considered, the most striking finding is that quota women have more previous electoral experience than nonquota representatives. In examining the elitism critique, the analysis indicates that while the educational and occupational backgrounds of the quota representatives do differ substantially from those of their constituents, they are no more elite than their nonquota counterparts. Finally, while only limited conclusions can be drawn from the data, the analysis fails to support the concern that reserved seats are used only to bolster the governing regime. Taken together, these results expose the contradictions inherent in defining a qualified candidate, while also demonstrating that the common criticisms of quota women may not always hold when subjected to empirical verification.

GENDER QUOTAS AND POLITICS IN UGANDA

The Ugandan National Assembly currently includes 332 representatives. Among these members are 215 county representatives who are directly elected through single-member districts via a first-past-the-post system and seventy-nine women who are directly elected to district-level seats reserved for female representatives. The remaining seats are designated for various special interest groups, including ten representatives of the armed forces, five representatives for trade unions, five representatives for the disabled, and five youth representatives. Finally, in addition to the voting members, there are thirteen ex officio positions appointed by the president and held by ministers without voting rights.

The inclusion of reserved seats for women in parliament dates back to 1989, when Uganda became one of the first African countries to adopt a quota for women. The quota policy resulted from both the lobbying of women's organizations and the political considerations of the ruling National Resistance Movement (NRM), following years of conflict and political instability. Influenced by the principles emerging from the 1985 United Nations Nairobi Conference on Women, Ugandan women returned from Kenya with a greater focus on women's participation in government. Following Yoweri Museveni's ascension to power, leaders of the women's movement advocated the inclusion of larger numbers of female representatives in government.

Museveni, in turn, viewed the creation of reserved seats as a political opportunity to solidify support among female voters, using the inclusion of female representatives as a quid pro quo for women's loyalty to the NRM (Tamale 1999; Tripp 2000). He mandated the reservation of a seat in each district for a female representative, creating thirty-four seats for women in the National Resistance Council. While the previous election in 1980 resulted in the inclusion of only one woman in the 126-seat National Assembly, following the implementation of the gender quota in 1989, women filled, but did not exceed, the quota, resulting in female parliamentarians holding 12.2 percent of seats. As the number of districts grew, the number of seats reserved for women increased in tandem, and in 1996, women gained fifty of the 276 parliamentary seats. This number increased again following the 2001 election, in which female parliamentarians won seventy-five of 304 positions (Inter-Parliamentary Union 1995; Inter-Parliamentary Union 2009).

Following Museveni's rise to power, all representatives to the new National Resistance Council were selected via an electoral college. However, in subsequent elections, county representatives were chosen through universal adult suffrage, while other interest groups—including youth, workers, and the disabled—began selecting representatives through their own organizations. As opposed to these special interest groups, women elected to reserved seats (hereafter, women district representatives) were considered not representatives of women but, instead, female representatives of the district. This distinction precluded their selection by women's organizations. Yet women district representatives were also excluded from direct elections. Instead, they continued to be selected via electoral colleges made up of members of both women's and local councils (Tamale 1999; Tripp 2003).

Because of their selection via electoral colleges, candidates campaigning for reserved seats had to garner the approval of a small number of elites rather than a districtwide constituency. These candidates were not vetted by women's organizations, nor were they screened based on the strength of their electoral platforms (Goetz 2002). There was, therefore, no mechanism for ensuring that the women selected were qualified to serve in parliament. The system also advantaged elite women who could use their wealth to procure the support of electoral college members (Goetz 2002; Tripp 2006) and easily fell victim to patronage politics. The use of the electoral college thus resulted in the election of several female NRM loyalists who owed their seats to Museveni (Goetz 2003; Tamale 1999; Tripp 2003; Tripp 2006). Because of the candidate selection mechanism, the Ugandan reserved seats system provided a quintessential example of the criticisms launched against quota policies by both politicians and scholars. The electoral colleges failed to ensure that quota women possessed qualifications comparable to those of other representatives, while also promoting elitism and cronyism.

Given the obvious limitations of this system, it was widely criticized by both scholars and members of the Ugandan women's movement. For many years, women campaigned for universal adult suffrage and for the election of quota women, but Museveni continuously thwarted these efforts (Tripp 2003; Tripp 2006). Despite repeatedly refuting these demands, in 2006, women district representatives were directly elected to office for the first time (Electoral Commission of Uganda 2006). The transition to direct elections was part of a broader set of constitutional reforms. Internal conflicts between factions within the NRM led Museveni to reverse his long-held opposition to a multiparty system, and in a July 2005 referendum, more than 90 percent of voters approved a return to multiparty politics (Makara, Rakner, and Svåsand 2009). The 2006 elections thus heralded the end of twenty years of "no-party democracy" and introduced universal adult suffrage and the election of quota women. Comparatively speaking, women were successful in these elections, gaining 31 percent of seats in parliament. In addition to the seventy-nine women district representatives, at the time of data collection in 2009, there were also sixteen female county representatives, six female special interest representatives, and one female ex officio representative, bringing the total number of women in the Ugandan National Assembly to 102.

DATA AND METHODS

The historical context and design of the quota policy make Uganda an ideal case for an analysis of the qualifications of quota women. The Ugandan National Assembly implemented a quota policy long before most other states. In comparison with studies that examine quota women in the elections directly following the policy adoption, assessing parliamentarians' qualifications several elections after the quota was first implemented provides results that are less subject to the variability inherent in the initial implementation period. Beyond the longer time horizon, the use of electoral colleges historically made Uganda a most likely case for demonstrating the veracity of antiquota criticisms. Although the direct election of quota women mitigates many of these previous concerns, the history of the reserved seats policy makes analyzing the qualifications of current quota women particularly salient in the Ugandan case.

Beyond the historical context, the reserved seats policy also allows for the comparison of quota women with both nonquota men and nonquota women, allowing for the distinction between quota and sex effects. In contrast to legislative quota policies that apply to the candidate slate, reserved seats policies allocate positions for women in legislative assemblies that men are ineligible to contest. Legislative quotas make it difficult to distinguish between quota and nonquota representatives, since following their implementation, all female candidates became quota women. In Uganda, however, there is a clear distinction between women who are vying for reserved seats and women who are running against men for seats as county representatives. Comparing the qualifications of the seventy-nine quota women with those of the 199 male and the sixteen female county representatives elected without the assistance of affirmative action provides clear comparisons between quota and nonquota representatives. It also distinguishes the influence of the quota policy from the broader effects of sex differences between politicians.

In order to compare quota women with other parliamentarians, data were gathered on the 294 directly elected members of the current Ugandan National Assembly.[1] Members of the eighth parliament of Uganda, serving from 2006 until 2011, were selected for several reasons. Given the extensive research conducted on the reserved seats system prior to the electoral reforms, analysis of the quota policy after this transition represents a new contribution to the literature on women's representation in Uganda. Focusing on these representatives also allows for the assessment of the consequences of the quota policy under the new electoral framework, rather than examining data from a system that is no longer in place. Moreover, analysis based on the parliamentarians elected in 2006 provides the groundwork for comparisons between pre- and postreform periods, allowing for the reevaluation of earlier criticisms within the new electoral environment. Finally, focusing on the postreform period enables this research to address a broader set of literatures concerned with the qualifications of quota women who are directly elected to office in multiparty systems.[2]

The analysis in this chapter is conducted on an original data set constructed from online biographies posted on the Web site of the Ugandan parliament.[3] These biographical sketches include information on party identification, seat type, constituency, committee membership, education and work histories, relevant prior political experience, and special interests.[4] Using these data, the qualifications of district representatives are compared with those of male and female county representatives using the nonparametric Fisher's Exact Test with 100,000 Monte Carlo simulations and Cochran-Mantel-Haenszel tests. The comparisons generated from these simple statistical analyses provide an initial test of the veracity of the claims concerning the qualifications of quota women.

DEFINING AND OPERATIONALIZING QUALIFICATIONS

While the Ugandan quota has dramatically increased the number of women in office, it has also been criticized for elevating candidates who do not possess the merits to hold office, advantaging elite women, and promoting loyalists who owe their seats to the governing regime. Although these concerns are particularly salient in the Ugandan case, they reflect a broader set of criticisms levied against quota women cross-nationally. The first argument, which is more commonly voiced by politicians, claims that the women elected via quota policies do not merit their positions in office. The other critiques, which are more frequently articulated by activists and scholars, claim that quotas promote representatives who fail to represent women's interests as a result of their elite status and loyalty to the governing regime. Although these three criticisms highlight different aspects of the definition of a qualified candidate, each is fundamentally based on the fear that quotas bring the wrong candidates into office.

Despite the prevalence of these concerns, existing research provides mixed evidence in support of these criticisms. A number of case studies reveal differences between quota women and other politicians on demographic indicators that shape perceptions of merit, including age, educational level, and employment history (see, for example, chapters 2 and 3 in this volume). Merit is also typically defined in terms of prior political experience. While several studies find that quota women have less experience than nonquota legislators (Kolinsky 1991; Sater 2007), others find only marginal differences between the two groups (chapters 2 and 3 above).

Although scholars and female activists reject the argument that there are not enough qualified women to serve in political office, they remain concerned that electoral affirmative action disproportionately benefits elite women. Several studies criticize quotas for promoting women whose only qualification is their personal relationship with powerful men (Chowdhury 2002) or whose socioeconomic status does not adequately mirror the characteristics of their female constituents (Pupavac 2005; Rai 1999). In other cases, however, the accusations of nepotism are largely unwarranted (Franceschet and Piscopo 2008), and quota women are no more likely than other candidates to be promoted because of family ties (Zetterberg 2008).

Since quota women owe their place in office to the elites who either select them for the designated seats or control their position on the slate of candidates, there is also a concern that they have no incentive to deviate from the demands of the party leadership. Existing research indicates that quota women are often selected because of their loyalty to political parties (chapter 5 in this volume) and that these policies result in the co-optation of female legislators (Rai 1999). These concerns are particularly prevalent in those countries using reserved seats, where scholars have found that these seats have been offered as a quid pro quo for loyalty to the party (Bauer 2008; Tripp 2006) and are used to increase the strength of the ruling party (Matland 2006).

Drawing on these critiques, three competing metrics by which to evaluate the qualifications of quota women emerge: possession of the attributes that traditionally define a meritorious candidate for office, elite status, and loyalty to the governing regime. These claims indicate that the definition of a qualified candidate remains contested. The inherent subjectivity in defining qualifications for office is reflected in the contradictory expectations placed on candidates by different factions. For many politicians, a qualified candidate is one who possesses the characteristics held by the existing political elite. In contrast, for activists and scholars, a qualified candidate may be one who brings a more diverse background to office and is not constrained by the existing regime. Consequently, the social and political attributes that define conventionally meritorious candidates may simultaneously identify candidates as elites or patrons of the ruling party.

ANALYZING QUALIFICATIONS

Given the contradictions inherent within the definition of a qualified candidate, instead of conducting a single analysis, this chapter evaluates quota women on each of these three metrics. To examine the first claim, it compares quota and nonquota representatives on both demographic attributes, such as educational level and occupational background, and political characteristics, including previous experience in the bureaucracy and elected office, which are traditionally used to define merit. Elite status is evaluated by comparing the educational and occupational backgrounds of quota women with both nonquota parliamentarians and the Ugandan population. Finally, in order to assess the third claim about loyalty to the governing regime and the co-optation of quota women, this chapter evaluates incumbency, party identification, and commitment to women's issues. Together, these analyses examine not only whether Ugandan quota women are more or less qualified than their counterparts but also along which of the competing dimensions of qualification these differences appear.

Educational Background

A parliamentarian's educational background not only influences whether she is perceived as capable of governing but also reveals whether she can be considered more elite than her constituents and fellow parliamentarians. The Ugandan constitution (article 80, section 1) stipulates that in order to be eligible to serve in parliament, candidates must have "completed a minimum formal education of Advanced Level standard or its equivalent."[5] This requirement obviously limits the range of educational backgrounds of parliamentarians, and all of those listing their educational level report at least a postsecondary certificate. While a higher percentage of county representatives have bachelor's and advanced degrees, the difference between quota and nonquota representatives is not statistically significant (p = .152). Further analysis also fails to indicate a difference between the educational attainment of reserved seats representatives and female county representatives (p = .316).[6]

Occupational Background

Like education, occupational background is a key determinant of perceptions of both merit and elitism among parliamentarians. Highly skilled careers generally hold more prestige than low-skilled work, and absence from the labor force may preclude one from gaining political office by limiting public sphere participation. The majority of parliamentarians provided detailed career histories, with more than 85 percent of county representatives and approximately 90 percent of women district representatives reporting their occupational backgrounds. While for the remaining parliamentarians it is impossible to distinguish nonparticipation in the labor force from simply choosing not to report prior occupational experience, given the high percentage of women district representatives who reported a work history, it is clear that the vast majority of quota women are not just the wives and daughters of powerful men but, instead, have ample professional experience.

In order to compare the employment history of quota and nonquota representatives, the occupations of Ugandan parliamentarians are categorized using two classification schemes: the first uses career categories identified by the Ugandan Bureau of Statistics for the national census; the second uses the most frequently listed careers of representatives in the previous parliaments to devise a classification scheme for current legislators. For both the census and the alternative coding schemes, there is a statistically significant difference in the occupations pursued by county and women district representatives (p < .001).[7] Further analysis of the data based on the second coding scheme indicates that the difference is primarily driven by membership in the field of education (p < .001).[8] While only 11 percent of county representatives were educators, 38 percent of district representatives reported working in this field. A one-sided Fisher's Exact Test indicates that the percentage of educators among quota women is also significantly greater than among female county representatives (p = .040).

While the disparity in occupational history is greatest in the field of education, the one-sided Fisher's Exact Test also indicates that county representatives are more likely to come from the field of law than are women district representatives (p = .037). However, there is no difference between quota women and female county representatives (p = .463). Rather, male parliamentarians are simply more likely to come from the legal profession than are female legislators (p < .001). Beyond these two career types, there is neither a statistically significant distinction between the quota and the nonquota representatives generally nor one between the quota women and female county representatives specifically in any other field.

Party Identification

Given that the position of district representative has often been awarded to NRM loyalists, it is important to examine whether after the transition to the multiparty system, reserved seats continue to be controlled by the movement. The NRM may have an incentive to seek to maintain control of these positions in order to bolster parliamentary support for Museveni, and this dominance may in turn offer some support for the argument that reserved seats policies are used to strengthen the ruling party. The data indicate that of the county representatives, 65 percent are NRM members, while 73 percent of women district representatives identify with the movement. Although a slightly greater percentage of quota women are affiliated with the NRM, the difference in party membership between these two groups is not statistically significant (p = .202), nor is there a difference between women reserved seats and women county representatives (p ≈ 1).

Incumbency

Status as an incumbent can be considered both a positive and a negative attribute in assessing the qualifications of quota women. For those concerned primarily with the question of merit, having previously served in the National Assembly indicates that a quota woman has the experience necessary to warrant her position in office under the multiparty system. Those concerned about elitism and patronage, however, may argue that incumbency indicates that quota positions continue to be filled with candidates who gained their positions via their elite status and loyalty to the NRM under the electoral-college/no-party system. Forty-six percent of the women district representatives serving in the seventh parliament were reelected to the eighth parliament, and although a smaller percentage of women district representatives are incumbents—38 percent, as opposed to the 46 percent of county representatives—the difference is not statistically significant (p = .269).[9] As was the case for county representatives broadly, the percentage of parliamentarians serving multiple terms also failed to differ significantly between reserved seats women and women county representatives (p = .785). Thus, despite the limits on the conclusions that can be drawn from these data, the results do indicate that turnover among quota women does not differ dramatically from that among nonquota representatives.

Prior Political Experience

Whereas previous research suggests that quota women have less political experience than their nonquota counterparts, these results do not generalize to the Ugandan case. First, there is no difference in the reported levels of bureaucratic experience of county and women district representatives (p = .598), nor is there a difference in the experience levels of quota women and nonquota women (p = .285).[10] Although the data do not indicate a significant distinction between rates of prior service in the bureaucracy among county and district representatives, there are differences in the previous electoral experiences of these groups. In contrast with expectations, however, the data indicate that women district parliamentarians report significantly *more* experience as elected officials than do nonquota legislators (p < .001). Whereas only 21 percent of county representatives claim to have served in another elected office before winning election to the National Assembly, 43 percent of quota women report having been previously elected to office. The distinction is even greater when comparing reserved seats women with women county representatives, as less than 13 percent of nonquota women report having served in another elected office (p = .025).

Interest in Gender Issues

If the women elected to office are party loyalists who have been co-opted by the governing regime, they should be no more or less likely than other party members to express interest in women's issues. In contrast, if the reserved seats attract women who identify as feminists or create a feeling of obligation among female legislators to act on behalf of women, then quota women should be more likely than other parliamentarians to indicate concern for these issues. In order to evaluate commitment to women's issues, representatives are compared based on the articulation of interest in women's issues and service on committees explicitly concerned with gendered topics.

Parliamentarians are encouraged to list special interests in their biographies. From these interests, they are scored using an indicator variable, receiving a one if they explicitly express concern with women's or gender issues—such as "promoting girls' education" and "reproductive rights and health"—and a zero otherwise. Although claiming an interest in women's issues does not necessarily translate into the pursuit of similar legislative initiatives, it is a low-cost mechanism to signal a commitment to serving female constituents. Thus, while the measure does not capture a representative's propensity to act for women, it does demonstrate a desire to appear as if one is committed to doing so. In this respect, the measure captures the obligation that quota women may feel to present themselves as representatives of women, rather than just representatives of their party. Among quota women, 20 percent articulated an interest in women's issues. A smaller percentage of nonquota women made similar claims (only 12 percent), although the difference between the two groups is not statistically significant (p = .525). Of the 199 male representatives, however, only two express similar interests, and the difference between male and female representatives is statistically significant (p < .001). Thus, while quota women are more likely to express concern with women's issues, this interest is explained by sex rather than seat type.

Parliamentarians may also signal their commitment to gender issues through their committee membership. In Uganda's parliament, committee assignments are largely at the discretion of the representatives (Hanssen 2003), and committee membership thus reflects the preferences of the legislator. The primary committees associated with women's and gender issues are the Committee on Gender, Labor and Social Development and the Committee on Equal Opportunities. Obviously, because these committees have broad agendas, parliamentarians may be motivated to join them out of concern for nongendered issues. Despite this limitation, differences among legislators clearly emerge. Twenty-eight percent of female parliamentarians serve on a gender-related committee, compared with only 12 percent of male representatives. While there is a statistically significant difference between male and female parliamentarians (p < .001), membership rates do not significantly differ between quota and nonquota women (p = .507). As was the case with the articulation of gendered interests, differences in committee assignments are explained by sex rather than seat type.

EVALUATING CRITICISMS OF QUOTA WOMEN

While political opponents claim that quotas promote women who do not merit their positions in office, scholars and activists are more concerned about the elite status and loyalty to the governing regime exhibited by quota candidates. In light of the statistical analysis, these criticisms are reexamined to determine whether they hold in the Ugandan case. Although the data allow for stronger conclusions to be drawn about some of these claims than about others, when taken together, the empirical evidence provides significant insights into the common criticisms of quota women, suggesting that many of these are misplaced.

Quotas Promote Nonmeritorious Women

Data on Ugandan parliamentarians refute the assertion that quota women are less deserving of their positions than other legislators. Although many different measures of merit were considered, quota women always met the standards set by nonquota legislators. There were no statistically significant differences between women district and county legislators in educational level, rate of workforce participation, incumbency rate, or experience serving in the bureaucracy. The analysis does indicate that women holding reserved seats have pursued different career paths from those of other parliamentarians, as they are more likely to report a career in education than are both county representatives generally and female county representatives in particular. However, while a career in education may be less prestigious than a career in law, it fails to indicate that a legislator does not merit her position.

In considering qualifications for office, the most striking finding is that women district representatives are more likely to have previous electoral experience than both male and female county representatives. In this respect, quota women are actually more qualified than the nonquota legislators. There are several potential explanations for this disparity. While party leaders may be aware of viable candidates for county representative who have not previously served in office, it may be a norm that district representatives are drawn primarily from women who have served on local councils. Alternatively, there may be a smaller field of women who participate in politics, making these women more likely to win seats reserved for women at both the local and the national level.

Preliminary evidence does indicate that the elections for women district representatives draw fewer challengers, averaging 2.7 candidates per seat in the 2006 election, as compared with the 3.7 candidates running for the county representative seats. Without a qualitative case study analysis, however, it is impossible to do more than speculate about the causes of these differences. Nevertheless, it is clear that quota women are no less qualified to hold office than men on many of the conventional indicators of candidate merit and are more qualified on one of the most important attributes shaping perceptions of politicians' preparedness to serve in parliament. Thus, the Ugandan case provides no support for the political rhetoric that quotas promote undeserving women to office.

Quotas Promote Elite Women

In examining the veracity of the assumption that gender quotas promote elite women, the evidence is mixed. The women occupying the district seats undoubtedly differ from average Ugandan women in terms of educational and occupational background. While all of the quota women have some advanced education, census data indicate that 32 percent of Ugandan women older than fifteen have no formal education. Similarly, although most reserved seats women report a work history, labor force participation among females is only 51 percent in rural areas and as low as 43 percent in urban centers. Of those women participating in the workforce, more than 80 percent report farming as their source of livelihood, whereas only 5 percent of quota women report a career in agriculture (Uganda Bureau of Statistics 2006). These demographic differences indicate that on average, women district representatives are undoubtedly more privileged than the majority of their female constituents.

Although quota women are clearly of a higher social status than the majority of the Ugandans whom they represent, it is misleading to imply that quotas promote elite women at the expense of candidates who would more closely mirror the demographics of their constituents. The statistical analysis indicates that quota women are no more elite than their nonquota counterparts. First, there are no significant differences in level of education between the women district and county representatives, a finding that is unsurprising given that the requirements governing candidate selection explicitly exclude those who do not have the requisite educational experience. While there are some differences in occupational background—almost 40 percent of quota women are educators, whereas 40 percent of county representatives are concentrated in law and business—these differences indicate that quota women come from less prestigious careers than county representatives.

Second, like reserved seats women, county representatives also have markedly different educational and occupational backgrounds from those of the average Ugandan. While the vast majority of county representatives hold a bachelor's degree, only three out of every one hundred Ugandans has any postsecondary education. Similarly, although more than two-thirds of Ugandans report subsistence farming as their source of livelihood, less than 10 percent of county representatives are agriculturalists (Uganda Bureau of Statistics 2006). Thus, while quota women are more elite than their female constituents, it is also the case that virtually all parliamentarians are more elite than those they claim to represent. While quotas may bring elite women into office, on all measures considered in this analysis, quota women are no more elite than any other representatives.

Quotas Promote Party Loyalists

Beyond concerns about elite status, quota policies have also been charged with promoting party loyalists who are selected on the basis not of their competence but of their allegiance to the governing regime. Of the three claims, this is the most problematic to examine given the data available. It is difficult to quantify whether a candidate was selected simply because of loyalty to party elites, and additional research on parliamentary voting records is needed to establish whether quota women are less likely to deviate from the party agenda than other representatives. Despite these constraints, however, limited conclusions can be drawn from this analysis.

While quota women may be selected on the basis of their party loyalty, the data clearly indicate that this does not occur at the expense of their qualifications for office. On the many different measures of merit that were considered, women district representatives always met or exceeded the standards set by the county representatives. Analysis of party identification further indicates that quota women are no more likely to be NRM members than are nonquota representatives. As the percentage of opposition members and independents was similar across groups, it appears that reserved seats are no longer used solely to bolster Museveni's regime.

Finally, incumbency rates do not differ between quota and nonquota representatives, indicating that following the electoral reforms, the number of quota women who entered parliament under the electoral college system has remained no higher than the number of county representatives who entered office during the no-party system. Thus, even if women elected under the electoral college system were selected only because of their loyalty to the NRM, following the 2006 election, these women were no more likely than other parliamentarians to have retained their positions in office.

Much of the concern about party loyalty is centered on the assumption that quota women will be co-opted by the governing regime and will therefore fail to advocate for women's substantive representation. While analysis of bill introduction and adoption is beyond the scope of this research, the data do provide information on legislators' interest in women's issues. The analysis indicates that both female county representatives and quota women are more likely than male county representatives to list women's issues among their special interests and to sit on committees that deal with these issues.

Although these findings do not necessarily negate the possibility that quota women are selected because of their willingness to kowtow to party leaders, this preliminary analysis indicates that even if quota women are selected on the basis of party loyalty, this does not necessarily imply that they are less concerned with women's substantive representation. The reserved seats policy does not, on the other hand, appear to create an obligation for these representatives to articulate an interest in women's issues, as quota women do not demonstrate a greater propensity to express these concerns than female county representatives.

CONCLUSION

Expanding the concept of descriptive representation to account for the characteristics of quota women provides significant insights into the concerns raised about these policies. The analysis in this chapter presents two key lessons about the qualifications of quota women. The first, which is primarily theoretical, is that scholars may need to reexamine how they define a qualified quota representative. In operationalizing qualifications, it became clear that the expectations placed on quota women are often in tension with one another. The educational, occupational, and political characteristics that allow quota women to be perceived as meriting their positions in office also define them as elites or party loyalists. Moreover, while quota women are criticized for being selected only because of their loyalty to the political party, this loyalty is a key determinant in moving from the party rank-and-file into positions that allow women to become key actors in determining the party's policy agenda. Thus, when criticizing quota women for elite status or loyalty to the existing regime, scholars of women and politics should recognize that these characteristics may be necessary for a representative to be perceived as meriting her position or to be capable of forwarding women's substantive representation. They must be careful to ensure that they are not placing unrealistic demands on quota representatives.

Beyond this theoretical contribution, this chapter provides significant insights into the veracity of the criticisms often leveled against quota women. It has been argued that quotas promote women who do not merit their positions in office, elite women, and women who are selected based only on their loyalty to the governing regime. Traditionally, Uganda would have provided a most likely case for demonstrating the veracity of these criticisms, as the electoral college system used to select district representatives did not contain any checks on candidate quality and clearly facilitated elitism and cronyism. However, even with the negative history associated with reserved seats in Uganda, data on the parliamentarians gaining office in the 2006 election fail to support many of the commonly held assumptions about quota women. The analysis clearly dismisses the arguments that quotas promote women who are less meritorious than their quota counterparts, as district representatives always met or exceeded the standards set by the county representatives. Moreover, while quota women are more elite than their female constituents, on the measures considered in this analysis, they are no more elite than their nonquota counterparts. Finally, the data provide no evidence for the assertion that quota women are more likely to be party loyalists than other representatives are or that party loyalty comes at the expense of interest in women's issues. Taken together, this analysis exposes the conflicting expectations placed on quota women and negates many of the popular arguments against their presence in office.

NOTES

1. Since this chapter focuses on the qualifications of quota women as compared with nonquota representatives, the analysis excludes the special interest representatives and ex officio members.
2. Because of the significant electoral reforms between the election of the seventh and eighth parliaments, the decision to focus on current representatives precludes the inclusion of data from earlier parliaments, as aggregating data across time periods would be theoretically unsound.
3. Data were gathered in June 2009 from the Web site of the Ugandan parliament, www. parliament.go.ug.
4. Biographies are self-reported, and parliamentarians may provide as many or as few details as they wish. All profiles contain the representative's seat type, sex, political party, and committee membership. The vast majority of parliamentarians also provide more extensive curricula vitae. More than 96 percent, for example, include their educational background, while 87 percent report their career history. This response rate is higher than one might expect from a survey of parliamentarians and is arguably no more likely to contain false information.
5. This requirement refers to the Uganda Advanced Certificate of Education (UACE), which is similar to the Advanced Level General Certificate of Education (A-Level) in the United Kingdom. Students sit for UACE examinations following two years of upper secondary school, and successful completion of these exams is a prerequisite for admission to university.
6. This finding is robust to the exclusion of representatives who do not report their educational background.
7. This finding is robust to the exclusion of representatives who do not report their occupational background.
8. The alternative coding scheme derived from past parliaments was chosen because it maintains the integrity of the census coding while reducing the total number of categories and disaggregating the fields of business and law.
9. A Cochran-Mantel-Haenszel test confirms that these results are robust to controlling for party effects ($p = .196$).
10. A Cochran-Mantel-Haenszel test confirms that these results are robust to controlling for party effects ($p = .448$, $p = .393$, and $p = .576$, respectively).

REFERENCES

Bauer, Gretchen. 2008. 50/50 by 2000: Electoral Gender Quotas for Parliament in East and Southern Africa. *International Feminist Journal of Politics* 10 (3): 347–367.

Chowdhury, Najma. 2002. The Implementation of Quotas: Bangladesh Experience. Paper presented at the IDEA Workshop, Jakarta, Indonesia, September 25.

Electoral Commission of Uganda. 2006. Scores for the Candidates for the 2006 Elections of the District Women Representatives in Parliament. http://www.ec.or.ug/Elec_results/Women%20MPs%202006.pdf (accessed July 6, 2009).

Franceschet, Susan, and Jennifer M. Piscopo. 2008. Gender Quotas and Women's Substantive Representation: Lessons from Argentina. *Politics & Gender* 4 (3): 393–425.

Goetz, Anne Marie. 2002. No Shortcuts to Power: Constraints on Women's Political Effectiveness in Uganda. *Journal of Modern African Studies* 40 (4): 549–575.

———. 2003. The Problem with Patronage: Constraints on Women's Political Effectiveness in Uganda. In Anne Marie Goetz and Shireen Hassim, eds., *No Shortcuts to Power: African Women in Politics and Policy Making*, 110–139. New York: Zed.

Hanssen, Kari Nordstoga. 2003. Can You Really Fail to Support the One Who Feeds You? An Analysis of Female Representation in the Ugandan Parliament. M.A. thesis, University of Bergen, Norway.

Inter-Parliamentary Union. 1995. *Women in Parliaments: 1945–1995*. Geneva: Inter-Parliamentary Union.

———. 2009. Women in National Parliaments: Situation as of June 30, 2009. http://www.ipu.org/wmn-e/classif.htm (accessed July 13, 2009).

Kolinsky, Eva. 1991. Political Participation and Parliamentary Careers: Women's Quotas in West Germany. *West European Politics* 14 (1): 56–72.

Makara, Sabiti, Lise Rakner, and Lars Svåsand. 2009. Turnaround: The National Resistance Movement and the Reintroduction of a Multiparty System in Uganda. *International Political Science Review* 30 (2):185–204.

Matland, Richard E. 2006. Electoral Quotas: Frequency and Effectiveness. In Drude Dahlerup, ed., *Women, Quotas and Politics*, 275–292. New York: Routledge.

Pupavac, Vanessa. 2005. Empowering Women? An Assessment of International Gender Policies in Bosnia. *International Peacekeeping* 12 (3): 391–405.

Rai, Shirin M. 1999. Democratic Institutions, Political Representation and Women's Empowerment: The Quota Debate in India. *Democratization* 6 (3):84–99.

Sater, James N. 2007. Changing Politics from Below? Women Parliamentarians in Morocco. *Democratization* 14 (4): 723–742.

Tamale, Sylvia. 1999. *When Hens Begin to Crow: Gender and Parliamentary Politics in Uganda*. Boulder, Colo.: Westview.

Tripp, Aili Mari. 2000. *Women and Politics in Uganda*. Madison: University of Wisconsin Press.

———. 2003. The Changing Face of Africa's Legislatures: Women and Quotas. Paper presented at the Implementation of Quotas: African Experiences Workshop, Pretoria, South Africa.

———. 2006. Uganda: Agents of Change for Women's Advancement? In Hannah Britton and Gretchen Bauer, eds., *Women in African Parliaments*, 111–132. Boulder, Colo.: Lynne Rienner.

Uganda Bureau of Statistics. 2006. The 2002 Uganda Population and Housing Census, Education and Literacy. http://www.ubos.org/index.php?st=pagerelations2&id=16&p=related%20pages%202:2002Census%20Results (accessed July 14, 2009).

Zetterberg, Pär. 2008. The Downside of Gender Quotas? Institutional Constraints on Women in Mexican State Legislatures. *Parliamentary Affairs* 61 (3): 442–460.

5 Reserved Seats, Patriarchy, and Patronage in Morocco

James N. Sater

In 2002, the Moroccan monarchy made the landmark decision to institute a thirty-seat reserve list for women in parliament, thereby introducing an important change to the predominant male character of politics. That year, five women were able to win seats in locally contested constituencies outside the reserve list, resulting in a total of thirty-five female parliamentarians. While hopes were high in 2002 that the reserve list would help reshape the composition of parliament and lead to spillover effects in locally contested constituencies, such hopes have not materialized. In 2007, the number of female elected parliamentarians outside the list decreased from five to four. This chapter makes some broader suggestions about the types of women who were elected through the reserve list by analyzing the relevance of the concept of neopatrimonialism for the limitations inherent in increasing women's participation in an authoritarian Middle East state.

Examining the types of women elected poses some difficulties in political systems in which informal selection processes and political influence are often more important than formal processes such as elections, criteria such as electoral support, ideology, or qualifying attributes such as education or profession. Compared with the case of France (see chapter 2 in this volume), in Morocco it is difficult to provide data on the women themselves as a result of limited public information on parliamentarians, a small sample size, and the limited experience of only one full legislative period (2002–2007). Consequently, in addition to presenting data that the author obtained through a survey conducted in 2006–2007 among female parliamentarians, this chapter focuses on patron-client relations that underlie electoral processes that allow women to hold elected office, both on the reserve list and in directly elected positions.

The main argument is that neopatrimonial loyalties have undermined the de facto unity of women in parliament based on class, educational background, and the absence of strong ideological splits between more conservative and more liberal political parties. Such loyalties express themselves in recruitment and have had, inter alia, a limiting impact on what women do once they enter the parliament. This chapter will argue that the reason for this is that gender policies, such as the introduction of a quota, are not neutral but are embedded in existing power dynamics and debates. Thus, quotas as a means of empowerment have so far limited women's ability to alter broader trends in the political sphere.

While women's inclusion in the political process may increase the legitimacy and credibility of representative institutions among the more educated populace, the strategies through which women achieve this inclusion, in fact, reproduce the authoritarian state itself and, with it, the subordination of women. One of the reasons for this is that in Morocco, reserve lists tend to put women in positions of recipients of political favors. Consequently, instead of becoming a means of empowerment, reserve lists tend to put those selected into positions of dependency vis-à-vis centers of political power.

THE MOROCCAN POLITICAL CONTEXT

Morocco's monarchical system is autocratic in the sense that all main decisions are either initiated by the monarch, Mohamed VI, or need approval by him and a small group of loyal advisers and technocrats. It is also authoritarian in the sense that the monarch's position in the political system is not subjected to public criticism, and any criticism may be punished by the courts, which are also controlled by the monarchy (Desrues and Moyano 2001, 21–47). In spite of this, Morocco enjoys a political life outside the confines of monarchical control, partly because the monarchy can look back to centuries of rule. Together with Islamic credentials through his title Amir Al Mu'minin ("Commander of the Faithful"), this gives the ruling monarchy more legitimacy than many of its Middle Eastern counterparts.

Since independence was achieved in March 1956, numerous parties have been elected to parliament and local assemblies, partly because of widespread political activism in the nationalist Istiqlal (Independence) Party in the struggle against colonial rule from 1953 to 1955. Outside of the Istiqlal Party, many other parties have sought political office. To name but a few, there are leftist political parties such as the Socialist Union of Popular Forces (USFP) and the Party of Progress and Socialism (PPS); Islamist groups such as the Party of Justice and Development (PJD); and nonpolitical "administrative" or "royal" parties such as the Constitutional Union (UC) and Popular Movement (MP). These parties were often created as a result of party splits that the monarchy partly encouraged by appointing different leaders to ministerial positions. Those not appointed regularly criticized monarchical authoritarianism and autocracy (Willis 2002, 1–22).

To deal with such criticism and political activism, and thus challenges to their rule and position, Morocco's three postindependence monarchs—Mohamed V (1956–1961), Hassan II (1961–1999), and Mohamed VI (since 1999)—have developed a strategy that Deneoux and Maghraoui (1998) call "political dualism." Periods marked by a widening of the scope of political freedom have been followed and/or accompanied by resort to more traditional means of political leadership in the form of "arbitration" and, if necessary, coercion (Deneoux and Maghraoui 1998, 104–127). Consequently, women's activism inside and outside of political parties, in addition to women's rights questions, have proceeded amid tensions between parties and the monarchy, on the one hand, and political oppression and liberalization, on the other. As a consequence, activism has been increasingly expressed in nonpartisan civil society organizations, such that all leading reforms in the area of women's rights have had a significant public support network of women active in civil society (Sater 2002, 101–118).

This context is vital for understanding the adoption of the reserve list in 2002, as is the type of electoral system used in Morocco. Until the introduction of a thirty-seat reserve list, women's representation in parliament was close to nonexistent. Two women, Latifa Bennani-Smires (Istiqlal) and Badia Skalli (USFP), were exceptions, but they owed their participation to high-level support from political parties and the royal family. Both were elected in 1993, the first women to enter parliamentary politics. Until these elections, interference by Ministry of Interior officials resulted in widespread election rigging. On its own, however, the electoral system has also made it difficult for women to be elected.

The first-past-the-post system divided the country into constituencies, in which voters were to choose among different parties' representatives by a simple majority vote. Prospective candidates, therefore, had to overcome the hurdle of being nominated by the party in a particular constituency. For women, this was a major obstacle, with parties choosing "strong" (male) candidates over women. This preference was exacerbated by intraparty competition over candidacies, which had the effect of pushing women out of the public sphere, which in a conservative Arab-Islamic context is often defined as male. The result of these interactions was the selection of very few female candidates. For example, in the 1984 parliamentary election, there were fifteen women among a total of 1,333 candidates, and none was elected (Gribaa 2009, 59).

In addition, periods of sometimes extreme political violence discouraged women's participation in formal politics, as they compounded the male character of the political field. There were two attempted military coups in the early 1970s, plus kidnappings and killings of opposition leaders such as Mehdi Ben Barka in 1965 and Omar Benjelloun in 1975. Throughout the 1980s, opposition political parties and groups called for general strikes and political disobedience, which led to hundreds of deaths and imprisonments in a period that Moroccans call the "Years of Lead." The general strikes and riots of 1984 and 1990 in response to structural adjustment policies imposed by the International Monetary Fund and Morocco's support for the United States-led coalition against Iraq were particularly violent (Zoubir 1993, 83–103).

The poor female representation in Morocco's parliamentary institution, however, is not indicative of low political awareness among women in general. On the contrary, women played an important role especially in leftist and secular parties, such as the PPS, the National Union of Popular Forces (UNFP), and the USFP. The student organization National Union of Moroccan Students (UNEM), in which women were active since the 1970s, was also a focal point for political activity (Brand 1998, 50). The close association of these groups with the general policy of dualism that the monarchy pursued vis-à-vis these groups made female politicians particularly subject to party politics, rendering them ineffective at putting women's questions on the political agenda. This led to the development of women's activism outside the area of party politics, while close connections remained, as many of the most active militants had been active, high-level members of political parties.

Since the mid-1990s, Moroccan politics has gone through some important changes. The ailing Hassan II looked for a stable transition to his son, Crown Prince Mohamed, and he needed the support of the main political parties that were then still officially in opposition. He succeeded by making some concessions in the area of human rights and women's rights, such as freeing political prisoners, creating a human rights ministry, and abrogating some restrictive provisions that required women to obtain permission from their male guardians to obtain a passport and to work (Leveau 1997, 95–113). The most important concession was a new constitution in 1996, in which a lower house of the parliament was separated from an upper house. The lower house was to be the result of direct elections, whereas the upper house was to be elected indirectly by local chambers of commerce, local municipalities, and other administrative organizations. The lower chamber was deemed more democratic and transparent because of the lower levels of interference, in addition to the fact that opposition parties fared relatively better in directly contested than in indirectly contested seats.

The result of this reorganization was that in the 1997 parliamentary elections to the lower house, opposition parties could claim a victory, and Hassan II could ask the leader of the strongest party, Abderrahman Youssoufi of the USFP, to form his government. This was despite the fact that the diversity of parties elected to the parliament meant that the strongest party, the USFP, obtained only fifty-seven out of 295 seats. The extremely fragmented political field was the result of the first-past-the-post system, which was both strongly personalized and based on patron-client relations (Leveau 1985). The government that was formed, further, remained under the authority of the king, who could command loyal parties such as the Popular Movement to participate in it.

Despite these restrictions, the government of Alternance, as it was called, had political, social, and economic reform as its main point on the agenda. The promotion of this agenda for reform was aided by the subsequent death of Hassan II on July 23, 1999, and the accession to the throne of his son Mohamed VI. The Moroccan monarchy therefore underwent some major adjustments, further made clear to all actors by the new king's emphasis on a "New Concept of Authority" in November 1999 (Bennis 2000). This new focus also included women's rights, stemming from the involvement of the government in a program sponsored by the World Bank, the "Action Plan for the Integration of Women in Development," focusing on how to integrate women into the country's development efforts.

THE QUOTA, THE MONARCHY, AND THE "GENTLEMEN'S AGREEMENT"

This drive toward electoral reform and a gender quota suited the new king, Mohamed VI, very well, as he tried to mark a shift between his rule and that of his father. After all, Hassan II was domestically considered a harsh autocrat. The "Action Plan" provided a golden opportunity, as it included controversial reforms of Morocco's conservative family code from 1958, the Moudawana. In fact, the plan divided the country between feminist groups, on the one hand, and conservative Islamic elements in political parties and Islamic groups, on the other. In March 2000, demonstrations in Casablanca and Rabat in favor of and against the plan rocked the country. The Moudawana had been an attempt to apply divine sharia law to family matters. The conflict represented a core identity question of the Moroccan nation, as Islam is not only the religion of state but also the primary source of the king's legitimacy as the country's highest religious authority and protector of Islam.

As the Commander of the Faithful, the new king was able to stop the debate and propose a compromise in 2003, reflecting the monarch's self-definition as that of arbiter and "unifier" of Morocco's fragmented society (Waterbury 1970, 146). In order to depoliticize the issue and render it a royal domain, a nonpublic commission debated the issue for two and a half years behind closed doors. The compromise was rendered public in September 2003. It upheld polygamy as a Muslim right. However, it also gave women an equal right to divorce and formalized the right to oral divorce (repudiation) that men formerly enjoyed, and it abolished the principle of guardianship that had rendered women second-class citizens.

It was just a small step from this major reform of the family code to increasing women's participation in parliament. When women's rights activists organized with female members of the political parties to propose the introduction of a quota in 2002, their demands fell on the receptive ears of the monarch. From his point of view, changes to the composition of the powerless parliament could increase both domestic and international support for the monarchy in Morocco (Deneoux and Desfosses 2007, 79–108). In addition, Mohamed VI began to call on parties to reform themselves. He attributed increased support for Islamist parties and groups to parties' "divisiveness" and "jockeying for power," irrespective of citizens' wishes and priorities. In the monarch's words, through elections, he wished to create a "healthy, rationalized political landscape" that worked on behalf of the "general policies of the nation" and did not pursue "purely political, electoral calculations" (July 23, 2007). Consequently, a quota for women was well suited to his ambitions to pursue tangible political reforms.

As in Argentina in the early 1990s, when the Network of Political Women supported a comprehensive electoral reform (chapter 3), some NGOs and female members of mostly leftist parties organized in favor of a wide-ranging quota system. A brief campaign organized by the Network of Women Partisan Leaders during electoral reforms in spring 2002 was partially successful. The original reform introduced more proportionality at the constituency level. This was achieved by establishing local party lists that competed for multicandidate semiproportional constituencies. Seizing the opportunity for more substantive reforms, women called for the establishment of a 30 percent quota for women, arguing that according to international experiences, a real impact only becomes noticeable when women achieve this proportion. As existing male members of parliament would not agree to a quota that would come at the expense of their own seats, they converged on a proposal for a quota that would expand the size of the parliament from 295 to 325 members, adding thirty seats for women, which corresponded to a quota of about 10 percent. One reason for reducing the quota from 30 percent to 10 percent was that Morocco already had two chambers numbering 295 and 260 representatives each, a fairly large number of national parliamentarians for a population size of about 32 million.

However, the special reserve list was not an official reform but, rather, the result of a simple oral promise by party leaders, or a "gentlemen's agreement," as it was called. The official explanation for this was that a law instituting a real quota would violate the principle of gender equality and nondiscrimination as enshrined in Article 8 of the Moroccan constitution (Kingdom of Morocco 1996). The quota was to be implemented in the form of a national list. All parties participating in the elections were asked to produce a list of women, and voters were to choose among them in a second vote. A system of proportional representation at the national level would then distribute the seats depending on the women's ranks on their respective party list. This arrangement gave women two options for election: presenting themselves on the national list of their party and becoming elected if the party obtained a significant percentage of votes or presenting themselves at the constituency level on a party ticket and obtaining enough support from voters after a local campaign. Either way, as illustrated below, both the candidate selection process among political parties and royal consent to, and pressure toward, the quota affected women's position toward the party system and the authoritarian state.

OPERATIONALIZATION AND DATA COLLECTION

This chapter focuses theoretically on the phenomenon of patriarchy in politics, in particular on how an authoritarian neopatrimonial state uses patriarchy as a means of sustaining itself. It is argued that because of patriarchal structures in political parties that extend to the monarchy, women who are elected through the reserve list tend to be fairly disunited, in spite of the fact that they share quite a number of socioeconomic characteristics. This mechanism is relevant to the study of Middle Eastern authoritarianism, as it illustrates how patriarchal social structures are potentially overcome in modern political development but how neopatrimonial political rule may be reproduced through the very same process.

Max Weber's 1914 theory of patrimonialism draws a distinction between traditional (patrimonial) and modern (neopatrimonial) states based on a successful claim to the legitimate monopoly over the use of coercion. The lack of monopoly over the use of coercion no longer limits neopatrimonial states, while the means of rule remain granting grace and favors (Weber 1978, 232). This means that neopatrimonial states can extend inclusion to new social categories such as women without facing any risks of losing power as a result of organic family or religious ties characteristic of traditional rule.

Evaluating the meaning of women's political inclusion, however, is problematic. Most authors writing on the Middle East point to cultural patriarchy and the neopatrimonial characteristics of authoritarian states as the main impediments to both democracy and women's equality (United Nations Development Program

2003; Joseph and Slyomovics 2001). Features of patriarchy, though, are not gender specific; the entire male political class is also regulated by patron-client relations. As late as 2007, for example, the Moroccan prime minister, Abbas El Fassi, declared that his government's program was that of the king, not that of his party. Along similar lines, close advisers of the king have founded new political parties (1984 and 2007), winning overnight landslide victories and forming broad alliances in parliament. Connections to the king thus remain the single most important political asset in Morocco.

The creation of the reserve list has not disrupted these dynamics but, rather, appears to reflect and extend these trends in relation to the women elected. Indeed, female MPs have coined the term *parachuté* ("parachuted in") to refer to the wives, daughters, and other close female relatives of party bosses who suddenly appeared on the women's lists with the support of (male) patronage. Patriarchy in Morocco, however, extends substantially beyond formal political institutions and, in the process, provides actors with important resources for political action. In fact, Morocco's peculiarity lies in the combination of parliamentary and other nonstate actors' ability to define the agenda through a multifaceted combination of networks.

In order to examine women's participation in such relations and networks, the study examined the following features of female MPs. First, how are the relationships between female MPs and political parties characterized, and how do these relate to the establishment of the quota? Second, what do the socioeconomic backgrounds of the women elected via quotas reveal about representation and class membership? Third, how successful have female MPs been when forming cross-partisan collaboration on issues of mutual concern? Fourth, what have been these women's positions vis-à-vis women's rights organization and the state, and have women been able to establish, or been prevented from establishing, autonomous constituencies? While it is difficult to pursue all of these questions equally based on the data available, each touches on a different facet of women's descriptive representation.

With these questions in mind, a variety of approaches were employed in relation to data collection. Unfortunately, inside knowledge regarding candidate selection is largely inaccessible to outside observers, and furthermore, unlike the case in many Western countries, résumés and other materials on MPs are not accessible to the public. However, information on the types of women elected via the reserve list was gathered through several alternative means. An invaluable starting point for the analysis was a series of interviews with selected parliamentarians, in addition to program officials of international aid agencies such as National Democratic Institute. This was complemented by an anonymous written questionnaire on the socioeconomic backgrounds of female MPs sent by mail and followed up by Moroccan female interviewers, which was administered in 2006–2007 (Sater 2007). Finally, Moroccan newspapers were consulted for material that is regularly published on internal power struggles in political parties, while surveys of general political attitudes were used to draw some wider conclusions about how quota women are viewed by the general public.

Women elected through the quota share a number of characteristics. Some of these are the result of how the political field evolved in the last two to three decades. Others are more directly linked to the fact that the quota is constituted as a reserved list of party nominees. The survey conducted in 2006–2007 with female MPs revealed a high degree of education, with almost 50 percent of the women in the 2002–2007 parliament holding doctoral degrees. This sheds some interesting light on the debate to which other chapters in this volume refer regarding the often-cited risk of lower qualifications among quota women. In fact, in Morocco's political system based on neopatrimonialism, the general amount of education is fairly low in the Moroccan parliament, with some deputies even being illiterate. This disparity indicates that women tend to hesitate and doubt their own qualifications before entering politics. As one female parliamentarian explained: "Men fight to death in order to get into parliament. Women don't have the same culture, and prefer not to be at the front line. You can ask a cigarette vendor whether he believes that he is capable of representing public interest in parliament, and he will say yes. You ask a woman with a Ph.D. in economics, and she will say that she doesn't believe that she knows enough about politics" (Milouda Hazib, interview with the author, May 19, 2005).

Second, the women elected through the quota had very long periods of political socialization and apprenticeship in the political parties. Almost two-thirds declared that they entered politics more than twenty years ago, with only one-third entering politics after 1980. Such political experience extends to nonparty activities: the women had substantial links to the various women's rights associations, with about two-thirds being active as presidents of their local women's rights associations. This is linked to how the quota was achieved, which, as discussed above, grew out of the high level of involvement by women's groups in debates over electoral reform. At the same time, socialization and apprenticeship are not restricted to formally entering parties or other associations. Nearly all women surveyed viewed politics as a family tradition. Most often, either their fathers or their husbands were active in politics, illustrating the strong family ties that underlie many political parties in Morocco.

Further observations might be made concerning their professional and class backgrounds. The women elected through the quota had experience in similar professional fields, primarily as high-level civil servants and as university professors. Nearly 50 percent of the women reported an annual household income of more than $48,000 (Sater 2007, 738), which compares with an annual per capita gross national product in Morocco of about $1,200. The women thus not only share similar backgrounds but are also clearly part of Morocco's political class as it has evolved over the past forty years.

Because of these similarities in political and socioeconomic background, there were attempts as early as 2004 to create an integrated Women MP Forum. However, very few women in the survey expressed the view that cross-party collaboration was an important characteristic of women (Sater 2007, 736). This suggests that patrimonial practices within the parties diminish the potential for female solidarity. Given the class background and lack of strong ideological differences—with the exception of the Islamist

PJD—this may at first appear surprising. After all, women's backgrounds would suggest a similar perspective, and the lack of strong ideological currents might be expected to lead to a higher level of pragmatism. Also, as advanced in the literature on women in politics, a higher sense of diplomacy and pragmatism based on women's experience may lead to a greater sense of unity among female parliamentarians, especially based on practical and strategic gender interests (Nelson and Chowdhury1994, 18).

Lack of ideological orientation, though, is a double-edged sword, as it may extend to the activities of female MPs themselves. As previously noted, a fundamental characteristic of women in parliament—and MPs in Morocco more specifically—is their dependency on party bosses for recruitment. This is independent of whether they are on the national list or are candidates in individual constituencies; in both cases, approval is necessary from an internal "candidate commission" that is often handpicked by party bosses. The result is the *parachuté*, the female relatives of party leaders suddenly appearing out of nowhere to occupy the top tiers of the women's lists. However, at the local constituency level, the parties' power over nomination processes operates only for relatively new and "fresh" candidates. A locally powerful woman may switch her party allegiance if a party refuses to nominate her over a male candidate. In one case, conflicts over who was to be represented at the local constituency led Fatna El Khiel to change parties and win the ticket of a rival political party, the Popular Movement. Her story has nonetheless remained an exception.

Dependency on party leadership can be detected by comparing the lists of women elected in 2002 and in 2007. Of the thirty-five members who were elected in 2002, only about 50 percent (eighteen out of thirty-five) made it back to the 2007–2012 parliament. A closer look reveals that in two parliamentary parties, the Istiqlal and the Popular Movement, all of the female parliamentarians from 2002–2007 were reelected. In contrast, not a single female parliamentarian of the USFP was reelected.

The official reason was that the party tried to be more "democratic" by "choosing" different women as the heads of the lists, away from women such as Fatima Belmoudden, Fettoum Koudama, and Rachida Benmessaoud and toward Salwa Karkri Belakziz, Aïcha Lekhmass, and Latifa Jbabdi (*Aujourd'hui le Maroc*, June 22, 2007). Looking more closely, however, it appears that with a new party head, Mohamed El Yazghi, the party leadership chose different loyalties from those that prevailed under the preceding head, Abderrahman Youssoufi. By the same token, it may not be a coincidence that neither the Istiqlal nor the Popular Movement experienced a leadership change, and all incumbent women were reappointed to national lists. Loyalty to the continuing party leadership paid off.

These patterns illustrate the particularities of Morocco's party system, in which party membership interlinks with more traditional tribal, kinship, ethnic, and regional loyalties. Even if women have proven to be very educated, motivated, and active in parliamentary politics since the introduction of the reserve list in 2002, allegiance to leaders remains the ultimate source of political success. This is true whether women present themselves on the national list, where direct patronage seems more important, or at the constituency level, where local support is more crucial. In both instances, candidate nomination processes continue to be monopolized by party leaders.

The presence of the quota does not appear to have dramatically changed these practices in a more women-friendly direction. In 2007, the socialist USFP only presented three female candidates at the tops of their local lists for Morocco's ninety-two constituencies (*Aujourd'hui le Maroc*, June 22, 2007). Overall, the number of women who were listed as candidates in the election to the lower house only marginally increased, from 266 to 269, out of a total number of candidates that increased from 5,865 to 6,691 (Gribaa 2009, 56). This means that the actual percentage of women listed as candidates by the parties dropped from 4.5 percent to 4.0 percent, during a period when major reforms increased women's rights quite substantially. Not surprisingly, just one USFP woman was elected on the local list, while the number of directly elected women dropped from five to four.

Since the 2007 election, the process of increasing women's participation has taken the role of the monarch even more to the forefront of parliamentary politics. As a new power in parliament with monarchical backing, the Authenticity and Modernity Party (PAM) welcomed professional women and started recruiting many of Morocco's female parliamentarians onto its list as it merged with other parties. By including a substantial number of women on its local lists in the 2009 municipal elections, the PAM also became an active supporter of the introduction of a local constituency quota in 2009. It supported the election of one of its local municipality female councilors, thirty-three-year-old Fatima Zahra Mansouri, to become mayor of Marrakech in June 2009. She thereby became the second female mayor in Morocco, after Asmaa Chaâbi of the PPS, who was elected in Essaouira in March 2009 (*Jeune Afrique,* June 22, 2009).

A comparison between Chaâbi and Mansouri reveals some important features regarding the types of women who are selected to positions of political authority by either the PPS or the PAM. Chaâbi at first sight appears to represent an attempt by the socialists to include the business class in its ranks, as her father, Miloud Chaâbi, is one of the wealthiest businessmen in the country. However, Miloud Chaâbi is also a powerful parliamentarian of the PPS. The pattern of electing relatives of powerful economic and political actors thus continues to prevail in one of Morocco's oldest socialist parties.

In contrast, Mansouri represents a new class of women, not only because of her age. Her father was a low-level functionary (a pasha) in the Ministry of Interior in the Marrakech area with some basic authority. This relates to the fact that the PAM was founded by the country's second most powerful man after the king and has a fairly undisguised aim to undermine the second largest party in parliament, the Islamist PJD. The case of Mansouri illustrates that the quota has had the effect of pushing a new generation of technocratic women into the political field, women outside of the established political class who otherwise lack political experience, family networks, or a coherent ideology. Yet it also appears that these women's political fortunes depend on their ability to counter the increasing attraction of Islamist parties. Thus, the women who are elected continue to lack political support groups outside of the political elite and the monarchy.

WOMEN'S SENSE OF UNITY, MOTIVATION, AND POLITICAL ACTIVISM

Initially, the changes in the 2002–2007 parliament seemed quite drastic. Up from two representatives in 1997–2002 to thirty-five in the new legislative period, women seemed to constitute a new force. The fact that five women were elected directly also indicated that the move toward the list had the indirect result of enabling women to compete successfully for some of the 295 locally contested seats. Encouraging signs also came from women's activities within the parliament. One woman from the Islamist PJD, Soumaya Khaldoun, headed one of six parliamentary committees, the Foreign Affairs Commission. Another woman, Fatna El Khiel of the Popular Movement, was elected vice president of the parliament. The fact that ideological lines seemed fairly divided on first sight, with six women coming from the Islamist PJD, did not provoke any significant divisions.

On the contrary, the movement consisting of activists from the two main women's rights organizations that helped push for the quota aimed at transforming itself into a general interparty and inter-women's rights organization standing committee in order to coordinate all women's political activities. The idea illustrated the wish expressed by many not to get drawn into party conflicts. Yet the fact that the idea never materialized also showed how divisive political activities remained. According to a women's rights activist, "once these women entered the parliament through the quota, their allegiance to the women who supported them quickly diminished" (Latifa Jbabdi, interview with the author, May 5, 2007).

Even though women in parliament have been organized in a Women MP Forum since 2005, activities in this forum have been limited partly by the importance of party politics. Securing a place on the list, expressing loyalty to leaders, and strengthening party identity leave few resources for cross-party cooperation. As one parliamentarian put it, "You are not appreciated for what you do but rather for the loyalty that you express to the [male] chief" (Milouda Hazib, interview with the author, May 19, 2005). The approach of the 2007 parliamentary elections and, subsequently, the 2009 municipal elections further suppressed intraparliamentary cooperation across party lines.

Regardless of these complications, it became clear that women had a high degree of political awareness concerning the exceptional nature of their presence and potential threats to their political survival. Toward the middle of the 2002–2007 session, two such threats emerged. In 2005, women faced the threat of having other underrepresented groups, such as business leaders and members of the liberal professions, put on the national list, too. After all, the national list was a women's list based only on an oral promise by (male) political party chiefs. After intensive cross-party mobilization that included the Women MP Forum, the PPS proposal was rejected. This was an issue that would have potentially affected all women equally.

In contrast, a second threat that emerged in 2006, a debate over increasing the original 3 percent hurdle on the national list to 6 percent, would have affected only a handful of female parliamentarians. The measure was a move toward the creation of more cohesion in Morocco's extremely fragmented parliament: twenty-three political parties were represented in 2002–2007, with the smallest party obtaining just one seat. Because the increase of the minimum from 3 percent to 6 percent only affected women from smaller groups, it did not trigger cross-party collaboration among women, and the proposal was subsequently adopted.

By far the most important reform that was partially initiated by women in parliament has been the establishment of a 12 percent local quota for municipal elections in 2009. Overnight, 2,822 out of 23,367 local representatives were women, up from

127 elected in 2004. Morocco's municipal councils, however, have little power or budget. As in national politics, most local politics is decided by a royal parallel system consisting of royal representatives (*walis*) and governors who are linked to the centralized Ministry of Interior, headed by a royal appointee. Nevertheless, symbolism is highly important, as Moroccan women's quest for more equality has focused extensively on achieving equal representation and overcoming legal inequities.

Although opponents argued that there was a lack of qualified women at the local level, the main women's rights associations mobilized together with female MPs in favor of more balanced representation. Again, however, links to political parties were frequent. For example, Latifa Jbabdi, the president of the Feminine Action Union (UAF), one of the two most prominent women's rights associations, was appointed to the USFP local 2007 parliamentary list in the capital city of Rabat. Another group, the Democratic Association of Moroccan Women (ADFM), started as the women's section of the PPS. While links to parties are helpful, one consequence has also been rivalries among women's groups, again illustrating the role of patronage in shaping gender identity and representation.

The UAF initiated a "women helping women" network similar to the 2002 "women's leadership" network which mobilized for the thirty-seat reserve list. However, this network only partially harnessed support from other groups because of the UAF's links with the USFP. A similar campaign was initiated by the Movement of Thirds. Here, under the leadership of the ADFM with its close links to the PPS, women mobilized in order to increase the national quota from 10 percent to 30 percent, in addition to the new municipal quota. In this campaign, the main protagonists were PPS parliamentarians, such as Fatima Farhat (www.afrik.com, November 19, 2009). While both campaigns emphasized different aspects of the women's quota, the two mobilizations did not mutually reinforce each other and remained fragmented. In the end, only the municipal quota was adopted when the king announced on October 12, 2008, that "Our ultimate project is to guarantee a just representation of women at the municipal level."

CONCLUSION

This chapter suggests that political expedience and patronage have led to divisions among female MPs and groups in civil society in spite of the similar class and educational backgrounds of female MPs. While reform programs in the area of women's rights have become very important in Morocco's reformed political system since the accession of Mohamed VI in 1999, these reforms have been limited by such divisions. While these divisions limited the ability of these women to push for more substantial changes, it needs to be pointed out that they did not render women second-class politicians, a concern that other contributions in this volume have addressed. Rather, substantial divisions are a common feature of all parliamentarians in Morocco, rendering them all second-class politicians dominated by an alternative system of power, the monarchy. These limitations lead to a number of conclusions and implications with respect to how women's rights are addressed and how such activities and reforms are perceived by the Moroccan population.

First, despite the limitations caused by party politics, the symbolism of women's empowerment through quotas has clearly struck a nerve among Moroccan feminists and academics. Mohamed VI's "new" Morocco is more securely based on the perceived empowerment of women. Women's groups' strategy has been to influence debates and public awareness, as Khadija Errebah of the ADFM explains: "When the women's movement demands that the quota should be made a law and that a third of the seats should be reserved for women, we do not expect to be immediately successful. Instead, we want to increase pressure that will show its fruits sometime later on" (cited in El Azizi and Lamlili 2006). For such pressure to bear fruit, women invoke the king's support as the ultimate way of achieving any reforms. According to the current minister of social affairs, Nouzha Skalli, "A royal will often follow social pressure, and it is our role to articulate this pressure" (interview with the author, May 20, 2005). Consequently, women have used Morocco's established hierarchies inside and outside of political parties.

Second, the population's exclusion from such participation has not stimulated a general awareness with regard to questions of gender equality and justice. A nationwide survey published by *Le Monde* in France and *TelQuel* in Morocco in August 2009 offers some important clues in this respect. According to some of the results, despite the political elite's largely consensual approach to gender reforms that are led by the king, the population at large has so far remained fairly unreceptive to such ideas. The king's overall program of change received a 91 percent approval rating and was only tarnished with regard to one question: about 50 percent of those surveyed reported that the country had gone too far in the area of women's rights. While this is certainly more a result of the changed family law, the Moudawana, it also includes a general perception of women's empowerment and the role of women in leadership positions. Despite continuing inequalities both quantitatively and qualitatively, only 16 percent of the surveyed population believes that women should have more rights (*Le Monde*, August 3, 2009).

Third, the disparity between political changes and perceptions somewhat reflect extreme social disparities and the channels through which political changes are achieved. The social, cultural, linguistic, and tribal divisions between urban and rural areas remain immense. Although changes in women's rights have had strong roots in civil society, the organizations that pushed for most of the changes remain the realm of an educated elite with only marginal links to the urban and rural poor. The ADFM, for example, explicitly views itself as an intellectual organization. Consequently, the social space among lower-income groups is taken up by Islamist charity workers and Islamic movements, such as Jama'at Al Adl Wal Ihssane and Al Tawhid wa al Islah. Women's strategies reflect the fact that in Morocco's postcolonial history, political success has never been a result of mass mobilization. Instead, changes only occurred as a result of an interelite bargain focusing on the king as the primary distributor of favors. It appears that the consequence of this system and such strategies has been that the quota and some of the reforms that are associated with increased women's rights remain far removed from the everyday experience of Morocco's large pool of undereducated and traditional citizens.[1]

Finally, this leads to a major challenge faced by women's increased participation in politics through the quota. The aforementioned low approval rating of the symbolic changes of more women's rights needs to be understood within the Moroccan population's overall assessment of its political class. A 2007 survey conducted by Al Akhawayn University in Ifrane on attitudes toward parties indicates that the assessment of political parties has reached a historical low and that all electoral consultations are viewed as little more than a mechanism through which the country's political elite is enriching itself (Sater 2009, 392). This is related to the main nature of Moroccan political parties, adamantly described by Willis as "little more than large-scale interlinking patron-client relations" (2002, 8). One deviation of such patron-client relations has become vote buying, an activity that in some electoral districts is reported by about half of all voters (Zerhouni and Baboussa 2008, 67). As Moroccans' general attitude toward their political class is very negative, quotas and other instruments of women's empowerment may, in fact, only mean that women's rights are increasingly associated with a highly unpopular group of politicians.

NOTE

1. According to UNICEF statistics, only about 52 percent of Morocco's adult population is literate. See http://www.unicef.org/infobycountry/morocco_statistics.html.

REFERENCES

Bennis, Azzedine. 2000. A propos du Nouveau Concept de l'Autorité. *Alternatives, Lettre d'Information et de Réflexion*, no. 6 (January), Casablanca.

Brand, Laurie. 1998. *Women, the State, and Political Liberalization: Middle Eastern and North African Experiences*. New York: Columbia University Press.

Deneoux, Guillaume, and H. R. Desfosses. 2007. Rethinking the Moroccan Parliament: The Kingdom's Legislative Development Imperative. *Journal of North African Studies* 12 (3): 79–108.

Deneoux, Guillaume, and Abdeslam Maghraoui. 1998. King Hassan's Strategy of Political Dualism. *Middle East Policy* 5 (4): 104–127.

Desrues, Thierry, and Moyano, Eduardo. 2001. Social Change and Political Transition in Morocco. *Mediterranean Politics* 6 (1): 21–47.

El Azizi, A., and Nadia Lamlili. 2006. Sale Temps pour les Femmes. http://www.mediterraneas.org/article.php3?id_article=616 (accessed January 28, 2010).

Gribaa, Boutheina. 2009. *Renforcement du Leadership Feminine et de la Participation des Femmes a la Vie Politique et au Processus de Prise des Decisions en Algeria, au Maroc et en Tunisie*. Tunis and Santo Domingo: UN-INSTRAW and Centre de la Femme Arabe pour la Formation et la Recherche. http://www.womenpoliticalparticipation.org/upload/publication/publication1.pdf.

Joseph, Suad, and Susan Slyomovics. 2001. *Women and Power in the Middle East*. Philadelphia: University of Pennsylvania Press.

Kingdom of Morocco. 1996. Constitution. http://www.maroc.ma.

Leveau, Remy. 1985. *Le Fellah Marocain: Défenseur du Trône*. Paris: Fondation Nationale de Sciences Politiques.

———. 1997. Morocco at the Crossroads. *Mediterranean Politics* 2 (2): 95–113.

Nelson, Barbara J., and Najma Chowdhury. 1994. Patterns of Women's Political Engagement from a Global Perspective. In Barbara J. Nelson and Najma Chowdhury, eds., *Women and Politics Worldwide*, 3–24. London: Yale University Press.

Sater, James. 2002. The Dynamics of State and Civil Society in Morocco. *Journal of North African Studies* 7 (3): 101–118.

———. 2007. Changing Politics from Below? Women Parliamentarians in Morocco. *Journal of Democratization* 14 (4): 723–742.

———. 2009. Elections and Authoritarian Rule in Morocco. *Middle East Journal* 63 (3): 381–400.

United Nations Development Program (UNDP). 2003. *Arab Human Development Report 2003.* New York: UNDP.

Waterbury, John. 1970. *The Commander of the Faithful: The Moroccan Political Elite—A Study in Segmented Politics.* London: Weidenfeld and Nicolson.

Weber, Max. 1978. *Economy and Society,* Vol. 1. Berkeley: University of California Press.

Willis, Michael. 2002. Political Parties in the Maghrib: The Illusion of Significance. *Journal of North African Studies* 7 (2): 1–22.

Zerhouni, Saloua, and Abdelaziz Baboussa. 2008. Le Marketing Politique Face aux Realites Electorales. *Economia* 1: 60–70.

Zoubir, Yahia. 1993. Reactions in the Maghreb to the Gulf Crisis and War. *Arab Studies Quarterly* 15 (1): 83–103.

PART TWO
SUBSTANTIVE
REPRESENTATION

Substantive representation occurs when legislators pursue policy goals that align with the interests and priorities of their constituents. The composition and nature of women as a group, however, is the subject of controversy among feminists and non-feminists alike, with some proposing that women share important interests in common and others drawing attention to different facets of identity and ideology that divide women as a group. Debates over quotas reflect these concerns, but the sheer diversity of countries that have adopted quotas also highlights a number of thorny issues about how best to operationalize women's substantive representation and how to design research strategies that capture the various activities through which legislators seek to promote women's interests and priorities. The task is made more difficult by the inability in some cases to distinguish between quota and nonquota women, raising important questions about the effects of sex versus the effects of quotas.

Grappling with these questions, the chapters in this section offer a range of theoretical and methodological insights into how to gauge quotas' impact on substantive representation. First, the case studies show that the content of "women's interests" is contextual, fluid, and subject to contestation, rather than essential, static, and easily agreed on. In addition to levels of development, which can influence the women's-rights issues that are deemed central, there is also important variation in the issues that are settled in some countries while remaining hotly debated in others, such as inheritance laws or women's right to work. Second, the authors draw attention to the need to recognize the multiple stages of policy-making processes, which include agenda setting, deliberation, and decision making. The actions that legislators take during each stage may be public or may occur behind the scenes and be less visible. While some may question whether all of these activities should count as instances of substantive representation, the range of steps involved in transforming interests into policy outcomes poses a challenge for researchers in determining what legislators are actually doing, an issue that becomes especially complex in countries where promoting women's rights places politicians at risk.

More broadly, the chapters highlight a third challenge, which is to sort out how these dynamics are themselves connected to features of a country's political and institutional context. Legacies of dictatorship, genocide, or institutionalized racism have implications for constituency formation, identity construction, and the capacity and willingness of female legislators to act for women. Quotas implemented in new democracies or postconflict societies are thus limited in their ability to empower female legislators and affect dramatic policy changes. Institutional design may provide further constraints, as parliamentary rules restrict legislator autonomy and presidential systems concentrate power in the executive, both of which reduce the power of legislators over policy making. Finally, the analyses point to some of the complexities and even negative consequences of quota policies: quotas can legitimize the idea that women are a constituency with common political interests but thereby inhibit the expression of other collective identities. Quotas also signal political leaders' commitment to gender equality, masking efforts by these same leaders to marginalize legislators who pursue women's policy goals.

6 Labels and Mandates in the United Kingdom

Sarah Childs and Mona Lena Krook

Quotas for women in politics have a controversial history in the United Kingdom, with debates revolving around questions of merit and fairness (Squires 1996) and the relationship between central and local political party organizations (Childs and Cowley 2011). Different from quotas applied to party lists in countries with proportional representation, the structure of the British electoral system—majoritarian, with single-member districts—has required strategies focused on the composition of candidate shortlists, or the final lists of candidates considered in each district. Although smaller parties were the first to introduce compulsory shortlisting in the 1980s, requiring that one or two women be included, the Labour Party took a more dramatic step in 1993 by adopting all-women shortlists (AWS), mandating that only female candidates be considered in half of the vacant seats that the party was likely to win. While approved by the party conference, the AWS policy attracted strong criticism both within and outside the party once it had been passed (Lovenduski 1997). In 1996, two male party members sued the Labour Party in an industrial tribunal, arguing that their exclusion from candidate selection violated the terms of the Sex Discrimination Act (Russell 2000). The tribunal agreed, but after a drop in the number of female members of parliament (MP) in 2001, following a dramatic increase in 1997, the Sex Discrimination Act was amended in 2002, and use of AWS was reintroduced. Public discussions of quotas and women's representation have led to pressure on the Conservatives and the Liberal Democrats—the other two main parties—to increase the proportion of women they elect to parliament. Both parties have responded but stopped short of quotas in favor of designating "priority lists" that include women but do not compel local parties to select them as candidates.

Ambivalence about strict quota measures, whether by party leaders, local activists, the media, or the general public, revolves around questions about candidate quality, voter choice, and intraparty relations. These debates feed into concerns about electoral performance and legislative activity, namely that quotas would lead to substandard MPs who were overly loyal to party leaders and did not fully represent local interests (Childs and Cowley 2011). Doubts about the relation between quotas and electoral performance were raised in an acute form for Labour in 2005, when a disgruntled local male stood as an independent candidate in Blaenau Gwent on an explicitly anti-AWS ticket and beat the AWS candidate in a traditionally safe Labour seat. Although this result may be viewed as a one-off (Cutts, Childs, and Fieldhouse 2008), as there was no wider electoral cost for AWS candidates that year, that event reaffirmed concerns about the desirability of quotas, which continue to be raised within the party today (Mullin 2008). Such views are echoed among Conservative Party members, who stated in focus groups that using AWS invites charges that a woman "only got selected" because of her sex, suggesting that "she's not that good really" (Childs and Webb 2011). Quotas, they indicated, resulted in the election of women who lacked "experience" and were "ill-prepared" (see also chapters 2, 3, and 4 in this volume). When asked for examples, however, focus groups cited a number of female Labour MPs, only one of whom was actually selected via an AWS (Childs, Webb, and Marthaler 2009).

Ongoing skepticism thus reveals that despite being adopted by Labour almost two decades ago, the use of AWS remains contentious—and topical—both within and outside the Labour Party. Yet the tendency to elide quota women and nonquota women also raises the question of whether assessments of parliamentary behavior are accurately ascribed to AWS or whether these effects can instead be attributed to sex more generally. Existing research on quotas tends to overlook this distinction, often because a quota law governs the selection of all female candidates (Franceschet and Piscopo 2008; Murray 2010). The British case, however, offers an opportunity to examine these effects more closely, given that among the 101 Labour women elected in 1997, only thirty-five were selected via AWS. At the same time, the large group of new female Labour MPs were also known disparagingly as "Blair's Babes," a reference to Labour leader Tony Blair, which suggested that they all owed their positions to him in some way—and, at a minimum, highlighted the fact that they were women. Media attention, combined with party debates and criticisms over quotas, produced contradictory expectations regarding women's legislative behavior. Some anticipated that the newly elected Labour women would change the culture and policy outputs of parliament, because of the doubling of the proportion of women in the House of Commons from 9 percent to 18 percent (Childs 2004). Others predicted, in contrast, that they would simply toe the party line, as much as—or more than—male MPs (Cowley and Childs 2003).

To evaluate the validity of these competing accounts, this chapter draws on three waves of interviews with Labour women first elected in 1997. These women were interviewed after the 1997 election, just before the 2001 election, and prior to the 2010 election. Earlier analysis of the first two waves of this data focused broadly on the experiences of this parliamentary intake, exploring attitudes and behaviors in relation to the substantive representation of women (Childs 2004). These interviews are reanalyzed here, together with the new data from the third wave of interviews, to ascertain whether responses differed in any way between women who were selected on AWS and those who were not. Drawing on the distinction between "mandate" and "label" effects outlined by Franceschet and Piscopo (2008), the study explores whether, on balance, the women reported sensing an obligation to act for women or, alternatively, a stigma leading them not to pursue women's issues. The analysis classifies interview responses in each wave that are consistent with these two sets of effects, examines patterns in the responses given by quota and nonquota women, and compares trends among these groups over time.

Mandate effects are more common than label effects among both groups, but there are important differences in how quota and nonquota women experience pressures and opportunities to represent women, with label effects being more acute for women selected via AWS. By the third wave, more MPs report a mixture of mandate and label effects, but most switching over time occurs in the direction of mandates, suggesting that, despite some initial difficulties, label effects were gradually overcome and that Labour women sensed and responded to a mandate to act on behalf of women. These results indicate that there are, in fact, differences in how quota and nonquota women approach the policy-making process but also that the balance of effects may shift as legislators become more experienced and the perceived stigma attached to being a quota woman lessens over time.

ALL-WOMEN SHORTLISTS AND WOMEN'S POLITICAL REPRESENTATION

The earliest policies addressing women's selection as parliamentary candidates in the United Kingdom emerged in the Social Democratic Party and the Liberal Party in the early 1980s (Krook 2009). The Labour Party followed suit in 1987, deciding that in districts where women had been nominated, at least one woman had to be included on the final shortlist. Around this time, Labour women learned about gender quotas in other socialist and social democratic parties across Europe (Short 1996). At the party conference in 1990, where they distributed a pamphlet stressing the need for AWS, they secured commitment to a target of 50 percent women among the party's MPs within ten years or three general elections. While the party did nominate more women, however, most were placed in unwinnable seats (Russell 2003, 69).

After the party's third consecutive loss to the Conservatives in 1987, research by leading women within the Labour Party, circulated via a Fabian Society pamphlet (Brooks, Eagle, and Short 1990), advocated the introduction of AWS. Making the case for quotas, the pamphlet explicitly emphasized the electoral disadvantage the party faced because of its lack of female MPs. Research by the party, indeed, found that the public perceived Labour to be a "male" party and attributed many of its proposals on women's issues to the Conservatives, headed at that time by Prime Minister Margaret Thatcher (Brooks, Eagle, and Short 1990, 4). The authors argued, consequently, that electing female Labour MPs would finally bring women's concerns into the political discourse, leading to a "fairer and more equal society, the aim of every socialist" (Brooks, Eagle, and Short 1990, 5).

Party women concluded that the best policy would be to require that the AWS be used to select candidates in half of the party's "key" seats (winnable on a 6-percent swing), including seats where a Labour MP was retiring. This policy was viewed as a compromise solution that would increase the number of women in safe seats at the same time as it would preserve some discretion for local parties and opportunities for men. The proposal was presented to the 1993 party conference as part of a package of proposed changes to the party constitution. Since the main subject of debate revolved around relations between the party and trade unions, the proposal to adopt AWS did not receive much public attention. Once approved, however, AWS attracted strong criticism both inside and outside the party (Squires 1996).

Noting these objections, party leaders asked constituencies to organize consensus meetings to decide which seats would be subject to AWS. Most managed to comply, although the central leadership did compel one constituency to adopt an AWS (Russell 2003). The party abandoned the policy in early 1996, however, in light of a successful lower-court challenge by two male party members who had sought nomination in districts designated for AWS. The tribunal ruled that the policy violated the employment provisions of the Sex Discrimination Act, and the party leadership decided not to appeal the decision (Russell 2000). Doing so meant that the ruling only affected selections in these two constituencies, allowing nominations already made using AWS to stand. The result was the election of thirty-five women via AWS, approximately one-third of all Labour women elected to parliament in 1997.

During preparations for the next general elections, activists began to voice concerns that local parties would select only men in the seats where sitting Labour MPs were retiring. By early 2000, several MPs began to call for reform of the Sex Discrimination Act to allow parties to use positive action in candidate selection. While including this demand in the party manifesto, the party simply required gender-balanced shortlists for vacant seats, leading to a slight decrease in the numbers of women elected. Returned to office, the new Labour government submitted a bill that would reform the Sex Discrimination Act to exclude any act taken by a party to reduce inequality in the numbers of women and men elected at any level of political office. Because of the permissive nature of the bill, it passed all stages in both houses of parliament without a vote, a type of expedited enactment normally reserved for entirely noncontroversial bills on topics of low public salience (Childs 2002). With little media attention, the bill passed virtually unnoticed into law in February 2002. Unusually, however, the bill contained a sunset clause stating that the act would expire at the end of 2015—in time for at least three general elections to have taken place—unless a specific order was made to the contrary, which occurred under the Equality Act of 2010, setting a new sunset clause of 2030.

Leading up to elections in 2005, all three major parties considered whether to adopt measures to recruit female candidates. Labour agreed to apply AWS in at least half of all seats where incumbent Labour MPs were retiring, with the goal of electing at least 35 percent women. The Liberal Democrats considered AWS at their party conference in 2001 but rejected them in favor of a target of 40 percent female candidates in districts where sitting MPs were standing down and seats required a swing of less than 7.5 percent to win. Conservatives remained much more divided. Some members called on the party to adopt quotas, but even the mild efforts of the party chairman to persuade local parties to select women met with little or no response (Childs 2004; Russell 2003). Women's representation increased overall, however, from 17.9 percent to 19.5 percent, which compared favorably with the 1997 result of 18.2 percent (Krook 2009, 147).

Six months after the elections, the Conservatives chose a new leader, David Cameron, who in his acceptance speech noted that it was crucial to change patterns of representation in the party. He proposed and implemented a plan involving a "priority list" of aspirant candidates—consisting of at least 50 percent women and a "significant" proportion of black, minority ethnic, and disabled candidates—from which Conservative-held and target constituencies would be required to select their candidates (Campbell, Childs, and Lovenduski 2006). Because of a lack of response, six months later Cameron officially dropped the "A-list" policy but required local parties to consider gender-balanced shortlists at every stage. Yet in his submission to a special parliamentary committee in 2009, Cameron announced that some of his party's shortlists would use AWS from January 2010, although in actuality, there was none. Even so, his pledge was received negatively by many Conservative Party members and commentators, who argued that they would select inferior and nonlocal women over higher-quality men and against the wishes of local people (Childs and Webb 2011).

On election day in 2010, 143 female MPs—22 percent—were returned to the House of Commons, a historic high. Despite some interparty rebalancing, the long-observed asymmetry in women's descriptive representation in the Labour Party's favor continued. The Conservatives, the party with the highest number of MPs, elected forty-three women, more than doubling their number (up from seventeen), though not doubling their percentage of women, who account for less than 16 percent of Tory MPs. The Liberal Democrats, in contrast, saw a decline in terms of both the percentage and the number of female MPs: from 16 percent to 12 percent and from nine to seven women. The outgoing Labour Party saw its number of female MPs decline, too, from ninety-eight to eighty-one, but the percentage actually increased, to nearly 32 percent. The key to Labour's relative success, in an election where it lost some ninety seats overall, lay in its use of AWS in sixty-four constituencies. Just less than half of these candidates were elected, including for the first time five black and minority ethnic women (Ashe et al. 2010).

LABEL AND MANDATE EFFECTS IN WOMEN'S SUBSTANTIVE REPRESENTATION

There is little doubt that AWS have had a favorable impact on women's descriptive representation, especially in light of the challenges witnessed around the globe in terms of electing more women in countries with first-past-the-post electoral systems (Caul 1999). The controversies surrounding the use of gender quotas, however, led to heightened attention and often criticism of the new female Labour MPs for wearing the wrong clothes, voting the wrong way, and being concerned with the wrong issues. Above all, they were accused of not making a difference in policy making and thus having failed women (Childs 2004). These various charges, taken together, reflect two contradictory predictions regarding the behavior of quota women.

The first is what Franceschet and Piscopo (2008) describe as a "mandate effect," whereby female legislators perceive an obligation to act on behalf of women. Mandates emerge over the course of quota campaigns as a result of arguments that female representatives are needed in order to introduce a new perspective into policy making, raising expectations about the projected impact that increased numbers of female MPs will have on laws beneficial to women as a group. The second is a "label effect," stemming from stereotypes about quota women that negatively affect how female legislators are viewed by their colleagues and the public at large. In particular, accusations that women selected via quotas are less experienced, less capable, and blindly loyal to male party leaders create a stigma that some women may seek to overcome by rejecting any mandate to act for women, in an effort to demonstrate they are "serious" politicians. Franceschet and Piscopo propose that female legislators may respond to these two effects in different ways, shaping prospects for the substantive representation of women.

Although Franceschet and Piscopo develop this distinction as a means to theorize about how quotas affect policy making on women's issues, their empirical study is not able to distinguish between quota and nonquota women, because the quota law in Argentina applies to all women elected to the national congress. Their discussion of their results, moreover, is ultimately about the role of gender: women have been able to change policy agendas but not outcomes, because of the lack of change in "institutional features and gender bias in the legislative environment" (2008, 396). This raises the question of whether these effects are generated by quotas per se or are simply problems experienced by female politicians more generally because of their minority status, as suggested by literature on tokenism and women's legislative behavior (Dahlerup 1988; Kanter 1977). Because only some women were selected via AWS in the United Kingdom, a closer look at the British case presents a way forward in terms of assessing the role played by quotas in particular versus sex and gender more broadly. Restricting the focus to new Labour women elected in 1997 and tracking their views over time make it possible, further, to distinguish between quota and nonquota women while controlling for other features such as party and cohort.

The data for this study consist of three waves of interviews with female Labour MPs first elected in 1997. The original data set involved thirty-four interviews, a sample including more than half of all of the newly elected female MPs. These same women were invited to participate in the two subsequent rounds of interviews in 2000 and 2009, maintaining the group's cohesiveness over time. The initial project did not draw a distinction between selection mechanisms, and once compared with data on AWS, it emerged that nearly two-thirds of the sample had been selected on an AWS, thereby creating a skewed data set. While this sample is therefore not representative of all of Labour's newly elected female MPs in 1997, response rates among quota and nonquota women remain consistent over time (see table 6.1), allowing comparisons across samples, keeping the 2-to-1 ratio of interviewees in mind.

Table 6.1 Interviewed new Labour female MPs, by election and means of selection

Interview year	Women MPs selected by AWS	Non-AWS women	Total
1997	23 (68%)	11 (32%)	34 (100%)
2000	15 (65%)	8 (35%)	23 (100%)
2009	13 (68%)	6 (32%)	19 (100%)

A second challenge, given that the first two rounds of interviews were not designed with questions about mandates and labels in mind, is to devise a template for capturing these two sets of effects based on the specific questions posed in each wave. A typology of indicators was thus developed, drawing on the data available, to classify interview responses. Elaborating on the framework of Franceschet and Piscopo (2008), responses were viewed as manifestations of mandate effects when they reflected the belief that women were empowered to act for women, such that female MPs identified with or felt a positive association with women as a group and perceived an obligation to pursue women's issues in their legislative work. In contrast, answers were seen as exemplifying label effects when they suggested that women were disempowered to act for women, such that women sensed that they were negatively perceived or excluded from positions of power as women and reported taking steps to overcome this stigma by not acting for women as a group.

For the 1997 interviews, mandate effects included identifying as a feminist, sensing a responsibility to act for women, giving examples of female MPs acting for women, believing that women had a different perspective that they brought to politics, stating that there were issues important to women as a group, viewing their association with women's issues as positive, and reporting lessened resistance to women's presence in politics. Label effects were reflected in responses not identifying as a feminist, feeling constrained to act for women or downplaying their presence as women, refusing to act for women or remaining agnostic, rejecting the notion of a women's perspective, expressing skepticism at the concept of women's issues, viewing any association with women's issues as negative and as implying that they were not able to represent other interests, and recounting resistance to their presence in parliament as women.

The interviews conducted in 2000 were intended originally to serve as an opportunity to assess whether women's views on their representative roles had changed over the course of their first term in parliament. Consequently, the question guide was altered somewhat to focus on how the respondents described their legislative activity on behalf of women. While the questions were not exactly the same, there was substantial overlap, and answers can again be categorized in terms of the two effects. Those capturing mandate effects consisted of attending the meetings of the Parliamentary Labour Party's (PLP) women's group, finding value in the work of this group, sensing a responsibility to act for women, giving examples of female MPs acting for women, stating that there were issues important to women as a group, and reporting lessened resistance to women's presence in politics. Responses more in line with label effects included not attending the meetings of the PLP women's group, finding little value in the work of this group, feeling constrained to act for women or downplaying their presence as women, expressing a sense of having failed women, viewing any association with women's issues as negative, and reporting resistance to their presence in parliament.

The final round of interviews held in 2009 drew on many of the same questions as before but in addition asked the women which policies they viewed as their main achievements over the course of their tenure in parliament, the degree to which they worked with other female MPs in policy making, and their reaction to a female cabinet minister's charge that women merely served as "window dressing" in the Labour government headed by Gordon Brown. Answers classified as mandate effects involved attending the meetings of the PLP women's group, finding value in the work of this group, sensing a responsibility to act for women, listing policies on women's issues among their major achievements, giving examples of female MPs acting for women, working together with other female MPs, stating that there were issues important to women as a group, expressing skepticism about window-dressing claims, and reporting lessened resistance to women's presence in politics. Label effects were embodied in responses about not attending the meetings of the PLP women's group, finding little value in the work of this group, feeling constrained to act for women or downplaying their presence as women, emphasizing work on nongender issues among their main achievements, expressing a sense of having failed women, stating little contact with other female MPs, viewing any association with women's issues as negative, believing that women were indeed still outside circles of power, and reporting resistance to their presence in parliament.

After this template was developed, the interviews in each wave were reread, and a note was made about which interviewee expressed each sentiment. Because the interviews were semistructured and other topics were discussed that were not included in this analysis, interview content varied somewhat, and respondents did not always clearly articulate one view or the other. At the same time, interviewees also occasionally offered contradictory statements at different moments in the interview, saying, for example, that they felt obliged to act for women (mandate) but felt constrained to act and downplayed their presence as women (label). Mentions in both directions were recorded, recognizing that, as Franceschet and Piscopo (2008) point out, female MPs may experience both sets of effects simultaneously. The resulting data were then summed for each respondent, capturing how many times each individual offered statements that reflected mandate and label effects. These counts were analyzed to see whether there were any broad patterns, any differences among quota and nonquota women, and any changes in the balance of effects over time.

The key advantage of this approach, in addition to being able to distinguish between quota and nonquota women, is that it does not rely on speculations about the thoughts and motivations of female legislators. Rather, it asks them directly about their views on representing women and is able to track whether these views changed—or not—over time. A limitation of the analysis is that it does not take actual legislative activity into account. However, the importance of party discipline and the centrality of the government in proposing legislation render this a difficult task in the British case. The attitudes and actions of female MPs behind the scenes—as reflected in the interview data—may yield more accurate information on how women, in fact, contribute to the legislative process.

MODE OF SELECTION AND WOMEN'S REPRESENTATIVE ROLES

When the proportion of women in parliament doubled in 1997, as a result of the Labour landslide, expectations ran high that women's increased numbers would translate into improved substantive representation of women's issues. At the same time, concerns about candidate quality connected to the use of AWS, together with negative and demeaning media coverage of "Blair's Babes," projected a stigma onto the cohort of new Labour women elected. Interviews conducted with these MPs soon after their election reflected the tensions they perceived in navigating this mixed landscape of mandate and label effects. On the one hand, some reported anticipation that female MPs would "stand up for women" and "actively promote women's greater role in society, take an interest in women's issues, give them serious consideration." One made an explicit link between her selection on an AWS and the responsibility she felt to act for women by stating, "I feel it is a duty in a positive sense because the whole point, the whole argument I used to justify . . . my selection on an all-women shortlist was the need for a voice for women who had not had a voice previously." Many felt that there were issues important to women, although the specific issues mentioned varied enormously, and that female constituents needed to be able to see that parliament was "taking more account of women's issues and women's concerns."

On the other hand, other MPs explained that "in order to make progress in politics, . . . you can't be too much one of the girls," meaning that it was important for female MPs to look at "what is practical" and not be "too strident" or "rub all our male colleagues up the wrong way." One explicitly acknowledged the trade-offs between mandates and labels when she stated that her colleagues "do identify with women's interests" but that she was personally concerned that women would be "pigeonholed" if they associated themselves with these issues. Indeed, she argued that "women representatives who see themselves as MPs for women [are] causing a lot of women to turn off." Others complained that political commentators perpetuated the idea that women were only interested in conventionally defined women's issues when female MPs were "sick to death of child care." One noted, further, that she sought to avoid "go[ing] around saying publicly, 'oh, isn't it wonderful you have got a woman candidate,'" perceiving that if she was "too demanding," men in the party would report back unfavorably to local party organizations.

After dividing out these responses across quota and nonquota women and then comparing the number of mandate and label effects mentioned by each MP, it emerges that mandate effects are more common than label effects among both groups (see table 6.2). However, while there is a proportional split among AWS and non-AWS women in terms of those reporting more mandate than label effects, there are proportionately more non-AWS women who only perceive a mandate effect. In contrast, label effects are more acute among women selected via AWS, with only one non-AWS woman reporting on balance more label effects. There was little difference among those who experienced both effects evenly. The data suggest, therefore, that a majority of new female Labour MPs felt that they had a positive obligation to promote women's issues in policy making but that those selected with the help of quotas sensed a stigma attached to their mode of selection, negatively affecting their ability to act for women.

When many of these women were reinterviewed at the end of their first term in 2000, there were some notable changes in their response patterns. On balance, mandate effects were still more common than label effects in both groups. While label effects were still felt more strongly by quota women, however, a larger number—in both absolute and proportional terms—reported stronger label effects than previously. Only one nonquota woman gave answers leaning toward labels rather than mandates. In terms of those who switched position between 1997 and 2000, women in both groups were equally likely to do so, but the direction of the shifts were different: there were as many AWS women reporting stronger mandate effects as label effects, while non-AWS women more often moved toward greater label effects, including more even splits between the two effects (see table 6.3). Overall, these changes mean that the sample as a whole was more likely to express label effects than in the previous round of interviews, even if mandate effects prevailed, suggesting some tempering of the optimistic tone of the earlier sample.

To illustrate further, a large number of interviewees found value in the work of the PLP women's group and were able to give examples of female MPs acting for women on a wide range of issues, which they attributed to having "points of reference that a man couldn't have." One felt that such policies would not have been possible "without the 101 women," because "there are issues that affect women disproportionately and that unless women pursue them, nobody else will." Others, however, felt that the PLP women's group was not a "congenial group," nor was it regarded as "serious." When asked why they missed meetings, one said that "somewhere in my mind, I think that isn't important, I'm doing other things," while another stated that speaking about the "women's agenda" was "not something I'm really comfortable with." Some expressed disappointment regarding the extent to which they had been able to act

Table 6.2 Balance of mandate and label effects among female Labour MPs, 1997–2009

		Mentions only mandate	Mentions more mandate	Equal mentions	Mentions more label	Mentions only label
1997	AWS	5	16	2	5	1
	Non-AWS	4	8	2	1	0
2000	AWS	4	9	0	6	2
	Non-AWS	2	3	4	1	0
2009	AWS	0	7	4	2	0
	Non-AWS	0	4	0	1	0

for women but felt that women could not afford to act collectively without threatening their political careers and that by taking up women's issues, they would be stereotyped and marginalized as being only interested in women's concerns.

By 2009, after three terms in parliament, there were again perceptible shifts in the effects reported. As in the two earlier rounds, mandates were still more common than labels among both groups, but strikingly, there was a substantial reduction in the number of MPs emphasizing label effects overall, which was the result of changes among quota women exclusively. Significantly, though, there were no longer any respondents whose statements could be classified as reflecting only mandates or only labels: all MPs described some mixture of effects, regardless of mode of selection, although all of those in the split category were selected via AWS. Examining switches between 2000 and 2009, the absolute numbers of individuals moving across categories are the same, but proportionately, this movement is more common among nonquota women. For these MPs, nearly all of these shifts occur in the direction of mandates, whereas quota women switch to the even category more often, twice from a mandate emphasis and once from a label emphasis.

Looking at the whole twelve-year period, eight MPs were consistent over time, whether this was measured at two or three moments, depending on whether the final interview took place in 2000 or 2009. Fifteen individuals changed their position at some point, whether in 2000 or 2009 or both, nine of whom were selected via AWS and six of whom were not. Among those MPs interviewed three times, six reported a different stance in 2009 from that in 1997. Almost all of these were quota women, who, as in 2000, tended to move toward being more evenly split—three of them had initially expressed a greater mandate effect. Taken together, however, most switches across time occurred in the direction of mandates. When viewed alongside the general tendency to emphasize mandate effects, this suggests that initial difficulties with labels were overcome to a great extent over time, such that Labour women sensed that they had a mandate to represent women and that they fulfilled it at least in part, despite ongoing challenges and some backtracking in earlier policy gains.

For example, while slightly more MPs viewed their work on nongender issues to be among their main achievements, many pointed to their own policy successes on women's issues, and even more could point to instances of other female MPs acting

Table 6.3 Switches in effects among interviewees over time

		1997–2000		2000–2009		1997–2009	
		AWS	Non-AWS	AWS	Non-AWS	AWS	Non-AWS
Switches	Toward mandate	3	0	1	4	1	1
	Toward even	0	2	3	0	4	0
	Toward label	3	1	1	1	0	0

for women, on policies as diverse as domestic violence, forced marriages, pensions, child care, abortion, prostitution, and taxation on sanitary products. One noted, in this context, that although there were "overblown expectations of what the number of women elected in '97 could do, there's also been an underestimation of the impact that we've had." Many could recount moments when they worked together with other female MPs on issues important to women and when they had mobilized together with others to support female MPs—especially cabinet ministers—who were experiencing troubles. Nearly all felt, in comparison with the situation in 1997, that their presence had "normalized selecting women" and enacted a "cultural shift in the Labour Party, so that it's perfectly normal to be a Labour woman MP."

Others were more skeptical, arguing that "it was all very naïve to imagine that there was a women's group," with one explaining that she did not approach policy making in the vein that "I'm a woman politician and therefore I'm going to pursue issues or particular concerns in just that agenda." Another stated that middle-aged women had not received much attention: "the government's done something for our children, and it's done something for our parents, . . . but the women of that group are the ones who are giving on all sides, but actually we haven't done very much for them." Female MPs were divided, however, on the window-dressing question, although many sensed that the Brown government was less open to promoting women to real positions of power. A large number shared the opinion that "politics is more macho, more aggressive, more bullying than it's ever been in my experience," even going so far as to state, "I feel a bit despondent about it all, to be honest. I mean, I thought we'd really broken through the glass ceiling in '97, and I really thought there was going to be continuous progress."

While the vast majority of respondents expressed support for AWS as a mechanism for increasing women's representation, with little difference between quota and non-quota women, there was no consensus across the interviews regarding the experiences of women selected this way. One quota woman, for example, claimed that her AWS status had "never, ever, ever been mentioned to me," and another observed that "you don't hear the grumbling about women-only shortlists in the way that there used to be. . . . It's not controversial. And you do find, I think, amongst Labour MPs, people are very relaxed." Another, however, talked about how she had been made to feel like "some sort of . . . excuse of an MP, some sort of second-class MP," and "the Tories will bring it up forever, because that's how I was originally selected." Along similar lines, a different MP recalled, "I was elected on an all-women shortlist, and I've had Tories say to me, 'Oh, you weren't, you're too good.'" Such remarks suggest that there is still a stigma associated with being selecting on an AWS and a tendency to equate all new Labour women elected in 1997 with quota women. The evidence presented here indicates that mode of selection has had an impact on how these MPs have viewed their representative role and how their experiences in parliament have evolved over time.

CONCLUSION

Together with the other chapters in this part of the book, the study undertaken here seeks to determine whether quotas have altered prospects for the substantive representation of women. In contrast with earlier work on this question, the nature of the quota policy in the British case affords an opportunity to assess whether outcomes are shaped by the use of quotas per se or whether similar dynamics are witnessed among all women elected, making sex and/or gender the primary explanatory factor regardless of the mode of candidate selection. Given recent limited moves by the other main parties toward greater acceptance of positive action, answers may be particularly welcomed by observers of British politics concerned with knowing whether quotas enable substantive representation or may, in fact, be counterproductive to improved policy outcomes for women.

The analysis utilizes data from three rounds of interviews with Labour women elected for the first time in 1997, when the number of women in the House of Commons doubled, in part because of the introduction of a party quota. Responses of women elected with and without AWS were compared to explore whether either group was more likely to sense mandate or label effects. The findings indicate that there were indeed differences across groups, with women selected via AWS more often expressing sentiments associated with labels—although, overall, responses of both quota and nonquota women tended to be more closely aligned with mandates. While configurations of effects varied across interview rounds, the power of labels appeared to diminish over time. All the same, stories told by interviewees also suggest that MPs continue to have diverse perceptions, even if, by the final round, the shared trend was for all interviewees to report a mix of mandate and label effects.

Quotas thus do appear to heighten some of the challenges and opportunities that women face in political office. However, with time, some of the stigma connected to quotas may erode, bringing the experiences of women elected with and without these measures more in line with one another. The data, unfortunately, do not permit consideration of *why* these shifts in effects have occurred. In addition to greater acceptance of quotas by MPs and the public at large, a role may be played by incumbency, in the sense that a woman first elected in 1997 standing in 2010 would have been subsequently selected by her party and reelected several times. For a woman originally selected via AWS, in particular, this process may reduce possible criticism for being a quota woman, while enabling her to gain electoral legitimacy and greater confidence in acting for her constituents and other interests. Further, media representations may have evolved over time, shaping how the public—and MPs—perceive such women and their cohort more broadly, although more research on this question would be required.

REFERENCES

Ashe, Jeanette, Rosie Campbell, Sarah Childs, and Elizabeth Evans. 2010. Stand by Your Man: Women's Political Recruitment at the 2010 UK General Election. *British Politics* 5 (4): 455–480.

Brooks, Rachel, Angela Eagle, and Clare Short. 1990. *Quotas Now: Women in the Labour Party.* London: Fabian Society.

Campbell, Rosie, Sarah Childs, and Joni Lovenduski. 2006. Women's Equality Guarantees and the Conservative Party. *Political Quarterly* 77 (1): 18–27.

Caul, Miki. 1999. Women's Representation in Parliament: The Role of Political Parties. *Party Politics* 5 (1): 79–98.

Childs, Sarah. 2002. Concepts of Representation and the Passage of the Sex Discrimination (Election Candidates) Bill. *Journal of Legislative Studies* 8 (3): 90–108.

———. 2004. *New Labour Women MPs: Women Representing Women*. London: Routledge.

Childs, Sarah, and Philip Cowley. 2011. The Politics of Local Presence: Is There a Case for Descriptive Representation? *Political Studies* 59 (1): 1–19.

Childs, Sarah, and Paul Webb. 2011. *Gender and the Conservative Party*. Basingstoke, U.K.: Palgrave.

Childs, Sarah, Paul Webb, and Sally Marthaler. 2009. The Feminisation of the Conservative Parliamentary Party: Party Members' Attitudes. *Political Quarterly* 80 (2): 204–213.

Cowley, Philip, and Sarah Childs. 2003. Too Spineless to Rebel? New Labour's Women MPs. *British Journal of Political Science* 33 (3): 345–365.

Cutts, David, Sarah Childs, and Edward Fieldhouse. 2008. "This Is What Happens When You Don't Listen": All-Women Shortlists at the 2005 General Election. *Party Politics* 14 (5): 575–595.

Dahlerup, Drude. 1988. From a Small to a Large Minority: Women in Scandinavian Politics. *Scandinavian Political Studies* 11 (4): 275–297.

Franceschet, Susan, and Jennifer M. Piscopo. 2008. Gender Quotas and Women's Substantive Representation: Lessons from Argentina. *Politics & Gender* 4 (3): 393–425.

Kanter, Rosabeth Moss. 1977. Some Effects of Proportions on Group Life. *American Journal of Sociology* 82 (5): 965–990.

Krook, Mona Lena. 2009. *Quotas for Women in Politics*. New York: Oxford University Press.

Lovenduski, Joni. 1997. Gender Politics: A Breakthrough for Women? *Parliamentary Affairs* 50 (4): 708–719.

Mullin, Chris. 2008. *A View from the Foothills*. London: Profile.

Murray, Rainbow. 2010. Second among Unequals? A Study of Whether France's "Quota Women" Are Up to the Job. *Politics & Gender* 6 (1): 93–118.

Russell, Meg. 2000. *Women's Representation in UK Politics*. London: Constitution Unit.

———. 2003. Women in Elected Office in the UK, 1992–2002: Struggles, Achievements and Possible Sea Change. In Alexandra Dobrowolsky and Vivien Hart, eds., *Women Making Constitutions*, 68–83. New York: Palgrave.

Short, Clare. 1996. Women and the Labour Party. In Joni Lovenduski and Pippa Norris, eds., *Women in Politics*, 19–27. New York: Oxford University Press.

Squires, Judith. 1996. Quotas for Women: Fair Representation? In Joni Lovenduski and Pippa Norris, eds., *Women in Politics*, 73–90. New York: Oxford University Press.

7 Policy Priorities and Women's Double Bind in Brazil

Luis Felipe Miguel

Redemocratization in Brazil opened up new spaces for political experimentation. After twenty-one years of military dictatorship, civilian rule was reestablished in 1985. Despite the multiple pressures of the transition to democracy, new forms of citizen participation flourished, including the participatory budget process adopted in many cities and the councils for public policies, stimulated by the new constitution adopted in 1988. A new political force, the Workers' Party (PT), was intimately linked to the social movements that had emerged during the dictatorship to demand democracy, and it became increasingly influential. But in spite of all of this, women's presence in formal politics remained minimal. Brazil has one of the lowest rates of women in parliament, ranking 106th according to the Inter-Parliamentary Union, the second-lowest score among South American countries. This is despite the adoption of a national quota law in 1997.

Brazil's quota law has been ineffective because of the combined effect of the electoral system (open-list proportional representation) and the absence of sanctions for parties that fail to comply with the quota law. As a result, women hold less than 10 percent of seats in the lower house, a figure only slightly higher than before the adoption of the quota. In this chapter, I show that women's scant presence in congress undermines the substantive representation of women in Brazil.

By substantive representation, I mean the ability to promote women's interests in decision-making arenas. "Interests" is a complicated concept, especially because women do not agree about what constitutes women's interests. Thus, most of the demands for political presence are made in the name of an identity or, better, according to Iris Young (2000), women's distinctive social perspective. Yet the notion of conflicting interests lies at the heart of politics. The distinctive female perspective is thus a point of departure around which women can construct their interests. I argue that the scant presence of women in congress undermines the advancement of the (differently understood) interests of women in Brazil.

The analysis in this chapter relies on several sets of data about legislative behavior and congressional politics in Brazil in the last two decades. Some of these data were gathered through earlier studies, and other data were drawn from the existing literature. The data include legislative initiatives, participation in congressional commissions, and interventions in plenary sessions. On the one hand, the data show that women's presence makes a difference. Although they are few in number, the presence of female representatives leads to changes in the policy agenda and even in the behavior of male representatives. On the other hand, the Brazilian case also reveals that presence is not enough. There are a number of obstacles that complicate the effectiveness of actions undertaken by female representatives in pursuit of women's interests.

Access to positions in representative bodies—the aim of the quotas—is an important step, but it is not sufficient. If politics is understood as a *field* in Bourdieu's terms (1979; 2000), it is a hierarchical space. Although they are formally equal, two representatives may differ in terms of prestige, influence, and ability to legislate successfully. Which parliamentarian introduces a bill makes an enormous difference to its trajectory and eventual success. In other words, different representatives occupy distinct positions in the political field. Women still face barriers in reaching high-status positions in the field of politics, and their effectiveness is therefore limited.

One aspect of these positions is defined institutionally. Brazil's lower house, the Chamber of Deputies, has a directorate with broad powers for internal management of in-house resources in addition to setting the legislative agenda. This board, elected every two years, is made up of a chairperson, six other officially appointed members, and four substitutes. No woman has ever held a seat on it. A female deputy, Luiza Erundina (Brazilian Socialist Party), proposed a constitutional amendment that would guarantee the presence of at least one woman in each parliamentary committee and on boards of directors in the Chamber of Deputies and the Senate. It has not been approved, however.

Another significant body is the Collegiate of the House of Leaders, which brings together the leaders of political parties and the leaders of partisan blocs from the majority, the minority, and the government. The Collegiate helps the board of directors carry out their roles and draw up agreements before they are voted in the plenary. Before 2009, no woman had served on the Collegiate of the House of Leaders. That year, a new regulation expanded the number of board members and included the coordinator of the female bloc in the house of representatives.

We also encounter sex differences beyond key positions, however. Parliamentarians without formal leadership posts may nonetheless exert greater influence than their peers. In short, some legislators have more political capital. A crude but useful indicator is the list of the "best 100 heads in the National Congress," elaborated since 1994 by the Departamento Intersindical de Assessoria Parlamentar (DIAP, "Interunion Department of Parliamentary Aides"), based on criteria that include formal posts held, influence in crucial decision making (or non-decision making), and reputation among other members of congress. In 2009, there were only five women on the list, three senators and two deputies. During the sixteen years of producing the list, the number of women has oscillated between three and six, with an average of 4.9. In other words, women's participation in the congressional elite remains low and is growing very slowly.

While some may argue that this situation is caused by women's lack of parliamentary experience, this is not, in fact, accurate. Rather, women's access to leadership positions in the congress is hampered because women's issues are accorded less political importance. Women in politics are thus prisoners of a dilemma. Ideas about gender create expectations about women's distinct contributions to politics. They are expected to pay greater attention to social issues and behave in a style that is less competitive and less aggressive. However, if women conform to these expectations, then their very actions undermine their access to leadership positions in politics. Women thus face two choices: they can either avoid conforming to gender stereotypes, thereby prompting resistance and criticisms for being insufficiently "feminine," or they can accept the niches available to them, thereby limiting their chances for advancing in their political careers.

This dilemma is made all the more stark by the fact that demands for a greater presence of women in politics are often supported by the idea of a feminine difference in the exercise of power. Maternal characteristics have been extended to the political arena, leading to assumptions that women will be less competitive and more concerned with vulnerable and marginalized groups. This discourse occurs frequently among women in politics who perceive maternal values as a way to affirm a positive difference in relation to their male competitors. Even their inexperience in political life gains a positive connotation, since women are thereby distant from traditional politics practiced by men, a style of politics characterized by dishonesty and neglect of societal concerns (Pinheiro 2007). This position is known as maternal thinking, or care politics, and has been developed most extensively by thinkers such as Sara Ruddick (1989) and Jean Bethke Elshtain (1981). Different patterns of socialization experienced by women engender a certain sensitivity and specific moral value judgments, different from masculine ones. This thought trend is based on literature from sociologist Nancy Chodorow (1978) and psychologist Carol Gilligan (1982). It both affirms unique feminine traits and extrapolates them to the political arena.

But the claims that women possess distinct moral attributes is questionable based on two perspectives, one that is political and another that is empirical. From a political perspective, as noted by Susan Okin (1989, 15), it is risky for feminists to propagate a type of discourse that can be appropriated by reactionary forces, such as the Catholic hierarchy, in order to trap women in the domestic sphere. Moreover, it is empirically possible to contest the association between women and any specific way of practicing politics. In fact, most women who are successful in their political careers tend to conform to a "masculine" standard of political behavior.

Indeed, within the parliamentary context, there is evidence that women are more likely to take up issues related to social affairs than those linked directly to the control of state resources and distribution of power. The question that this chapter addresses is whether this is a genuine option or, on the contrary, the result of a lack of choice for women. Stated another way, might women's actions be reflections of the lack of possibilities available to them in the political field (Delphy 1994)? At the same time that social issues are more open to women, such themes are associated with less prestigious positions in politics. Maternal politics thereby risks perpetuating a gendered division in political work, confining women to the ambit of social issues while giving men the right to administer tasks that have greater social recognition (L. F. Miguel 2000; 2001).

In the first section of this chapter, I summarize the data about women's participation in Brazil's Congress, followed by a brief discussion of the minor impact of the quota law. The second section compares women's and men's legislative initiatives and participation in congressional commissions. The third section analyzes the differences between women's and men's choices of issues to discuss in the plenary sessions. The fourth section focuses on the speeches delivered on International Women's Day on March 8 to reveal how male and female representatives perceive the condition of women. A brief conclusion summarizes the interpretations developed in the chapter.

WOMEN IN RECENT BRAZILIAN POLITICS

Although trends of exclusion and discrimination continue to be widespread, women's participation in Brazilian political life in recent decades has nonetheless been significant. Women's marches, especially linked to the Catholic church, played a key role in generating support for the 1964 military coup. Women also participated in protests against the subsequent dictatorship by leading movements against the high cost of living and in favor of political amnesty for prisoners. Women participated in an array of different social movements, at both base and leadership levels. Women's presence has also been felt in new participatory spheres that were initiated during redemocratization in 1985: administrative councils for public policies and participatory budgets.

But women's involvement in institutional politics—in political parties, elections, and legislative bodies—remains low. There are very few women elected for positions in the executive or legislative bodies. Brazil is a federal republic, led by a president who is elected by popular vote through two electoral rounds to serve a four-year mandate, renewable for one term. The federation is made up of twenty-six states and the federal district. Each state is headed by a governor, also elected by popular vote and in two electoral rounds. The states are divided into a varying number of municipalities. There are almost six thousand municipalities in Brazil, whose mayors are also elected by popular vote.

In 2008, 9.1 percent of elected mayors were women. At the state level, a woman, Roseana Sarney from the state of Maranhão, was first elected governor in 1994 (she was reelected in 1998). In 2002, two female governors were elected, and by 2006, there were three women among twenty-seven state governors. This number increased to four when the electoral court suspended Maranhão's governor's mandate because of campaign irregularities, and the candidate in second position, Roseana Sarney, was appointed. While the women elected from 1994 to 2002 represent the old model for female political appointees (they are a daughter, a wife, and an ex-wife of governors), the female governors elected in 2006 are examples of new criteria for political appointment:

social-movement militancy and visibility as professionals with specific expertise. It is not just a matter of women's growing presence in power, but there is also a change in the profile of women in politics. This is also perceptible in the congress—and it is probably the most important trend related to gender and political representation in Brazil in the last two decades. Yet this is by no means a consistent progression. In 2010, the same year in which a woman was elected to the presidency, the number of female governors shrank to two, and both of them had family ties to male political leaders.

Women's presence in Brazil's national parliament was small throughout the twentieth century. In the lower house, the Chamber of Deputies, and in the federal Senate, the upper house, women were absent or practically so for quite a long time. Since women were first enfranchised in 1932 until the end of military dictatorship in 1985, in eleven elections, only thirty-one female federal representatives were elected to the lower house. There were no female senators. Women's presence in parliament has become slightly more noticeable since the 1986 elections, although it is still less than 10 percent (see table 7.1).

From the 1998 elections onward, women have benefited from a legal provision that guarantees reserve vacancies for their candidature to the Chamber of Deputies. It determines that 20 percent—soon after raised to 30 percent—of the list of each party, or coalition of parties, must be female candidates. A quota law was introduced in Brazil in 1995 by Marta Suplicy. Law 9100 then regulated the following year's elections for mayors and municipal houses of representatives. In 1997, Law 9504 extended the principle to the state legislative assemblies and the federal Chamber of Deputies. The congressional debate about the adoption of electoral quotas was surprisingly weak (S. M. Miguel 2000). All political parties were in favor of the law. The only exception was the small Popular Socialist Party, which spoke out against the quotas, drawing on arguments about republican equality. This consensus was possible because of the relative innocuousness of the law.

Table 7.1 Women elected to the Brazilian National Congress, 1974–2010

	1974	1978	1982	1986	1990	1994	1998	2002	2006	2010
Chamber of Deputies[a]	1 (0.3%)	4 (1.0%)	8 (1.7%)	26 (5.3%)	29 (5.8%)	32 (6.2%)	29 (5.7%)	42 (8.2%)	46 (9.0%)	44 (8.6%)
Federal Senate[b]	—	—	—	—	1 (3.2%)	4 (7.4%)	2 (7.4%)	5 (9.3%)	4 (14.8%)	8 (29.6%)

(a) The total number of representatives varied throughout the period: they were 364 in 1974, 420 in 1978, 479 in 1982, 487 in 1986, 503 in 1990 and 513 from 1994.

(b) The Senate is renewed by a third and two thirds alternately over each election. Due to changes in the number of federal units and the introduction of "interim mandates", 22 senators were elected in 1974, 44 in 1978 (22 by popular vote and 22 by federal government appointment), 26 in 1982, 52 in 1986, 31 in 1990, 54 in 1994 and 2002 and 27 in 1998 and 2006.

Source: the author, from data by Tribunal Superior Eleitoral (TSE – Superior Electoral Court) and Instituto Brasileiro de Geografia e Estatística (IBGE – The Brazilian Institute of Geography and Statistics).

Three peculiarities of the Brazilian law must be highlighted. First, the quotas are for candidacies, not for seats in parliament. And in open-list systems like Brazil's, parties do not determine a preferential order of candidates. All candidates compete for the popular vote. On the one hand, newcomers, as most of the women are, lack guarantees of campaign resources or airtime and are thus disadvantaged. On the other hand, in this system, there are no quota women who are perceived to lack merit for their mandates as is common in other countries with legislated quotas (see, for instance, chapters 2, and 3 in this volume). Second, at the same time as it instituted the quota for women, the law also increased the number of candidacies each party or coalition may put forward. That measure guarantees that higher numbers of female candidates do not reduce the number of spaces for male candidates. Finally, parties and coalitions are not required to fill all the vacancies allotted to women; it is just that they are not allowed to replace them with men. Taken together, these three peculiarities substantially reduce the impact of the quota law on the composition of the legislature (Miguel 2008).

LEGISLATIVE PROJECTS AND COMMISSIONS

Brazil's political parties are relatively weak. As the open-list system favors personal campaigns, parties generate little popular loyalty. It is common for politicians to change party affiliation many times in the course of their careers. Parties have a monopoly over contesting elections, yet they cannot discard candidates with potential to attract votes. While they have some prerogatives in congressional action, on the whole, politicians enjoy considerable freedom to determine their legislative priorities. In contrast with other countries where strong party discipline prevails, if women's issues are not a prime concern to female representatives in Brazil, we cannot blame the parties (see chapter 8 on South Africa in this volume).

Looking at women's legislative behavior, in the form of legislative initiatives and proposals for constitutional amendments, is thus a good measure of women's preferences. The data reveal that when compared with male representatives, women are more likely to focus on social issues than on issues related to the economy and infrastructure. Existing research lends further support to this conclusion (Santos, Brandão and Aguiar 2004; Pinheiro 2007; Biroli and Mello 2008), even if the studies use different forms of categorization of propositions and in many instances produce data only for female representatives, with male behavior inferred from other sources.

What is more, the success rate of women's legislative initiatives, that is, the proportion of proposals that are passed into law, is lower than that of men, although there are some discrepancies in the data. Santos, Brandão and Aguiar (2004, 88) calculate a 1.5 percent success rate for legislative initiatives introduced by women for the period between 1984 and 2004. Pinheiro (2007, 136) finds a 4.5 percent rate of approved proposals for a slightly different period (1987 to 2002).[1] For representatives from both sexes, the success rate is estimated to be between 5 percent and 7 percent. Also relevant is that among women, 19 percent of the projects approved refer to paying homage, giving names to public institutions or places, and instituting commemorative dates, while for both sexes, this percentage is only 3.8 percent (Pinheiro

2007, 137). In other words, not only are a smaller portion of bills introduced by female representatives approved, but a higher proportion of their successful bills are concerned with less significant issues. Available data do not allow us to see if there is an independent trend that reduces the effectiveness of women's legislative initiatives or if it is a secondary effect because of their fewer years of congressional experience. After all, there is a significant correlation between time in congress and the success rate of a representative's legislative initiatives (Amorim Neto and Santos 2003, 687).

Another indicator of women's status in the Chamber of Deputies is their participation in parliamentary standing commissions. Virtually all initiatives and legislative proposals must go through commissions, which then issue their own analyses. In most instances, commission approval can be conclusive; that is, the project will be automatically approved without having to pass through the plenary. In 2005, 90.5 percent of all bills adopted as law had been conclusively approved through the commissions.

To analyze women's participation and gender roles in commissions and parliamentary discourses, three categories were devised. The "hard politics" category relates to the core of the political process, including partisan politics, occupation of positions in the state apparatus, economic and tributary politics, economy, productive infrastructure (communications and energy), defense, security, and foreign relations and international politics. The "soft politics" category addresses more social issues: health, education, culture, family, housing, human rights, environment, poverty, consumer rights, and reproductive rights. Finally, the "middle politics" category covers themes that allow for drawing up mixed approaches, such as social welfare (including such concerns as pensioners and public accounts), mass media, science and technology, and the civil service. Categories for parliamentary discourses also include "irrelevant questions," an item that incorporates homage paid in plenary sessions (to municipalities, public institutions, civil society organizations, and celebrities), which are very frequent in speeches; and "others," covering miscellaneous themes with a low observation frequency that could not be included in an existing category. As a hypothesis, it was expected that women's participation would be greater in activities falling under the soft rather than hard category.

The analysis included the fifty-first and fifty-second legislatures, covering parliamentary activity from 1999 to 2006. In condensing commissions' participation according to categories, it is possible to observe clearly the relation between gender and themes. Women are overrepresented in soft politics commissions: 85.9 percent of women compared with 55.4 percent of men took part in these commissions. In the hard politics commissions, the proportions are inverted: 74.5 percent of the men and 46.9 percent of the women participated. Gender differences are greater for commission participation than for legislative projects or parliamentary discourses. The difference can be partially explained by the fact that participation in commissions is decided by political parties. While parliamentarians decide for themselves which issues to introduce or discuss in plenary, participation in a commission depends on the space that a political party concedes to a representative. Thus, a stereotyped perception of feminine inclinations within parties contributes to the likelihood that women will be relegated to soft politics.

This does not mean than female representatives would prefer to be in other commissions and are impeded by party leaders, although in some instances, this does occur.[2] Women's preferences are influenced by the opportunities open to them in the long term. The option for an education commission, for example, instead of an infrastructural one, can reflect the fact that the electoral body, the media,[3] and their own peers in politics will be more receptive to women's work in the social area. That is, women can be more effective and generate greater symbolic dividends by working in *favor* of gender stereotypes rather than against them.

PLENARY DISCOURSES

While the bulk of research on parliamentary work assumes that its main, if not sole, product is the law (see, for example, Arnold 1990), I believe that it is necessary to give attention to discourses; the production of meaning in the social world is an essential element in political activity. Parliamentary discourse is destined for multiple publics. First, it is a moment of debate among peers. However, often it is also directed to an external public, be it public opinion in general or a specific group.[4] It is up to each representative to define the target (or targets) when constructing their discourses. The issues that are chosen can also indicate priorities in a representative's mandate. Such priorities do not arise merely from individual convictions. Priorities are also strategic, linked to the existing opportunities for advancing one's political career.

The data set is composed of a random sample of 11,830 discourses in plenary sessions from representatives of both sexes between 1999 and 2006.[5] It is an oversized sample, reaching almost 37 percent of the universe of discourses in the period, that aimed through a great volume of data to make more accurate inferences about female and male representatives with different trajectories. As one of the characteristics of parliamentary discourse in plenary sessions, in contrast with speeches made in the commissions, is the tendency to look at a multiplicity of issues over a short period of time, each discourse could be considered according to several themes simultaneously.

The 11,830 discourses were pronounced by 790 different orators. The most active was responsible for 318 speeches. Most speakers (624 representatives) have between one and twenty discourses in the sample. It is important to observe that proclivity to speak does not correlate with leadership positions in parliament: of eleven representatives with more than one hundred discourses in the sample, only two were among the "congress heads" according to the DIAP. Women are responsible for only 840 (7.1 percent) discourses in the sample, 5.1 percent of the discourses in the fifty-first legislature (a little less than the percentage of those elected, 5.7 percent) and 8.4 percent of discourses in the fifty-second legislature (a little more than the percentage elected, 8.2 percent). Among the most assiduous orators, the first woman to come into the spotlight occupies twenty-fourth position, with sixty-eight discourses in the sample.

The debate in the chamber is thus a male discussion. The data indicate clearly that there are different working profiles for men and women, with women concentrating on social issues. Both men and women give preference to the issues included in the hard politics category, thus reinforcing the impression that such issues are a major focus of political debate, rendering more visible those who are concerned with them. Concentration on issues of hard politics is slightly greater among male representatives; themes from this category are present in 73.3 percent of male and in 67.3 percent of women's discourses. The situation is inverted when the middle politics category is analyzed (19.5 against, or 22.6 percent). Nevertheless, the more significant difference is in soft politics, present in 46.8 percent of female discourses and only 30.8 percent of male discourses. The association between women parliamentarians and issues related to social issues is clear.

It must be pointed out that the dominance of men in the chamber is so great that even in "feminine" themes, they are the majority. Human rights serve as an example: although 71.9 percent of female representatives spoke about human rights in at least one of their discourses included in the sample (while 72.5 percent of the men never addressed the issue), these percentages indicate only forty-six women in a universe of 246 parliamentarians who speak about this issue. There were 122 discourses from female representatives on human rights in contrast with 451 from male representatives. In other words, given the overwhelming number of men in the plenary, even when there is a concentration of female discourses on specific issues, the predominant masculine nature of the debate cannot be denied.

Contrary to expectations, as women gain greater experience in the legislature, they contribute fewer rather than more discourses (see table 7.2). The trend is far less marked for men. A possible hypothesis for this phenomenon is that women representatives go through a disenchantment process wherein they perceive symbolic obstacles to exercising their mandates in the chamber.

In thematic terms, the legislative experience is even more illuminating. First-term representatives focus their discourses on issues linked to soft politics, and as they gain experience, they begin to change focus. There is a substantial decline in the soft politics category in statements from parliamentarians found in the third legislature and onward (see table 7.3).

The correlation between women and soft politics may be spurious given their membership in leftist parties, which tend to be more sensitive to social issues. Nevertheless, the data do not corroborate this viewpoint. Affiliation with a center or right-wing party does not have significant impact on parliamentarians' willingness to focus on soft or hard political issues.

Table 7.2 Discourse average as provided in the sample from the parliamentary representatives according to sex and legislative experience

	First legislature	*Second legislature*	*Third legislature or more*
Women	10.6	6.7	6.0
Men	9.9	11.8	9.6

Source: Miguel and Feitosa (2009).

Table 7.3 Thematic discourse areas in accordance with the orator's parliamentary experience

	First legislature	Second legislature	Third legislature	Fourth legislature or more
Hard politics	73.2%	71.0%	73.8%	74.2%
Middle politics	19.9%	18.7%	20.4%	20.7%
Soft politics	35.9%	31.5%	28.1%	26.2%
Irrelevant and others	18.5%	19.1%	19.8%	18.9%
Total	$n = 4,804$	$n = 3,366$	$n = 1,723$	$n = 1,937$

Source: Miguel and Feitosa (2009).

Multiple answers were allowed. Dependence among variables is very significant. Chi^2 = 48.65, dl = 9, 1-p = > 99.99%.

There is also evidence of a relationship between legislators' thematic focus and their membership in the parliamentary elite. In the period analyzed, 144 different representatives were included in at least one annual DIAP listing of the most influential members of congress. Only six were women. In other words, women made up 8.1 percent of parliamentarians analyzed in the study but only 4.2 percent of the most influential. Data clearly indicate the thematic priority among members of the legislative elite. Those on the DIAP list contributed 23.0 percent of the discourses in the hard politics category, and 17.4 percent offered discourses on soft politics. Thus, there is an association between themes considered to be male and positions of major influence in the political field.

At the same time, women who do manage to enter the chamber's elite have profiles that are much closer to those of their male peers than their female colleagues who remain in less prestigious positions (see tables 7.4 and 7.5). Within this last group, men deal more with hard politics in their discourses (a difference of 7.0 percentage points) and less with soft politics (a difference of 16.1 percentage points). On the slate of most influential congress members, women deal a little more with hard politics than men (difference of 3.6 percent), Women still deal more than men with soft politics, but the difference (10.2 percentage points) is significantly smaller than the difference between the less influential parliamentarians.

Analysis of tables 7.4 and 7.5 indicates that the distance that separates a more influential female representative from a less influential one in terms of their discourses is much greater than what separates two male representatives. Accumulating political capital for a woman implies taking on "masculine" themes. In fact, the data clearly indicate that as political capital grows, parliamentarians tend to focus on hard politics. Social issues or soft politics occur as an interesting thematic niche for beginners or for those who generally are at the periphery of the political field, seeking their visibility with issues that are less contested or where the dispute has competitors who are less strong. However, what is merely one level in a political career for a man

Table 7.4 Thematic discourse areas of representatives who are not listed in the DIAP, according to the orator's sex

	Women	Men	Total
Hard politics	65.3%	72.3%	71.7%
Middle politics	22.8%	18.5%	18.9%
Soft politics	48.6%	32.5%	33.8%
Irrelevant and others	14.0%	20.3%	19.8%
Total	n = 729	n = 8,515	n = 9,244

Source: Miguel and Feitosa (2009).

Multiple answers were allowed. Dependence among variables is very significant. $Chi^2 = 70.75$, dl = 3, 1-p = > 99.99%.

Table 7.5 Thematic discourse areas of representatives who are listed in the DIAP, according to the orator's sex

	Women	Men	Total
Hard politics	80.2%	76.6%	76.8%
Middle politics	21.6%	22.9%	22.8%
Soft politics	35.1%	24.9%	25.4%
Irrelevant and others	11.7%	16.0%	15.9%
Total	n = 111	n = 2,475	n = 2,586

Source: Miguel and Feitosa (2009).

Multiple answers were allowed. Dependence among the variables is not significant. $Chi^2 = 5.09$, dl = 3. 1-p = > 83.46%.

appears to be a more permanent location for a woman's parliamentary action. Thus, the interplay of sex and status in politics reinforces the argument of this chapter: women's propensity to focus on soft issues relegates them to less prestigious and less influential positions.

Even with a more effective quota law that actually increased the number of women elected, this dynamic might persist. But the presence of more women would also expand and diversify their participation in different commissions and spaces of the house. They would be—potentially, at least—in a better position to challenge the established hierarchies of themes and concerns in political action.

REPRESENTATION OF THE FEMININE CONDITION

In the Brazilian Congress, what is the impact of women's presence, even if small, in defending women's interests or in advancing a feminist agenda? The women elected hold different political views, and some adopt frankly conservative positions with respect to gender relations. Even when there is a commitment to feminist ideas, they are never a priority, given the competition with other interests and identities. Professional interests, links to social movements, and geographical location tend to be more influential in determining the policy agendas of female representatives.

Out of the two most visible laws in favor of women's rights, one of them—gender quotas—was initiated by a female parliamentarian. The other, the "Maria da Penha Law" adopted in 2006, addresses domestic violence and was initiated by the executive branch. Sometimes questions that are of vital importance to women remain absent from the congressional agenda. One issue, namely the right to abortion, remains almost taboo in the Brazilian Congress. From 2003 to 2008, only 519 speeches made during plenary sessions of the Chamber of Deputies (in a universe of 124,318) included the word *aborto* ("abortion") or the expression *interrupção da gravidez* ("interruption of pregnancy"); 14.5 percent were made by women. Only forty-seven of the 519 speeches were favorable to the decriminalization of abortion or at least to expanding the instances for legal abortion. Recently, the two most active representatives in favor of the right to abortion were men: the late José Pinotti from the right-wing Liberal Front Party and José Genoíno from the left-wing Workers' Party. Although it has been noted that "with the country's redemocratization, there were changes regarding abortion . . . especially in terms of the theme's visibility . . . and in the expansion of the debate" (Rocha 2006, 373–374), congress remains reluctant to discuss this issue given the resistance of certain segments of the electorate, especially those linked to churches.

Despite the relative silence on issues such as abortion, women have nonetheless come together to form a bloc in the chamber, a form of collective action that first emerged in the National Constituent Assembly (1987–1988) to pressure for legal equality. All female representatives belong to it. Since its inception, the women's caucus has played a role in several legislative achievements for women, such as the juridical equality between the sexes in the new Civil Code, approved in 2002, and the establishment of provisions in practicing abortion in cases permitted by law (rape or risk to the life of the pregnant woman) through the public health system.

A distinct angle to address the impact of women's presence in the chamber is to observe the unfolding of the debate on women's issues, more precisely how female and male representatives contextualize gender relations and represent women's condition through their speeches. The March 8 sessions tend to concentrate discourses on the theme during commemoration of International Women's Day. Analysis of discourses on this day thus affords an opportunity to see how representatives comprehend the feminine condition.[6]

International Women's Day has become the moment for attempts at appropriation, when female consumers receive roses in supermarkets and kitchen appliance brands promote "homages to women" through newspaper advertisements. Different approaches to acknowledging women are represented by the discourses of parliamentarians of both sexes. An analysis of March 8 speeches between 1975—International Women's Year, as declared by the United Nations—and 2006 indicates the changes in approaches to the theme in the chamber. In the forty-fifth legislature (1975–1978), the issue of women was hardly seen as significant; toward the mid-1990s, it became present in most speeches (see figure 7.1).

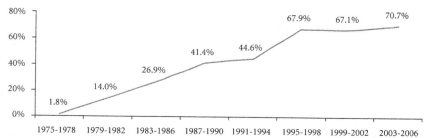

FIGURE 7.1 Proportion of the discourses that deal with the feminine condition in the March 8 sessions in the Chamber of Deputies, per legislative term (1975–2006).
Source: Campose Miguel (2008).

These sessions include 893 discourses. Female representatives were responsible for 14.3 percent of them—still a small percentage but more than double the proportion of female representatives in the chamber during the period analyzed. Women are also responsible for 28.1 percent of the discourses that deal with the feminine condition. In fact, 92.2 percent of female representatives who spoke at the March 8 sessions addressed the theme, in contrast with 39.5 percent of male representatives.

In more than thirty years, the number of women in the chamber has increased. There is no correlation between the percentage of women who have gone through parliament and the percentage of those who expressed their opinions on this issue in the March 8 sessions (r = -.306). Nevertheless, there is a high correlation between the percentage of women in the chamber and the percentage of discourses on this issue by both men and women representatives (r = +.961). In other words, the presence of more female representatives in the plenary encourages men to give greater attention to women's issues.

The speeches were grouped into three sets. Most of them are limited to a ritual greeting on International Women's Day, after which the orator goes on to other issues. Other speeches lean toward the glorification of women's "beauty" or "greatness" through relatively conventional praise of their "virtues" and their role in family life, the economy, or even politics. They form a set of discourses dedicated to an uncritical and depoliticized exaltation of woman. A second set of discourses deals with public policies geared toward women, gives recognition to some movement or personality, or comments on the history of women and feminism. Finally, the third set includes more critical discourses that raise problems of sexism, inequality, and violence against women.

Table 7.6 shows how female and male representatives differ in their approach to gender issues. While the mere exaltation of women dominates the discourses, a great number of female discourses incorporate a critical approach.

At the same time, men's discourses on March 8 in most instances (57.4 percent) reproduce the traditional stereotypes of woman as mother, homemaker, and companion, characterized by her generosity and goodness. Female representatives, in turn, give marked preference to militant representation of women either as fighters or as victims of patriarchal society, as is evident in 77.8 percent of their speeches.

Table 7.6 Relative presence of approach groups in discourses based on the representative's sex

	Women	Men	Total
Ritual greeting or depoliticized praise of women's virtues	42.2%	60.1%	55.3%
History and public policies	45.9%	38.5%	40.5%
Critiques and demands	86.2%	53.4%	62.2%
Total	$n = 109$	$n = 296$	$n = 405$

Source: Campos and Miguel (2008).

Multiple answers were allowed. The category "other approaches" was omitted, having only fifteen reports.

CONCLUSION

Gender socialization mechanisms play a key role in establishing female political practices. The association between women and the domestic sphere and the concomitant affirmation of public space as exclusive male territory remains operative, although women have broken numerous barriers to become involved in politics. The data analyzed in this chapter indicate that political women in Brazil have opted to work with issues linked to their traditional role and that this reinforces their less prestigious position in politics.

In all areas of women's actions in the Chamber of Deputies, their involvement in soft politics is evident. However, once they gain more visibility and prestige, they tend to shift their focus to issues linked to hard politics. It becomes clear, then, that there is a link between giving preference to specific themes in parliamentary activity—themes associated with men—and opportunities for greater and faster ascension in political life.

The mere presence of women in parliament, as necessary as it may seem, does not represent equal capacity for policy formulation and for producing representations of the social world. The link between women and themes of lesser importance in the political sphere keeps women on the periphery and demands of those who have already managed to ascend in the field the onus to break loose from the expectations regarding their behavior.

This obviously does not mean that masculine issues are essentially more important. It is, in fact, possible to argue the contrary. What is relevant here is to acknowledge that the predominant association between issues and gender works against women's rise to key positions in political power—a complex process in which, at the same time, male representatives benefit from the prestige of their preferred issues and concede prestige to these issues by defining them as masculine.

Given that men have more autonomy to establish their strategies, women in politics see themselves above all as faced with a shared dilemma. If they confront stereotypes by ignoring the social expectations about "appropriate" behavior, they are considered misfits, deviants, or masculinized. But if they opt to conform to gender stereotypes, they confine themselves to positions of lesser prestige in the political world. In this way, a type of feminine ghetto is created within male politics. This reinforces traditional gender roles and thus delegates to women, and not men, responsibility for dealing with social issues.

If gender quotas, as a means of broadening women's participation in public spaces, are sustained based on an essentialist argument, then we are sabotaging the possibilities of equal political representation. The defense of the expansion of subaltern social groups' political action relinquishes any essentialist argument that presents differentiated objective interests or a distinct moral character (Miguel 2001). What sustains this demand is the recognition of social inequality and the need to expand the spectrum of voices present in public debate—a requirement for full democracy, understood as a political regime in which norms are determined by those who will be submitted to them.

Nonetheless, numbers do make a difference. The increase in the number of women makes it more difficult to isolate them in specific thematic niches or to place them in a bloc separate from major positions in the field. Even with the reduced percentages in Brazil, the presence of a contingent of female representatives has drawn attention—including that of male representatives—to women's problems, as seen in the discussion of discourses in the March 8 sessions and the exponential increase in legislative propositions about women's issues, authored by both men and women since the 1990s (Santos, Brandão, and Aguiar 2004, 45).

Extending political equality is not just a problem for women or any other subaltern groups. It is a challenge to be faced in any society that seeks to be democratic. Confronting this issue requires institutional measures such as electoral gender quotas but also demands cultural changes that guarantee recognition of these groups and the redistribution of material resources that allow for political action, among them free time, to use Nancy Fraser's (1997) terms. Further, it also requires transformations in the day-to-day functioning of representative institutions by preventing them from simply reproducing already established hierarchies.

In short, the case of Brazil tells us that quotas, even if relatively ineffective in numeric terms, can make a difference. But they are not a panacea. The political field has its own rules which undermine the representation of subaltern groups. On the one hand, quotas, by themselves, can make the isolation of such groups more difficult, if they reach a substantive proportion of representative bodies, but this has not been the case in Brazil. On the other hand, women's subordination has roots in society as a whole and cannot be confronted in the political field alone. These challenges must be faced at the same time.

NOTES

1. Pinheiro nevertheless does not clarify if propositions that would in the future undergo presidential vetoes—and therefore cannot be changed into legal norms— are or are not counted among the approved.
2. See accounts from representatives reproduced in Pinheiro (2007, 162–165).
3. For an analysis of the role of political news in reinforcing gender stereotypes in politics, see Miguel and Biroli (2011).

4. It is not common for plenary discourses to be reported in the main media vehicles, although local or special interest newspapers do so. But there is TV Câmara, the television channel that transmits chamber debates by cable, and *A Voz do Brasil*, a one-hour daily program with official information, including a summary of events in the congress, which is compulsorily broadcasted by all radio stations around the country. Moreover, representatives use their speech records in promotional material sent to voters.

5. All of the data from the research can be found in Miguel and Feitosa (2009).

6. Complete results of this research can be found in Campos and Miguel (2008).

REFERENCES

Amorim Neto, Octavio, and Fabiano Santos. 2003. O Segredo do Ineficiente Revisto. *Dados* 46 (4): 661–98.

Arnold, R. Douglas. 1990. *The Logic of Congressional Action*. New Haven, Conn.: Yale University Press.

Biroli, Flávia, and Janine Mello. 2008. Gênero e Representação Política. Paper presented at VI Encontro da Rede Brasileira de Estudos e Pesquisas Feministas, Belo Horizonte.

Bourdieu, Pierre. 1979. *La Distinction*. Paris: Minuit.

———. 2000. *Propos sur le Champ Politique*. Lyon: Presses Universitaires de Lyon.

Campos, Luiz Augusto, and Luis Felipe Miguel. 2008. O Oito de Março no Congresso. *Cadernos Pagu* 31: 471–508.

Chodorow, Nancy. 1978. *The Reproduction of Mothering*. Berkeley: University of California Press.

Delphy, Christine. 1994. Feminismo e Reconstrução da Esquerda. *Revista Estudos Feministas* 2 (1): 187–199.

Elshtain, Jean Bethke. 1981. *Public Man, Private Woman*. Princeton, N.J.: Princeton University Press.

Fraser, Nancy. 1997. *Justice Interruptus*. New York: Routledge.

Gilligan, Carol. 1982. *In a Different Voice*. Cambridge, Mass.: Harvard University Press.

Miguel, Luis Felipe. 2000. Teoria Política Feminista e Liberalismo. *Revista Brasileira de Ciências Sociais* 44: 91–102.

———. 2001. Política de Interesses, Política do Desvelo. *Revista Estudos Feministas* 9 (1): 253–267.

———. 2008. Political Representation and Gender in Brazil. *Bulletin of Latin American Research* 27 (2): 197–214.

Miguel, Luis Felipe, and Flávia Biroli. 2011. *Caleidoscópio Convexo*. São Paulo: Editora Unesp.

Miguel, Luis Felipe, and Fernanda Feitosa. 2009. O Gênero do Discurso Parlamentar. *Dados* 52 (1): 201–221.

Miguel, Sônia Malheiros. 2000. *A Política de Cotas por Sexo*. Brasilia: Centro Feminista de Estudos e Assessoria.

Okin, Susan Moller. 1989. *Justice, Gender and the Family*. New York: Basic.

Pinheiro, Luana Simões. 2007. *Vozes Femininas na Política*. Brasilia: Secretaria Especial de Políticas para as Mulheres da Presidência da República.

Rocha, Maria Isabel Baltar da. 2006. A Discussão Política sobre Aborto no Brasil. *Revista Brasileira de Estudos Populacionais* 23 (2): 369–374.

Ruddick, Sara. 1989. *Maternal Thinking*. Boston: Beacon.

Santos, Eurico, Paulo Henrique Brandão, and Marcos Magalhães de Aguiar. 2004. Um Toque Feminino. In Comissão Temporária do Ano da Mulher do Senado Federal, *Proposições Legislativas sobre Questões Femininas no Parlamento Brasileiro, 1826–2004*. Brasilia: Senado Federal.

Young, Iris Marion. 2000. *Inclusion and Democracy*. Oxford: Oxford University Press.

8 Party Centralization and Debate Conditions in South Africa

Denise Walsh

Over the past fifteen years, scholars, leading international organizations, and international, regional, and local activists have advocated women's greater presence in politics.[1] The results have been impressive in Africa, where women moved into legislatures in large numbers as the result of quotas. Several African countries now have the highest rates of women representatives in the world, and the continent approximates the world average of 19.3 percent (Inter-Parliamentary Union 2011).

Before the South African democratic transition in 1994, the renowned dissident Helen Suzman was often the sole woman in the National Assembly. That changed when the African National Congress (ANC) implemented a 30 percent voluntary party quota for women candidates in the country's first nonracial election. Although the ANC was the only party to adopt a quota, it won 62.6 percent of the vote, and 27.7 percent of members of parliament (MP) were women. In 2009, women made up 44.5 percent of parliament as a result of continued ANC electoral dominance and its 50 percent quota. In 2011, only Rwanda, Andorra, and Sweden had a larger proportion of women in their national legislatures (Inter-Parliamentary Union 2011).

The first nonracial parliament (1994–1999) not only brought a large number of women into the legislature, but it also advanced women's rights. The new government ratified the Convention on the Elimination of All Forms of Discrimination against Women (CEDAW) in 1995, repealed numerous discriminatory laws, and legalized abortion in 1996 with strong ANC support. The 1995 Labour Relations Act, the 1997

Basic Conditions of Employment Act, and the 1998 Employment Equity Act improved women's employment status. In 1998, parliament passed the Domestic Violence Act, ended the minority status of women in customary marriages, and reformed the maintenance law. However, during the second nonracial parliament (1999–2004), women's rights legislation stalled despite continued need for action. Female legislators did little to alter that outcome. Why?

Scholars of South African gender politics point to several factors obstructing substantive representation, meaning the advancement of women's interests in policy making. They point to the collapse of the national women's movement after the 1994 election, tensions between women in civil society and the state, the increasing professionalization of female MPs, ANC discipline of outspoken female MPs, and a proportional representation (PR) system that encourages politicians to heed party bosses instead of constituents (e.g., Britton 2005; Hassim 2006; Gouws 2005). Scholars of democratization point to an additional problem: in countries with dominant parties, bosses threaten democratic accountability and responsiveness (Przeworski 1991; Diamond and Plattner 1999).

Few of these problems can explain the precipitous decline in substantive representation and the stall in women's rights after 1998, because they remained constant or decreased over time. ANC dominance, the PR system, and the quota existed at the birth of the new nation and persist to this day. The women's movement collapsed at the outset of the first South African nonracial parliament and did not revive. Moreover, single-issue women's organizations rebounded after the collapse of the women's movement, and their working relations with female MPs strengthened over time. The latter should have proved beneficial for substantive representation. The only factors that changed in the expected direction were ANC discipline of outspoken female MPs and their increasing professionalization. I argue that these two factors were linked to a broader pattern of ANC centralization that accounts for the decline in substantive representation and the stall in women's rights.

Through a structured, focused comparison of the first and second nonracial South African parliaments, I find that ANC governing elites used the party's electoral dominance, PR system, and quota in different ways that had far-reaching effects on substantive representation and women's rights.[2] Initially, ANC elites used these tools to pack parliament with talented leaders, to increase the influence of parliamentary committees, and to encourage civil society to assist them in a common cause of transformation. Female MPs exploited this situation by drawing on their large numbers and talents to expand debate conditions in parliament, increasing their voice and capacity for contestation. As a result, they exercised substantive representation and advanced women's rights. However, by the second parliament, ANC governing elites were using the party's electoral dominance, PR system, and quota to strengthen the executive branch, strangle internal party debate, rein in independent MPs, and direct civil society. That repressed debate conditions, limiting women's diversity, voice, and capacity for contestation, and it prompted a decline in substantive representation that stalled advances in women's rights.

On the eve of the 1994 elections, the ANC was not a highly centralized political party poised to take power. On the contrary, when F. W. de Klerk stunned the nation in 1990 by unbanning opposition parties and releasing political prisoners, including Nelson Mandela, the ANC scrambled to create a unified party out of a dispersed liberation movement. Female politicians, activists, and academics capitalized on this fluid political moment to organize and promote women's rights. In 1990, ANC women reestablished the Women's League (ANCWL) and attempted to secure earlier ANC commitments to a quota in its National Executive Council (NEC), proposing a 30 percent quota. Their demand generated bitter debate before being sharply rejected. Soon afterward, leadership divisions engulfed the ANCWL, and its capacity to spearhead gender reform declined.

Undeterred, a group of female politicians, activists, and academics spanning the political spectrum founded the Women's National Coalition (WNC). The WNC led 2 million South African women in a consciousness-raising campaign and wrote a National Charter. It also helped win a quota for women at the transition negotiations, a gender equality clause in the interim constitution, and extensive gender machinery in the new state. These successes, along with public concerns about the new government's inclusivity, pressured ANC leaders to advance women up the ranks: they placed a woman on each ANC committee and adopted a 30 percent quota for the multimember, closed-list PR system.

Given the chaotic status of the ANC in 1994 and the immense pressures of the transition, the party's selection of candidates in the first election was "haphazard" (Feinstein 2009, 24). Indeed, ANC candidates were diverse, and few had formal government experience. Women candidates included the powerful insider and leader of the WNC Frene Ginwala, the singer Jennifer Ferguson, ardent trade union organizer Pregs Govender, and rural activist Lydia Kompe. The majority of ANC women were concentrated at the bottom of the party lists, but ANC electoral dominance and pressures from the ANC's quota prompted other parties to advance women as candidates. As a result, 111 women swept into parliament. Their success siphoned leadership from the WNC, which collapsed after ruling MPs could not hold positions in its organization. Women's political dynamism thus shifted from civil society to parliament.

Female MPs took office under an interim constitution committed to inclusivity, accessibility, and transparency. The ANC endorsed these ideals as the majority of the population, which had long been excluded from formal politics, was mobilized and supported them. However, ANC support for participatory politics eroded as the party grappled with the challenges of governing the postapartheid nation and holding together a vast party. After the National Party resigned from the Government of National Unity (GNU) in 1996, ANC governing elites exploited their control of the executive branch by discouraging parliamentary autonomy and oversight and pursued party centralization.[3] They tightened candidate selection in 1998, controlling the final decisions for the party lists while competing with one another to ensure positions for favored candidates (Feinstein 2009, 73).

As the grip of governing elites over ANC MPs tightened, party leaders trumpeted women's descriptive representation and increased the quota. In 1999, women occupied every third slot on the party lists and made up 38 percent of the total.[4] President Thabo Mbeki extolled women's numbers as an indicator of the party's inclusivity and promised to expand the quota to 50 percent for the 2009 elections. In 2007, the populist Jacob Zuma defeated Mbeki in a battle over the presidency of the ANC. The change in leaders did not lesson elite control of the party. Although branches nominated candidates in 2009, party leaders ruled that all candidates must be free of "ill-discipline," with no history of "fostering divisions and conflict."[5] Despite Zuma's questionable commitments to women's rights, he honored Mbeki's promise to increase the quota.[6] The celebrated liberation movement that had struggled against daunting odds to end apartheid had become a centralized political party with few electoral challengers. Instead, internal rivals vied for leadership positions and used women's presence in parliament to display inclusivity.[7] This transformation had profound consequences for substantive representation and women's rights.

ANALYTICAL FRAMEWORK AND METHODS

As Miguel (chapter 7) and Larson (chapter 9) in this volume note, an increase in women's descriptive representation does not secure comparable advances in women's rights. This is hardly surprising, as women find that their efforts at proposing and debating gender legislation have a limited effect when parties and legislatures are undemocratic and sexist (e.g., Duerst-Lahti and Kelly 1995; Hawkesworth 2003). How parties and legislatures produce and maintain informal exclusions varies by political context. In this chapter, I provide a framework for analyzing the openness and inclusiveness of parliamentary politics that explains how female MPs can be prevented from engaging in substantive representation even when they make up a significant proportion of the legislature.

Drawing on critical deliberative theory (Fraser 1996; Young 2000), I hypothesize that if female MPs have access, voice, and capacity for contestation, they can engage in substantive representation and advance women's rights. *Access* refers to women's numerical presence, positions of rank, and diversity by class, race, and political ideology. Although access is not sufficient, as Miguel's discussion of Brazil in chapter 7 of this volume demonstrates, a diverse group of women with some rank can provide a basis for articulating and acting on shared gender interests. *Voice* refers to women's ability to speak out and be heard with respect on a wide range of issues and in a variety of styles.[8] Access without voice suggests tokenism: woman as audience. *Capacity for contestation* indicates that women can organize and challenge parliamentary norms and procedures that inhibit their effectiveness, often by establishing counterpublics, meaning groups in which members discover and articulate common concerns, debate collective goals, hone their organizational and public-speaking skills, make alliances across differences, and develop strategies for advancing their interests (Fraser 1996; Walsh 2006; Walsh 2011). Depending on the political context, a number of factors can prevent women from expanding debate conditions. In South Africa, the problem was not a lack of female MPs with rank but, rather, a highly centralized political party.

Figure 8.1 illustrates my argument, which I test through a structured, focused comparison of the first two nonracial South African parliaments. To develop my argument, I draw on qualitative sources such as newspapers, government documents, and interviews. My interview strategy was saturation rather than maximizing sample size. I conducted fifteen semistructured interviews of activists and researchers associated with parliament and ten semistructured interviews of a diverse group of female MPs. I used coding and memoing to collect and analyze the data and cross-checked my sources to ensure adequacy, scope, and consistency (Miles and Huberman 1984). As coding and memoing advanced, I fine-tuned my "general questions" (George and Bennett 2005, 67). For centralization, I ask: Did parliament have the capacity to question executive policies? Were women's organizations able to set their goals independently of government? For debate conditions, I ask: What were women's numbers in parliament? Were female MPs racially and ideologically diverse, and did they hold positions of power? Did women representatives speak out in committee meetings and debates, and did their colleagues listen to them with respect? Did female MPs challenge parliamentary norms and procedures, and did those challenges succeed? To assess substantive representation, I ask: What policy actions did female representatives take to promote gender-based violence (GBV) legislation, and were they successful? I focus on GBV because during both periods, South African women identified this as an important issue of common concern (Kola et al. 1999; Commission on Gender Equality 2005), and rates were extremely high (Jewkes, Levin, and Penn-Kekana 2002; Jewkes et al. 2006).

A comparison of the two parliaments holds constant several explanations for the variations in women's substantive representation and women's rights discussed in the introduction. Three additional contextual factors that might account for variation are also held constant: the type of party in power, the strength of the international women's movement, and the influence of traditional groups opposed to women's rights. Although ANC political leadership changed in April 1999 as Nelson Mandela stepped aside and the intellectual technocrat Thabo Mbeki took the helm, Mbeki's presidency signaled political continuity within the ANC.[9] The influence of the international women's movement in Africa remained high across both periods, too, so it cannot account for variation over time, either (Tripp et al. 2009). Finally, the influence of traditional chiefs on women's rights outcomes was constant, as they were aligned with the political opposition during both periods (Meer and Campbell 2007).

I cannot confirm here whether my causal chain explains variations in substantive representation and the passage of women's rights in widely different contexts. However, I do find that ANC centralization undermined debate conditions in the second

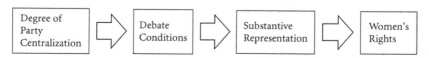

FIGURE 8.1 Party centralization and women's rights: The causal chain.

South African parliament, that descriptive representation contributes toward but is insufficient for substantive representation, and that variations in debate conditions shaped substantive representation and outcomes on women's rights in South Africa.

THE FIRST NONRACIAL SOUTH AFRICAN PARLIAMENT, 1994–1999

The 1994 parliament had considerable clout, as MPs were tasked with writing the final constitution. Indeed, parliament was a site of vibrant political debate, even on controversial issues such as HIV/AIDS (Feinstein 2009). MP autonomy was enhanced by ANC inexperience in formal governing. For example, ANC party whips were unfamiliar with parliamentary procedures and became overwhelmed with mundane tasks such as providing housing and parking for ANC MPs, limiting their ability to enforce party discipline (Jacobs 1997). MP autonomy coupled with a quota that ensured a significant presence of talented women leaders enabled female MPs to expand debate conditions, facilitating substantive representation and the advancement of women's rights.

Women's access to parliament was impressive. The quota and ANC electoral dominance ensured that ANC women made up more than 80 percent of the total number of female MPs in parliament. The ANC was a heterogeneous party. ANC female MPs reflected the country's class, ethnic, and racial diversity and the party's wide-ranging political commitments (Britton 2005; Geisler 2004).[10] Female MPs also held important positions in the new parliament. Frene Ginwala and Baleka Mbete were speaker and deputy speaker, respectively, ten women were chairpersons in the thirty-five powerful portfolio committees, and women were the majority in a number of committees (Hassim 2003, 89; Myakayaka-Manzini 1998, 175).

Women's remarkable access did not mean that debate conditions in parliament were open and inclusive. Women MPs complained about the "cut-throat" culture of parliament, likening it to "a boys' high school debating club" (Serote et al. 1996, 69). When their style of speaking and working in parliament differed from the male norm, it was not respected. As the *Cape Times* reported: "Jennifer Ferguson, ANC MP, still smarting after her 'poems to music' were declared inappropriate to Parliament while all around her 'fighting games' were being played out, suggested that women's broad goal ought to be to correct the imbalances in society."[11] Female MPs with less education and other structural disadvantages were the most disempowered. Mahau Phekoe of the Women's National Coalition noted: "At the last budget speech, three women commented on the budget. One read a speech written in English. She struggled with what she had to say. . . . Comments were made on her bad delivery. The other two had done no research. This discredited these women" (Meer 1998, 163). ANC MP Lydia Kompe, the charismatic leader of the Rural Women's Movement, admitted: "I cannot see myself making any input never mind impact here" (as quoted in Mtintso 1999, 41).[12]

Some male MPs obstructed women's ability to speak out and be heard. ANC MP Naledi Pandor remarked: "I have noticed sometimes that, when women put up their hands to speak, the male chairperson will look at them as if a bolt of lightning has struck."[13] Several women reported that men ignored them altogether when they asked to speak, while others would leave the room; sometimes men blocked women's entry to meeting rooms (Britton 2005, 75). A number of male MPs commented on women's appearance when they were making a speech; sexual harassment was common (Geisler 2000; 2004).

Debate conditions improved as women leaders established counterpublics.[14] In 1994, female MPs formed the cross-party Parliamentary Women's Group (PWG) to make parliament more women-friendly. Because parliament did not officially recognize the PWG, it had difficulty scheduling meetings and lacked a budget. Nonetheless, the group won some changes. For example, the parliamentary calendar was altered to match the school schedule, and meetings ended before the dinner hour.[15] The PWG lost momentum, however, as its successes meant that women's shared interests gave way to party ideology.

Additional counterpublics were forthcoming. Young black ANC women established an ANC Women's Caucus. Ginwala secured international funds for a Women's Empowerment Unit (WEU) that offered skills training. ANC women, along with those in opposition parties such as Sheila Camerer and Dene Smuts, helped to establish the Commission on Gender Equality (CGE) through public admonishment and by bringing men "on board" with workshops and training.[16] Additional challenges to the status quo succeeded by building on these victories. For example, Ginwala used the resources of her office, a position she won with backing from the ANC Women's Caucus, to secure a Joint Standing Committee on the Improvement of the Quality of Life and Status of Women (JMC) (Britton 2007, 73). That committee promoted a Women's Budget Initiative to expose gendered fiscal policy. Of all of these institutions, the JMC was the most dynamic, although it operated without a budget, lacked a full-time administrator, and was initially an ad hoc committee.

This array of counterpublics helped women to speak out and be heard. ANC MPs such as Brigitte Mabandla, Mavivi Manzini, and Thenjiwe Mtintso insist that men became more receptive over time and that women's contributions in committees and debates were increasingly valued (Geisler 2000; Mtintso 1998). Many women reported greater assertiveness and comfort by the end of their first term (Geisler 2000; Mtintso 1999). As debate conditions improved, female MPs took greater initiatives on gender legislation. On most issues, they differed more over details than passage. Women worked together, often using the ANC Women's Caucus, the JMC, and the PWG to prioritize legislation, network with other politicians and grassroots organizations, hold workshops and public hearings, and press for revisions in committee.

Reports and parliamentary records confirm that female MPs often raised GBV as an important issue. Working with women's groups in civil society, female MPs used National Women's Day and debates over the Human Rights Commission, educational spending, and pornography to highlight the issue (e.g., Hansard 1994; 1995). The ANC Women's Caucus initiated the Joint Civil Society-ANC Parliamentary Women's Caucus Campaign to End Violence against Women and Children to raise awareness of GBV within South African legal institutions and in their own constituencies. They organized a march on parliament and blanketed MPs with reports that facilitated debate (Shifman, Madlala-Routledge, and Smith 1997). The JMC priori- tized the issue, holding hearings on violence against women. The Second Women's Budget highlighted the costs of violence against women (Budlender 1997). With JMC chairperson Pregs Govender leading the charge, female MPs gained the support of government leaders and overrode objections for more "gender-neutral language" in their bill (Govender 2007; Meintjes 2003, 155).[17] The ANC then fast-tracked the 1998 Domestic Violence Act (DVA) through parliament over the objections of its feminist authors, who argued that it was still incomplete.[18] The groundbreaking leg- islation passed without controversy.

The DVA significantly expanded the definition of domestic relationships and the types of violence included, increased burdens on the police, and sanctioned arrest of abusers without a warrant. It also contained clear legal directives and instructions to bureaucratic administrators and provided monitoring indicators. During a pe- riod of party fluidity, the ANC quota and ANC electoral dominance helped female MPs gain access to the first parliament in which they used their leadership skills to pry open debate conditions and advocate and then pass seminal domestic-violence legislation. The second parliament offers a different story.

THE SECOND SOUTH AFRICAN PARLIAMENT, 1999–2004

By the second parliament, the effects of ANC centralization on the party, civil so- ciety, and parliament were unmistakable. Former ANC MP Andrew Feinstein argues that by 2000, the ANC was "a party fearful of its leader, conscious of his power to make or break careers, conscious of his demand for loyalty, for conformity of thinking" (2009, 111). As one scathing critic put it, "By 2001 . . . the ANC would no longer permit even internal debate about its lack of internal debate" (Butler 2005, 732). Ranking ANC members complained that the National Executive Council had become a "rubber stamp" packed with Mbeki loyalists (Gumede 2005, 295).

ANC governing elites also curbed the autonomy of civil society, pressuring NGOs to be service providers rather than government watchdogs. This was true of the ANCWL, which had returned to its role as a women's wing. NGOs working on violence against women suspected that bureaucratic red tape was being used to block money for organizations critical of ANC policies (Britton 2006). Activist Michelle Festus insists that NGOs' programming and selection of the boards of di- rectors were "driven by ANC politics" and had to "be in line with government policy to get funding."[19] From the perspective of opposition parties, civil society had become an extension of the ruling party. Remarking on the ANC pipeline of funds to favored organizations, Democratic Party MP Sandra Botha quips that the entire NGO sector was "an ANC jamboree."[20]

ANC centralization also undermined the role of parliament, as party elites used the PR system to quell dissent. Dependent on superiors for their jobs and deeply loyal to their leaders, few MPs challenged the executive. Chief whip Tony Yengeni became a "centre of discipline and the dispenser of patronage"; Ginwala complied with executive authority to the point of "intentionally obstructing parliamentary processes on behalf of the executive"; and ANC MPs desisted from criticizing the executive or his advisers, preferring instead to caucus, stall, and exonerate (Congress of South African Trade Unions 2006; Feinstein 2009, 76, 179). As president of the ANC, Mbeki controlled parliamentary committees (ANC MPs chaired all but two) and obstructed parliamentary debate over government corruption and his notorious HIV/AIDS policies.[21]

In 1999, these problems were not yet perils, and female MPs were optimistic that they could build on recent gains. As Inkatha Freedom Party MP Suzanne Vos explained, "I didn't come into politics naturally . . . the first time was daunting. . . . But we did get used to it and those of us who have come back are confident. Many of us have specialized, and this time we are not groping our way."[22] In addition to greater experience, women's numbers and leadership positions modestly increased. Women made up 39 percent of the ANC electoral lists. Out of the 120 women elected to parliament, ninety-seven were from the ANC. Together, women made up nearly 30 percent of MPs. Ginwala and Mbete continued as speaker and deputy speaker; women headed thirteen committees (26 percent), including Defense.[23] However, women's diversity, voice, and capacity for contestation declined. ANC elites began using the PR system and quota to discipline independent-minded female MPs. Although more women were distributed throughout the party lists and several garnered top spots in 1999, Pregs Govender (chair of the JMC) and Nozizwe Madlala-Routledge (chair of the ANC Women's Caucus) were not rewarded with rankings on the party list commensurate with their talents. That sent a clear signal that careers would be jeopardized if MPs persisted in advancing an independent gender agenda (Coetzee 1999).

Governing elites also narrowed the class, regional, and ideological diversity of ANC women. Thirty-four percent of the women from the first parliament did not return. The largest group that left was the poorest black women who lacked professional skills essential for parliamentary work. Their replacements were more likely to have mastered English, were more affluent, were younger, and had fewer children. They had experience in law and business; few had been grassroots activists (Britton 2006, 77; Geisler 2000; Hassim 2006). Newcomers were less interested in transformation than in professional advancement (Britton 2005). A third set of female MPs were mocked by colleagues and the press for their lack of merit and excessive party loyalty. Rightly or not, rural black women were identified with this group (*Noseweek* 2002).[24] Although women's numbers remained impressive, the quota and PR system enabled the ANC to prioritize professionalism and loyalty among MPs, making it more challenging for independent-minded women to rally support for gender reform.[25]

As ANC centralization increased and MPs became professionalized, parliamentary culture did not improve. Women who persisted in using different speaking styles continued to be rebuffed. When Govender asked listeners "to close their eyes and focus on the power of love and courage within their hearts" or invited them to take part in a "game" to illustrate a key point, her colleagues took her to task (Govender 2007, 206). Yet men's style of speech did not conform to conventional standards of professionalism. Some made catcalls in parliament and told sexist jokes at the expense of women colleagues. Despite Ginwala's successful attacks on sexual harassment during the first parliament, it reemerged as a serious problem (Govender 2007; *Noseweek* 2002).

ANC female MPs flatly denied these problems, signaling the extent to which party discipline was curtailing their voices. Denials came from previously outspoken feminist leaders, such as the deputy speaker Baleka Mbete, who had become a "fervent Mbeki loyalist" (Gumede 2005, 292).[26] In contrast, female MPs in opposition parties acknowledged that despite improvements, problems remained. As IFP MP Suzanne Vos insists, men dominated parliament, ensuring that female MPs were insecure and "Because we have a patriarchal society, women depend on men for patronage in terms of their places, because . . . the men are the bosses of the parties."[27] Female MPs from other parties stated for the record that they had been denied important decision-making roles, circumscribing their effectiveness (*Noseweek* 2002). If ANC female MPs expressed their discontent, it was done anonymously, signaling ANC disapproval of criticism.

Women's counterpublics founded during the first parliament also declined. Governing elites limited funding and marginalized women's groups. The PWG was moribund; the WEU restricted its work to skills assessment. The CGE continued to be severely hobbled by infighting, government co-optation, and limited funding (Manjoo 2005). The ANC women's caucus worked with the JMC, but ANC elites assiduously undermined it. The JMC was the last committee reconvened in the second parliament, its budget was reduced in 2001, and attacks on the chair's credibility intensified as she spoke out against the arms deal and HIV/AIDS.[28] In 2002, after being stalked and having her car dismantled, Govender resigned (Govender 2007).[29] The ANC then gutted the Women's Budget Initiative.

With ANC centralization intensifying, talented women in parliament considered leaving. They included Ginwala, who threatened to resign several times because the ANC-dominated Rules Committee attacked her power base.[30] She left abruptly in April 2004, admitting, "We [the ANC] need to reopen the dialogue we had in the eighties and the early nineties instead of going into our laagers and defending our ideas" (as quoted in Gumede 2005, 297). Ginwala's exit underscores how centralization and eroding debate conditions taxed party loyalty and undermined even the fiercest feminist MPs.

Constrained voice and capacity for contestation in the second parliament did not eliminate substantive representation on GBV, but women's efforts declined considerably. After the 1999 elections, the government neglected to set an implementation date for the DVA. In response, the CGE and the JMC joined NGOs in criticizing government delays; they won a December implementation date (Meintjes 2003, 157; Usdin et al. 2000). Soon thereafter, the commissioner of police reported a dearth of funding for enforcing the DVA (Mattes 2002, 28). A lack of itemization on costing, targets, training, and interdepartmental jurisdiction—missing from the DVA because it had been fast-tracked—became a critical problem. To prompt government action, the JMC, still under Govender's guidance, took investigative trips throughout the country and worked with the CGE and civil society to hold public hearings in 2002 (Manjoo 2005). Govender's successor did not lead the JMC in similar directions. Indeed, no further action on the issue occurred during the second parliament.

In January 2003, the South African Law Reform Commission (SALRC) completed its review of the law on sexual assault, begun during the first parliament. The SALRC recommended that all forms of sexual penetration irrespective of gender be included in the bill, along with a framework for implementation and medical treatment. The

Cabinet and Portfolio Committee on Justice and Constitutional Development rejected these costly provisions and introduced a clause requiring that complainants prove that the sex was not consensual (Artz and Smythe 2008). The government then shuttled the bill between departments and committees for the remainder of the period. The JMC did not make a single recommendation on the bill.[31] The lack of action by the JMC, government stalling, and the elimination of the bill's most progressive elements stand in stark contrast to the seminal, fast-tracked Domestic Violence Act of 1998.

CONCLUSION

Although the grip of ANC governing elites over the party has recently slipped, the ANC's electoral dominance, PR system, and quota enable it to maintain MP loyalty and to control the legislative agenda. Debate conditions in parliament remain constrained, substantive representation limited, and women's rights stalled.[32] When divisions within the ANC led to the election of Zuma as party president in 2007, Mbeki remained president of the country. Zuma's allies promptly claimed parliamentary leadership positions. The split revived parliamentary autonomy from the executive. One of Zuma's allies was Mbete, who deftly switched her political allegiances. She was named both speaker and chair of the ANC's Political Committee. As the committee shapes ANC strategy in parliament, the dual appointments presented a serious conflict of interest, signaling that parliament was under party control (Feinstein 2009). In 2008, the ANC expelled Mbeki from office and installed Kgalema Motlanthe as interim president, reviving executive dominance.

Women's numerical access to parliament increased with Zuma's presidency, but their voice and capacity for contestation has remained constrained. In 2009, half of all ANC candidates were women, alternating with men on the party lists. As a result, 130 out of 172 female MPs were from the ANC (Lowe Morna, Rama, and Mtonga 2009). Yet women's access to leadership positions fared poorly under Zuma: in 2009, the speaker and most party whips and leaders were men; deputy speaker Nomaindia Mfeketo was the sole exception (Lowe Morna, Rama, and Mtonga 2009).

Moreover, women's counterpublics declined precipitously. The ANC Women's Caucus did little to prevent debate conditions in parliament from becoming abusive. The caucus did demand the immediate suspension of chief whip Mbulelo Goniwe when he was accused of sexual harassment in 2006 but took little subsequent action as Goniwe relentlessly pursued reinstatement.[33] The problems in the CGE deepened as corruption allegations crippled the organization.[34] The new Ministry of Women, Youth, Children and Disability, established in 2009, failed to consult with women's groups, suffered from "departmental chaos," and proved incapable of running the 2009 Sixteen Days of Activism Campaign.[35] The JMC failed to meet regularly during the third parliament; a portfolio committee for the new Ministry of Women, Youth, Children and Disability replaced it.[36] Although Zuma was not as successful as his predecessor in controlling the party, ANC electoral dominance, the quota, and the PR system have been sufficient to maintain executive control over parliament, limiting debate conditions and curtailing pressures for continued advances in women's rights.

As women's presence increased in the third and fourth parliaments, substantive representation and advances in women's rights were rare. ANC female MPs did take some action on GBV but with limited results. The JMC declined to act on the stalled 2003 Sexual Offenses Bill, but it did hold hearings on GBV in 2006, as did the Portfolio Committee on Women, Youth, Children and Persons with Disabilities in 2009.[37] During the 2009 hearings, civil society presented incontrovertible evidence of the DVA's poor implementation and offered detailed recommendations for improvements, advocating strong government denouncements, increased funding, and specialized courts (Public Hearings 2009). Although the committee wrote a sympathetic report, tabled in October 2010, it has had limited effect: no amendment to the DVA has been forthcoming, despite demonstrated need and scandalously high levels of violence against women (Strategic Report 2009; Vetten et al. 2010). In 2007, parliament belatedly passed the Sexual Offences Act. Activists did not celebrate its passage, noting that it had been "unacceptably watered down" by the elimination of key victims' rights provisions (Artz and Smythe 2008, 7–8). The contrast with the Domestic Violence Act of 1998 could not be sharper.

In 1994, ANC electoral dominance and a PR system that facilitated a 30 percent quota brought a talented number of ANC women into parliament during a remarkably inclusionary moment. Capitalizing on that opportunity, female MPs established a number of counterpublics that helped them pry open debate conditions, and they exercised substantive representation and advanced women's rights. However, by the second parliament, a strong executive centralized the party. ANC governing elites used their electoral dominance, the PR system, and the quota to undermine women's counterpublics and discipline female MPs. That led to a decline in debate conditions that eroded substantive representation and stalled advances in women's rights. An expansion of the ANC's voluntary quota to 50 percent has not resolved these problems. Instead, elites continue to herald the quota, claiming a commitment to participatory politics and women's rights that no longer exists.

NOTE

1. This chapter has benefited immensely from comments on earlier drafts by many colleagues, including Shireen Hassim, Gretchen Bauer, anonymous reviewers, and the editors. Its remaining faults are my own. I would like to thank the University of Witwatersrand Political Science Department, the University of Virginia, and the Dickey Center for International Understanding at Dartmouth College for research support.

2. ANC governing elites during the second parliament included President Thabo Mbeki, Trevor Manuel, Tito Mboweni, Essop Pahad, Mojanku Gumbi, Frank Chikane, Titus Mafolo, Cunningham Ngcukana, and Wiseman Nkuhlu (Calland 2006).

3. The GNU included cabinet positions for all parties that won at least 5 percent of the vote and executive power sharing for the second-largest electoral winner.

4. Julie Ballington, as cited in "Moving Slowly Up the Gender Ladder," *Star*, May 14, 1999.

5. As quoted in Verashni Pillay and Liezel de Lange, "A Few Surprises in ANC Lists," News24.com, January 28, 2009.

6. In 2005, Deputy President Jacob Zuma was accused of rape. His notorious statements about sex, consent, and HIV/AIDS during his sensational trial exposed widespread acceptance of male domination and sexual violence.

7. The strongest opposition party, the Democratic Alliance (DA), captured 16.7 percent of the vote in 2009. The splinter party, Congress of the People (COPE), siphoned some ANC support, claiming 7.4 percent of the vote that same year. COPE is the only other party with quotas; they mirror those of the ANC.

8. Iris Marion Young suggests a wide range of speech, including protest and storytelling (2000).

9 Adam Habib and Roger Southall, "Different Men, Same Mission," *Financial Mail*, May 7, 2004.

10. No statistics exist on women in parliament by race. The apartheid regime categorized people as black, colored, Indian, and white. I use the term *black* to refer to the first three groups.

11. "Women Stake Their Claim to a Fairer Place in New South Africa," *Cape Times*, March 10, 1995.

12. Nevertheless, Kompe became a skilled MP.

13. As quoted in Susan Segar, "Still Largely a Male Domain," *Natal Witness*, July 5, 1998.

14. For a profile of women leaders, see Britton 2006, chap. 4.

15. Additional changes included a relaxed dress code, gender-sensitive language in legislation, more toilets for female MPs, and women's showers in the gym.

16. Mavivi Manzini, as quoted in "Where Is the Gender Equality Commission?" *Mail & Guardian*, May 5, 1995. The CGE is a constitutionally mandated body charged with monitoring and investigating gender equality.

17. Ian Clayton, "Key Challenges Lie Ahead for Women," *Mail & Guardian*, April 30-May 6, 1999.

18. Former CGE commissioner Rashida Manjoo, interview, Charlottesville, Va., February 4, 2010.

19. National Land Committee gender coordinator Michelle Festus, interview, Johannesburg, July 29, 2003.

20. Democratic Alliance MP Sandra Botha, interview, Cape Town, July 25, 2003.

21. In 1998, the government finalized its purchase of $4.8 billion in armaments. A series of corruption accusations followed, implicating then-deputy president Jacob Zuma (see Feinstein 2009 for a detailed discussion). Mbeki insisted that HIV did not cause AIDS, severely hampering government response to the disease.

22. Leanine Dickerson, "Female MPs Get Out of Grey Suits," *Sunday Independent*, August 8, 1999.

23. Female MPs continued to predominate on "soft" committees. Andile Noganta and Vusi Mona, "Loading the Dice in This Man's Game," *City Press*, April 25, 1999.

24. Inkatha Freedom Party MP Suzanne Vos, interview, Cape Town, July 23, 2003.

25. Ibid.

26. ANC deputy speaker Baleka Mbete, interview, Cape Town, July 24, 2003.

27. Vos interview.

28. "Government Slammed for Prioritising Defence over Gender Equity," *Mail & Guardian*, August 14, 2001.

29. Several CGE commissioners I interviewed reported similar problems; at least one received death threats. The deputy minister of health, Nozizwe Madlala-Routledge, a prominent women's rights advocate who criticized Mbeki's HIV/AIDS policies, was denied access to crucial information, harassed, and dismissed in 2007. Anso Thom, "Fired for 'Doing My Job'—Madlala-Routledge," Health-e News Service, August 13, 2007, http://www.csa.za.org/article/articleview/447/1/1/ (accessed May 6, 2009).

30. Jeremy Michaels, "'Too Powerful' Frene Replaced as Speaker," *Star*, April 23, 2004, http://www.iol.co.za/index.php?set_id=1&click_id=13&art_id=vn20040423041051744C460511 (accessed May 6, 2009).

31. Christi van der Westhuizen, "Fix the Gender Machine," *Mail & Guardian*, May 25, 2009, http://www.boell.org.za/web/104-370.html (accessed January 10, 2010); "Zuma Case Reveals SA Rape Problem," BBC News, February 15, 2006, http://news.bbc.co.uk/2/hi/africa/4713172.stm (accessed January 10, 2010).

32. By the fall of 2009, Zuma's inability to dominate the party was evident, prompting nostalgia for Mbeki's firm hand by mid-2010. For example, see Richard Calland, "Flag Waving Won't Fix the Widening Cracks," *Mail & Guardian*, June 13, 2010, http://www.mg.co.za/article/2010-06-13-flag-waving-wont-fix-the-widening-cracks (accessed June 13, 2010).

33. He was found guilty twice. "ANC Must Purge Sex Pests," *Independent Democrats*, December 15, 2006, http://www.id.org.za/newsroom/press-releases/press-release-archive/press-releases-2006/december-2006/lance-greyling-2013-2018anc-must-purge-sex-pests2019/?searchterm=mps (accessed August 1, 2009).

34. Manjoo interview, and see the corruption saga involving former commissioner Nomboniso Gasa in Sello S. Alcock, "Gasa Accused of Graft," *Mail & Guardian*, March 8, 2009, http://www.mg.co.za/article/2009-03-08-gasa-accused-of-graft (accessed June 17, 2010); and Nomboniso Gasa, "Mr. President, I Stand Accused . . .," *Mail & Guardian*, June 17, 2010, http://www.mg.co.za/article/2010-06-15-mr-president-i-stand-accused (accessed June 17, 2010).

35. Manjoo interview and Sheila Meintjes, personal communication, February 4, 2010. "2000 Report Card: Muddling Along in the C Class," *Mail & Guardian*, December 23, 2009, http://www.mg.co.za/article/2009-12-23-2009-report-card-muddling-along-in-the-c-class (accessed January 10, 2009).

36. Christi van der Westhuizen, "Fix the Gender Machine," *Mail & Guardian*, May 25, 2009, http://www.boell.org.za/web/104-370.html (accessed January 10, 2009).

37. Ibid.

REFERENCES

Artz, Lillian, and Dee Smythe, eds. 2008. *Should We Consent? Rape Law Reform in South Africa*. Cape Town: Juta.

Britton, Hannah. 2005. *Women in the South African Parliament: From Resistance to Governance*. Urbana and Chicago: University of Illinois Press.

———. 2006. Organising against Gender Violence in South Africa. *Journal of Southern African Studies* 32 (1): 145–163.

———. 2007. South Africa: Mainstreaming Gender in a New Democracy. In Gretchen Bauer and Hannah Britton, eds., *Women in African Parliaments*, 59–84. Boulder, Colo.: Lynne Rienner.

Budlender, Debbie. 1997. The Women's Budget. *Agenda* 33: 37–42.

Butler, Anthony. 2005. How Democratic Is the African National Congress? *Journal of Southern African Studies* 31 (4): 719–736.

Coetzee, Alice. 1999. Gender Activists Too Low on Party Lists. *Election Bulletin* 1 (1).

Commission on Gender Equality. 2005. *National Gender Opinion Survey*. Johannesburg: Commission on Gender Equality.

Congress of South African Trade Unions (COSATU). 2006. COSATU Secretariat Report to the Ninth National Congress, September 18–21, Gallagher Estate, Midrand. National Congress Reports.

Diamond, Larry, and Marc F. Plattner, eds. 1999. *Democratization in Africa*. Baltimore, Md.: Johns Hopkins University Press.

Duerst-Lahti, Georgia, and Rita Mae Kelly, eds. 1995. *Gender Power, Leadership, and Governance*. Ann Arbor: University of Michigan Press.

Feinstein, Andrew. 2009. *After the Party*. London: Verso.

Fraser, Nancy. 1996. *Rethinking the Public Sphere*. In Craig Calhoun, ed., *Habermas and the Public Sphere*, 109–142. Cambridge, Mass.: MIT Press.

Geisler, Gisela. 2000. "Parliament Is Another Terrain of Struggle": Women, Men and Politics in South Africa. *Journal of Modern African Studies* 38 (4): 605–630.

———. 2004. *Women and the Remaking of Politics in Southern Africa: Negotiating Autonomy, Incorporation and Representation*. Uppsala, Sweden: Nordiska Afrikainstitutet.

George, Alexander L., and Andrew Bennett. 2005. *Case Studies and Theory Development in the Social Sciences*. Cambridge, Mass.: MIT Press.

Gouws, Amanda. 2005. Shaping Women's Citizenship: Contesting the Boundaries of State and Discourses. In Amanda Gouws, ed., *(Un)thinking Citizenship: Feminist Debates in Contemporary South Africa*, 71–90. Cape Town: UCT Press.

Govender, Pregs. 2007. *Love and Courage: A Story of Insubordination*. Auckland Park, South Africa: Jacana Media.

Gumede, William Mervin. 2005. *Thabo Mbeki and the Battle for the Soul of the ANC*. Cape Town: Zebra.

Hansard. 1994. Debates in the National Assembly, 1st Session, No. 15. November 14–16: 4415.

———. 1995. Debates in the National Assembly, No. 3. March 28-April 6: 230.

Hassim, Shireen. 1999. The Dual Politics of Representation: Women and Electoral Politics in South Africa. *Politikon* 26 (2): 201–212.

———. 2003. Representation, Participation and Democratic Effectiveness: Feminist Challenges to Representative Democracy in South Africa. In Anne Marie Goetz and Shireen Hassim, eds., *No Shortcuts to Power*, 81–109. London and New York, Cape Town: Zed Books and David Philip.

———. 2006. *Women's Organizations and Democracy in South Africa: Contesting Authority*. Madison: University of Wisconsin Press.

Hawkesworth, Mary. 2003. Congressional Enactments of Race-Gender: Toward a Theory of Raced-Gendered Institutions. *American Political Science Review* 97 (4): 529–550.

Inter-Parliamentary Union. 2011. Women in National Parliaments. http://www.ipu.org/wmn-e/world.htm .

Jacobs, Sean. 1997. Whips "Vital Cog" in the Wheel. *Parliamentary Whip*, February 2: 7.

Jewkes, Rachel, Kristin Dunkle, Mary P. Koss, Jonathan B. Levin, Mzikazi Nduna, Nwabisa Jama, and Yandisa Sikweyiya. 2006. Rape Perpetration by Young, Rural South African Men: Prevalence, Patterns and Risk Factors. *Social Science & Medicine* 63: 2949–2961.

Jewkes, Rachel, Jonathan Levin, and Loveday Penn-Kekana. 2002. Risk Factors for Domestic Violence: Findings from a South African Cross-Sectional Study. *Social Science & Medicine* 55: 1603–1617.

Kola, Soraya, Debbie Budlender, Zaid Kimmie, and Ann Kushlick. 1999. *Gender Opinion Survey*. Cape Town: Community Agency for Social Enquiry.

Lowe Morna, Colleen, Kubi Rama, and Lowani Mtonga. 2009. *Gender in the 2009 South African Elections May 11*. Johannesburg: Gender Links.

Manicom, Linzi. 2005. Constituting 'Women' as Citizens: Ambiguities in the Making of Gendered Political Subjects in Post-apartheid South Africa. In Amanda Gouws, ed., *(Un)thinking Citizenship: Feminist Debates in Contemporary South Africa*, 21–54. Hants, U.K.: Ashgate.

Manjoo, Rashida. 2005. South Africa's National Gender Machinery. *Acta Juridica* 17: 243–272.

Mattes, Robert. 2002. South Africa: Democracy without People. *Journal of Democracy* 13 (1): 22–36.

Meer, Shamim. 1998. *Women Speak: Reflections on our Struggles 1982–1997*. Cape Town: Kwela and Oxfam GB.

Meer, Talia, and Craig Campbell. 2007. *Traditional Leadership in Democratic South Africa*. Durban and Cape Town: Democracy Development Program. http://www.ddp.org.za/contact-us (accessed May 1, 2009).

Meintjes, Sheila. 2003. The Politics of Engagement: Women Transforming the Policy Process—Domestic Violence Legislation in South Africa. In Anne Marie Goetz and Shireen Hassim, eds., *No Shortcuts to Power: African Women in Politics and Policy Making*, 140–159. London: Zed.

Miles, Matthew B., and A. Michael Huberman. 1984. *Qualitative Data Analysis: A Sourcebook of New Methods*. Newbury Park, Calif.: Sage.

Mtintso, Thenjiwe. 1998. Access, Participation and Transformation. Entrenching Democracy & Good Governance through the Empowerment of Women Report, November 13–15.

———. 1999. *Women and Politics: A Conceptual Framework. Redefining Politics*. Johannesburg: Commission for Gender Equality.

Myakayaka-Manzini, Mavivi. 1998. Women Empowered—Women in Parliament in South Africa. In Azza Karam, ed., *Women in Parliament: Beyond Numbers*, 175–180.

Strategic Report on Public Hearings on Implementation of Domestic Violence Act. 2009. November 18. http://www.pmg.org.za/report/20091118-strategic-report-public-hearings-implementation-domestic-violence-act (accessed September 1, 2011).

Stockholm: International Institute for Democracy and Electoral Assistance.

Noseweek. 2002. Women in Parliament. August (40): 8–11.

Public Hearings on the 11-Year Implementation of the Domestic Violence Act. 2009. October 29. http://www.pmg.org.za/report/20091029–11-year-implementation-domestic-violence-act-public-hearings (accessed January 10, 2010).

Przeworski, Adam. 1991. *Democracy and the Market: Political and Economic Reforms in Eastern Europe and Latin America*. Cambridge, U.K.: Cambridge University Press.

Serote, Pethu, Nozipho January-Bardill, Sandra Liebenberg, and Jacqui Nolte. 1996. What the S.A. Parliament Has Done to Improve the Quality of Life and Status of Women in S.A. Report released by Office of the Speaker of the National Assembly of South Africa, Cape Town. March 8. Photocopy.

Shifman, Pamela, Nozizwe Madlala-Routledge, Viv Smith. 1997. Women in Parliament Caucus for Action to End Violence. *Agenda* 36: 23–26.

Tripp, Aili Mari, Isabel Casimiro, Joy Kwesiga, and Alice Mungwa. 2009. *African Women's Movements: Changing Political Landscapes*, New York: Cambridge University Press.

Usdin, Shereen, Nicola Christofides, Lego Malepe, and Aadielah Maker. 2000. The Value of Advocacy in Promoting Social Change: Implementing the New Domestic Violence Act in South Africa. *Reproductive Health Matters* 8 (16): 55–65.

Vetten, Lisa. 2007. Violence against Women in South Africa. In Sakhela Buhlungu, John Daniel, Roger Southall, and Jessica Lutchman, eds., *State of the Nation: South Africa 2007*, 425–447. Pretoria: HSRC.

Vetten, Lisa, Teresa Le, Alexandra Leisegang, and Sarah Haken. 2010. *The Right & The Real: A Shadow Report Analysing Selected Government Departments' Implementation of the 1998 Domestic Violence Act and 2007 Sexual Offences Act*. Johannesburg: Tshwaranang

Legal Advocacy Centre. http://www.tlac.org.za/images/documents/The%20Righ%20 and%20The%20Real.pdf (accessed September 1, 2011).

Walsh, Denise. 2011. *Women's Rights in Democratizing States: Just Debate and Gender Justice in the Public Sphere*. New York: Cambridge University Press.

——. 2006. The Liberal Moment: Women and Just Debate in South Africa, 1994–1996. *Journal of Southern African Studies* 32 (1): 85–105.

Young, Iris Marion. 2000. *Inclusion and Democracy*. Oxford: Oxford University Press.

9 Collective Identities, Institutions, Security, and State Building in Afghanistan

Anna Larson

At its inauguration in November 2005, Afghanistan's lower house high numbers of female members of parliament, or Wolesi Jirga, was the subject of international acclaim—not only for its apparent embodiment of post-Taliban democracy but also for its extraordinarily high number of female members. Sixty-eight (27 percent) of 249 seats were and remain occupied by female legislators, as a direct result of a reserved seats system outlined in the 2004 constitution (Government of Afghanistan 2004, article 83). Almost reaching the UN-specified 30 percent critical mass of women in legislative bodies, then, the Wolesi Jirga ostensibly provides an environment conducive to the promotion of women's gender interests. In its first five-year term, however, women's considerable presence in parliament has not led to the substantive representation (or definition) of the interests of "women in general."

This chapter examines obstacles to the substantive representation of women's gender interests in the Wolesi Jirga. In using the term *women's gender interests* in this context, the study refers to the collective interests of women that emerge as a result of social constructions of gender roles and relations in Afghanistan (Wordsworth 2007, 3). These interests are distinct from (but often overlap with) those that arise from other aspects of women's identity. The term "substantive representation" is used to denote a form of representation that encompasses both the *means* through which women's gender interests are put forward in the legislature and the *outcomes* of this representation.[1] This chapter argues that as women's gender interests are in essence collective interests, often (and ideally) cross-cutting ethnic and regional divisions, their substantive representation requires collective action among gender activists (men or women). Furthermore, in terms of outcomes, substantive representation must result in potentially tangible gains for women in general. Although these gains can take a variety of forms, this study focuses primarily on achieving gender-sensitive legislation. It must be noted, however, that the mere existence of such legislation is no guarantee that it will be implemented or enforced.

The chapter first provides a background to the establishment of the reserved seats system in Afghanistan and its impact on existing political space for women at the national level. This background is characterized by Afghanistan's initially postconflict and now increasingly insecure context, in addition to various institutional factors that define the limits of political mobilization more generally in the country. Although current levels of insecurity in Afghanistan make it an unlikely case for the study of substantive representation, the context in which the reserved seats system was implemented—Afghanistan in 2006—was a different environment and one in which development actors were keen to promote institution building. Moreover, the notable absence of substantive representation in Afghanistan in 2010 emphasizes the extent to which gender quotas are not a panacea: their potential efficacy cannot be assumed on the basis of their merit as useful mechanisms alone. Quotas often do not achieve their intended goals (such as the promotion of women's policy interests) within expected time frames because of certain features of a political context.

The case study of female MPs' promotion of their gendered interests is based on research conducted for the Afghanistan Research and Evaluation Unit (AREU) between 2006 and 2010.[2] The chapter concludes with reasons for the limited substantive representation of women's gendered interests in Afghanistan to date.

Essentially, two key messages emerge from this study: (1) that the *means* of representation are fundamental—and collective action crucial—to the substantive promotion of women's gender interests, especially in societies divided by ethnic and other tensions; but (2) that the relationship *between* means and outcomes is not guaranteed. As with the Brazilian case outlined by Luis Felipe Miguel in chapter 7 of this volume, women's collective presence and mobilization alone are not enough in the uneven field of political engagement. Even if collective action is regularly mobilized, internal legislative procedures or the broader sociopolitical context can significantly limit or prevent efforts to represent these interests and produce tangible gains for women. This is especially the case in postconflict contexts, in which quotas have been initiated as part of external state-building and development programs—which, by their very nature, are designed toward the promotion of technical as opposed to political intervention.

QUOTAS AND THE POLITICAL CONTEXT IN AFGHANISTAN

Immediately before the fall of the Taliban, the plight of Afghan women was fast becoming the subject of international concern. As such, in the Bonn process—the joint international-Afghan state-building initiative which began with discussions and an agreement in Bonn, Germany, in 2001—considerable efforts were initially made to redress existing inequalities. With the strong encouragement of the international community, the interim and then transitional governments of Afghanistan made a series of commitments to Afghan women, including the reservation of 10 percent (of a total 1,600) seats in the 2002 emergency Loya Jirga ("Grand Council"), the establishment in 2002 of the Ministry of Women's Affairs (MOWA), the signing of the Convention for the Elimination of All Forms of Discrimination against Women (CEDAW) in 2003, and the unprecedented constitutional introduction in January 2004 of reserved seats for female candidates in legislative elections.

The Bonn Agreement required that a commission of nine members (including two women) be established to draft Afghanistan's new constitution using Zahir Shah's 1964 constitution as a basis. This commission was then replaced in May 2003 by a constitutional review committee, consisting of thirty-five members—nine of whom were women—and mandated to hold consultations with Afghans in all provinces and across ethnicities. While participatory in theory, however, this process was limited by the adherence to strict deadlines imposed by the Bonn process, and consultations were completed within two months. Nevertheless, during this time, women in civil society and female activists had some input into the content of the constitution. They were strongly supported by international NGOs and UN agencies that organized workshops and training for review committee members on the importance of a reserved seats provision (for more on the constitution-making process, see Brunet and Solon Helal 2003, 11–15).

The reserved seats system for the lower house of parliament determines that "from each province on average at least two female delegates shall have membership to the Wolesi Jirga" (Government of Afghanistan 2004, article 83). This creates a total pre-reserved space of sixty-eight seats across thirty-four provinces,[3] or 27 percent of the total 249 seats available in the Wolesi Jirga. Provincial seat allocation is determined by rough population estimates (in the absence of a recent census), and thus some provinces have more or fewer than two seats reserved for women, but all have at least one. Because of its status as a constitutional requirement, the system can only be altered by Constitutional Loya Jirga (CLJ)—a grand council called for issues of national significance or emergency.

Given the size and suddenness of the measure, the results of the first post-Taliban parliamentary elections in 2005 were somewhat surprising: women proved more successful than expected. Almost 30 percent of women won open (not reserved) seats (Wilder 2005, 1). In total, however, only sixty-eight women were allocated places in parliament, a number that coincided with the number of reserved seats. Women who won open seats had their seats incorporated into the allotted number of reserved seats. As such, the constitutional provision for "at least" sixty-eight seats was interpreted as a maximum or ceiling. This is evidenced in the interviews for this study, in which both female and male MPs made references to set numbers of "women's" and "men's" seats rather than "reserved" and "open" seats.

The subject of the reserved seats system reemerged in early 2010 when President Karzai issued a controversial decree altering the electoral law during a parliamentary recess. One notable change was assigning authority to the Independent Electoral

Table 9.1 Number of Wolesi Jirga seats per province

Province	Population	Wolesi Jirga seats	
		Total	Women
TOTAL	21,677,700	249	68
Badakhshan	790,200	9	2
Badghis	412,400	4	1
Baghlan	748,000	8	2
Balkh	1,052,500	11	3
Bamyan	371,900	4	1
Daikundi	383,600	4	1
Farah	420,600	5	1
Faryab	824,500	9	3
Ghazni	1,020,400	11	3
Ghor	574,800	6	2
Helmand	767,300	8	2
Herat	1,515,400	17	5
Jawzjan	443,300	5	1
Kabul	3,013,200	33	9
Kandahar	971,400	11	3
Kapisa	367,400	4	1
Khost	478,100	5	1
Kunar	374,700	4	1
Kunduz	817,400	9	2
Laghman	371,000	4	1
Logar	326,100	4	1
Nangarhar	1,237,800	14	4
Nimroz	135,900	2	1
Nuristan	123,300	2	1
Paktia	458,500	5	1
Paktika	362,100	4	1
Panjshir	127,900	2	1
Parwan	550,200	6	2
Samangan	321,500	4	1
Sar-i-Pul	463,700	5	1
Takhar	811,700	9	2
Uruzgan	291,500	3	1
Wardak	496,700	5	2
Zabul	252,700	3	1
Reserved for Kuchi (nomad)		10	3

Source: AREU 2009, 74–75.

Commission (IEC) to find measures to fill any reserved seats for women that were not won because of a lack of female candidates in a given province (Government of Afghanistan 2010, chapter 5, article 23). In 2005, the electoral law clearly stated that unallocated reserved seats should remain empty for a full parliamentary term (Government of Afghanistan 2005, chapter 6, article 22). Women's rights groups viewed this alteration as a way to appease conservatives opposed to the reserved seats system and a mechanism through which to provide an incentive to male candidates to prevent women from standing for office. The reform did not, however, have this effect; more female candidates competed for election in 2010 than in 2005, and in actual fact, one woman was elected outside of the sixty-eight reserved seats as a result of two women winning the two allocated parliamentary seats outright in Nimroz province. Their vote counts—3,480 and 3,369—stood more than a thousand votes ahead of the third candidate, a man, who gained 2,315 votes. Both seats were given to female candidates, despite only one of these being reserved for women. There are now sixty-nine women in the Afghan legislature. Nevertheless, this is an example of an exception rather than the rule, and there appears to be considerable opposition (as exemplified by the president's change to the electoral law) to the more widespread breaking of the sixty-eight-seat glass ceiling (for more discussion on this issue in general, see Dahlerup 2009, 35–36).

In terms of the political and institutional context, in 2001, Afghanistan was considered a postwar country. Thirty years of conflict had apparently concluded with the defeat of the Taliban, and by December 2001, a state-building and reconstruction program was being compiled in the Bonn discussions, complete with democratization initiatives—such as presidential elections—that would be the first of their kind in the country. While previous regimes had experimented with democratic practices on various occasions since the 1920s, none had gone as far as encouraging universal suffrage or the direct election of a premier.

Unfortunately, since this time, insecurity has increased, and the discourse of foreign policy is once again that of "winning the war" in Afghanistan. Even before security began to deteriorate nationwide, however, state-building programs in Afghanistan were coming up against a variety of problems. First, far from being a tabula rasa on which new institutions could be built, the remnants of Soviet, Mujahideen, and Talib attempts at forming administrative structures had created layers of overlapping institutional cultures in ministries, for example, which were entrenched to varying degrees and unreceptive to substantive replacement (Larson 2008, 48–65). Thus, the new post-2001 democratic machinery became in many ways another of these institutional layers, simply functioning at the surface without fundamentally changing the widespread reliance on earlier forms of administrative functionality (Kandiyoti 2007, 198). This is particularly evident in the case study of the parliamentary reserved seats system for women, as outlined below—which is often considered by its critics as merely another of the superficial, external impositions of the post-2001 era.

Second, various concessions were made in the formation of state and political institutions to accommodate the postconflict context. It was felt that a strong presidential system was necessary to facilitate decisive and productive leadership, which has since led to extensive executive influence over legislative affairs (not entirely dissimilar from those described in the South African case in chapter 8 of this volume), with debilitating effects on parliamentary procedures. It was also decided, after much discussion among high-level Afghan and international policy makers, that the simplest election system available would best suit the country's low literacy rates. Afghanistan is one of the few countries in the world to have adopted a system of single nontransferable vote, whereby individual citizens vote once for one candidate in multimember constituencies (provinces) and in which there are neither limitations on the number of candidates permitted to stand in a given province nor stipulations requiring candidates to be associated with political parties (Reynolds, Jones, and Wilder 2005, 7).

Indeed, another concession determined that marginalizing parties would circumvent potential ethnic tensions that could threaten the new "national unity." Thus, while parties exist in Afghanistan, often as factions based on ethnic identities (Ruttig 2006, 1), they are not formally recognized as necessary political players in the electoral system. Candidates for elections largely stand as independents, whether they are affiliated informally with parties or not. Ironically, within and outside of parliament, parties wield considerable influence but are not fixed entities, have no strong ideological basis, and tend to have shifting membership. As such, they do not provide solid platforms for the promotion of collective interests.

Linked to this is the overall lack of platform politics or a "politics of ideas" (Phillips 1995) in Afghanistan. During its first term, a considerable emphasis has been placed on *who* (i.e., particular social groups) is represented, rather than the ideas or platforms they intend to put forward. This corresponds to the way in which politics in Afghanistan is very much centered on clientelist networks of personalities and patrons, whether they be Mujahideen commanders, ethnic leaders, religious scholars, or prominent female MPs (Giustozzi and Ullah 2006; Roy 2003). Consequently, there is an absence of political platforms in parliament and very few issues-based alliances that cut across social groups.

Part of the problem is a "culture of political ambiguity" (Larson 2009a, 11), whereby there is an incentive *not* to formalize one's connections to a given party given the potential security risks that publicly labeling oneself might incur and given the benefits of bargaining with different political groups offering competing rewards for support on a given issue (Larson 2010, 1). This fluidity, while potentially advantageous to female MPs as individuals, undermines the consolidation of groups that could consistently promote an agenda for the substantive representation of women's gender interests.

METHODS AND DATA COLLECTION

This chapter divides the concept of substantive representation into two overlapping but distinct categories. First, in assessing the *means* through which women's gendered interests are represented, the chapter asserts that these interests cannot be put forward substantively without collective mobilization. Thus, evidence of such mobilization was sought throughout the data-collection process, and its frequency and longevity were analyzed. This is particularly important in the context of Afghanistan given the lack of ideas-based platforms transcending ethnic, linguistic, and regional divisions.

Second, the chapter claims that substantive representation is defined by *outcomes*, which, for the purposes of this study, are defined as the legislative results of collective action in parliament. While one could argue that passing legislation is not a tangible achievement for the majority of women in Afghanistan, given the central government's weak reach into the provinces and lack of power or political will to enforce laws, it is nevertheless an outcome that could potentially affect all women, as compared with the short-term practical needs of limited groups of female constituents addressed by individual MPs in the run-up to elections, for example.

The study triangulates the testimonies of MPs, along with members of the parliamentary secretariat, members of civil society, and international actors working in parliament, against formal documentation of parliamentary activities and the actual existence of legislation passed promoting women's gender interests. It also examines the relationship between these means and outcomes, testing the assumption that in theory, greater coordination among women and a more consolidated approach to the means of promoting women's gender interests would necessarily lead to the greater efficacy of that promotion and the production of more gender-sensitive legislation.

One limitation of this case study is that given the recent adoption of reserved seats, its link to external intervention, and indeed the lack of a functioning legislature at all in the thirty years before the Bonn process, there is little scope for comparison of pre- and postquota parliaments in Afghanistan. As such, it is difficult to separate the effects of the quota from the effects of women's presence more generally. However, as will be discussed below, most derogatory remarks made by male MPs about their female peers concern the apparently "unjust" way they were elected, rather than the presence of women per se. Thus, reactions toward female parliamentarians indicate to some extent the distinction between the effects of quotas and women's presence.

Initial data collection for this study took place between December 2006 and May 2007 but has been continually updated since. A sample of forty-two MPs (twenty-seven women and fifteen men) was primarily identified, chosen on account of their diverse ethnicities, backgrounds, and provincial constituencies. This has since been supplemented by many further interviews with different MPs, with the total reaching more than 120. A semistructured interview guide was used for all respondents, who were given a choice of three languages (Dari, Pashtu, or English) in which to respond to questions. All interviews cited were conducted by the author and a team of Afghan researchers. This chapter has been further updated since parliamentary elections in 2010 with interviews and informal conversations conducted by the author.

GENDER, IDENTITY, CONSTITUENCY: FACTORS PREVENTING WOMEN'S COLLECTIVE MOBILIZATION

The concept of critical mass implies that influence can be gained in quantitative terms. Yet many factors complicate the link between women's access to the political arena and their capacity to influence decision making. Critical mass also carries the implicit assumption of a link between women's presence and their ability or indeed willingness to promote gender interests (Tinker 2004). It is evident that in the Afghan parliament, as elsewhere, however, there are diverse interests and concerns among and between women which hinder the mobilization of female MPs as a collective bloc. This section discusses the competing identities held by women, the vague notion of constituency, personality politics, and the influence of extraparliamentary actors such as political parties and government officials.

Competing Identities

Advocates of affirmative action or the "politics of presence" often assume that members of a minority group share common interests (Phillips 1995, 24). Female MPs in the Wolesi Jirga are far from united as an homogeneous bloc and are instead divided across ethnic, class, linguistic, political, and regional lines. Thus, when discussing women MPs' propensity to represent women in general," it is necessary first to examine the extent to which they even identify with this group.

Interviews with female parliamentarians reveal that women are motivated to enter politics to represent specific group interests, not just gender interests. One woman from Wardak, echoing the concerns of a number of MPs, identified the needs of Hazara women from her province as those she intended to represent: "When I nominated myself, it was my goal to make a good situation for Hazara women in Wardak. During our history, we have had a very bad situation, and this is my chance to help them. . . . This was my most important goal in becoming an MP" (interview).

The respondent clearly identifies a limited group of citizens (from one ethnicity in a particular region) for whose interests she feels responsible, as opposed to women in general. Indeed, while she expresses concern for women's collective gender interests, there is no indication that these are prioritized over interests based on ethnicity or region.

The statement above also emphasizes the complicated nature of overlapping gender and ethnic identities. Indeed, the concept of multiple identities is important here, as people's interests are often determined by the particular aspects of their identities that they choose to prioritize at a given time. The relationship between gendered and ethnic identities is particularly complex and cannot be simplified to the point at which either one is considered "more important" than the other, but in analyzing the data set as a whole, it is clear that for both men and women, ethnic identity generates a greater sense of cohesion among individual MPs than does gender. Ethnicity influences the way female MPs construct their gendered identity. This kind of prioritization of other identities over gendered ones at a given point in time or to serve specific political purposes is not particular to Afghanistan. Yet the issue takes on a certain significance in this context given the country's history of shifting divisions and allegiances among ethnicities and the way in which ethnicity has been used over the last thirty years in particular by key power holders as a tool to generate and accumulate political capital and influence. Contrary to the actual divisions existing among them, however, in interviews, women often portrayed themselves as part of a male/female binary. Regardless of whether women do share interests on the basis of their gender, there is a general assumption that they ought to share these interests.

The Notion of Constituency

Related to the concept of multiple political identities is that of constituency—because, as stated above, the way in which MPs define themselves at a given time is linked to the group of people with whom they identify most closely and, by extension, represent. While an MP's official constituency in Afghanistan is his or her province, many MPs' self-articulated parliamentary priorities lie with district-level or even village-level, as opposed to provincial-level, interests. Several MPs acquired their seats in 2005 through the mobilization of district- or village-wide blocs agreeing to vote consensually (interviews with various MPs, 2007). Women in particular seemed to mobilize voter networks according to their own districts, as a way to minimize perceived security risks, reduce reputational slurs that might be incurred from contact with unknown men, and simultaneously maximize vote gains from *qawm* (wider family) and ethnic affiliations (Wordsworth 2006, 14–17).

As a result, the women's gender interests that are represented in parliament by these women may be specific to a very streamlined constituency. Furthermore, for citizens in villages or districts without elected representatives, the gap between people and government is widened, because residents have no familiarity, or *ashnai*, with the MP for their province. Voters in a more recent study on voting behavior during the 2009 elections referred to the concept of familiarity more explicitly, explaining that *ashnai* was necessary in order that they could hold representatives to deliver on promises at a later stage (Coburn and Larson 2009). This was described in terms of *ekhan gereftan*—literally, the ability to take someone by the collar and demand accountability. Essentially, then, MPs' de facto constituency is often considerably smaller than the de jure specification of province outlined in the constitution (Government of Afghanistan 2004, article 83). This has a direct effect on female parliamentarians' ability and desire to represent women in general. Combined with the lack of institutionalized, issues-based parties, which could potentially form a mechanism to generate cross-locational linkages within a given province, this accentuates the limited reach of MPs' constituent bases.

Personality Politics

A source of disunity among female MPs within parliament is personality politics, whereby the question of who is involved in a given initiative takes precedence over what it promotes. This was notable in the (internationally instigated) attempt to establish a women's caucus in parliament, as is evident from the following responses to interview questions on the subject: "This is the first time that I have heard of [the Women's Caucus]; I do not know who is involved in it" (interview, female MP for Balkh province). "I have not heard of [the women's caucus]; I do not know which women are members" (interview, female MP for Panjshir province). Rather than question the issues the caucus might raise in parliament, there is a stated concern about the personalities involved. This preoccupation with personalities was also a problem when a certain prominent female MP claimed to have instigated the establishment of the Women Parliamentarians' Resource Center, provided by UNIFEM.

Because of resentment on the part of many female MPs toward this individual, a number refused to use the center.

While appearing petty, however, this kind of personality politics is not merely an issue of women clashing; it demonstrates the perils of standing as a woman in leadership in the Wolesi Jirga. A certain responsibility is informally assigned to prominent women to uphold the reputations of other female MPs. Any "mistakes" made can bring on criticism by some male MPs of all female parliamentarians, as this statement made by a female MP from Nangarhar indicates: "When [one female MP] talks about *jihadi* leaders, men say very bad words to women, sexual words, and we get angry because we are also women" (interview). The resentment of women described here is directed at the woman in question and not at the men's sexually abusive comments. Indeed, a woman taking a stand in parliament may be marginalized by female colleagues if she does not accept responsibility for their reputations. The politics of personality played out among women and the divisions created by leadership "responsibilities" can thus prevent the substantive representation of their gender interests and indeed hinder the very discussion about what these interests actually are.

Influence of Extraparliamentary Actors

While formal, institutionalized parties do not technically exist in Afghanistan, as outlined above, many female MPs have informal connections to the factions or "proto-parties" (Ruttig 2006, 1) that wield significant influence in the political arena. Accordingly, MPs are often instructed from the sidelines in how to vote in internal plenary sessions, for example (interviews, 2007).[4] Nevertheless, the relationship between MPs and parties is far from straightforward, largely because of the fluidity of parties themselves. As there is rarely a formal membership system, female parliamentarians claimed membership in more than one party in different interviews, and it appears that they are able to manipulate different groups strategically to gain support or patronage. However, the lack of institutionalized party structures also hinders those who might use them to advance gender interests (Goetz 2002, 573). Furthermore, whether parties are able to dictate the actions of women in parliament or not, what is notable is the widespread dependence among MPs on these outside sources for (financial) support or patronage.[5]

More concerning is the practice of MPs receiving this kind of support from government sources. A number of parliamentarians interviewed for this study reported this practice as a common way to gain from the value of a vote: "Some MPs say bad things about [the leader of the opposition] because the government is giving them credit to do this; the government will then pay for their holidays to India" (interview, female MP, province in northeastern Afghanistan). "The government has used MPs by giving them cash, making them unable to monitor the cabinet, making deals with the parliament" (interview, male MP for Baghlan province). As the latter respondent indicates, this has serious implications for the ability of MPs to perform oversight functions. Additionally, it renders the concept of voting ideologically impotent if, as suggested, it is occurring on a large scale. The effect of this kind of activity on women's collective mobilization is also highly detrimental, as it provides financial incentive *not* to vote according to one's personal convictions. This is not to suggest that all MPs are mercenarily oriented but to demonstrate how informal (and often shifting) rules of the game often dictate the practice of politics and policy making in parliament.

LEGISLATIVE INERTIA, INSECURITY, AND SOCIAL CONSERVATISM: FACTORS AFFECTING OUTCOMES

Female MPs have encountered a number of debilitating obstacles that prevent the building of a cohesive bloc in parliament. Even when women have mobilized collectively over certain issues, however, other factors undermine the achievement of substantive outcomes. Contextual limitations, such as the way in which the Afghan parliament functions in a clientelist as opposed to broadly representational manner (Liddell 2009, 79) and in terms of the wider context of continuing conflict in Afghanistan, threaten to undermine gains that have been made on account of women's gender-interest representation. As James Liddell writes, "Since every parliament has its own power dynamics, any benefits to be gained by increasing the presence of women in politics are largely dependent on the nature of how such political institutions function in a local setting" (2009, 79). This section assesses the institutional conditions in parliament preventing the promotion of collective interests and then examines the broader security and political context in which MPs operate. These factors, along with the increasingly controversial intervention on the part of the international community, are affecting the representation and definition of women's gender interests and further obscuring the link between women's presence in parliament and their propensity to be agents of change.

Legislative Inertia

Given the newness of parliamentary procedures to most if not all MPs and members of the secretariat coming into the Wolesi Jirga in 2005, it is not surprising that the processes of passing and amending legislation have been somewhat slow across the board. Indeed, much of the first term has been spent establishing the roles and responsibilities of parliament, with international initiatives providing training in the format of workshops and conferences. These appear to have had limited effect, however, as a result of the frequent duplication of subject matter and the difficulty in persuading MPs to attend.

These initial problems explain the slow progress of legislative procedures, but there are other, more worrying obstacles. For example, while agendas for plenary sessions are supposed to be circulated to MPs in advance, in many cases, they are not disclosed until the day of a session itself, leaving parliamentarians little time to prepare. Agendas themselves are determined by a leadership committee, made up of the heads of eighteen parliamentary commissions, among whom are particular power brokers wielding significant influence. By far the most effective way to influence agendas is to persuade (legitimately or otherwise) key members of this group to act in favor of given interests. This is easier if MPs already have connections (on an ethnic, regional, political, or familial basis) with the most prominent personalities therein. In this context, raising women's gender interests requires persuading personalities to put forward an issue or bill for debate. This strategy often flounders, however, in the absence of political will to prioritize women's gender interests.

This dynamic is strikingly evident in the bill on the Elimination of Violence against Women, drafted jointly by the Ministry of Women's Affairs (MOWA); the Wolesi Jirga Commission for Women, Civil Society, and Human Rights; and civil society. The effort to devise a law of this kind was strongly supported by UNIFEM for a number of years. The law first appeared in parliament in July 2009 and stipulates: "Protection of women's Islamic and legal rights, and human dignity; preventing of violations against women; provision of information and public training about violations against women; and prosecution of perpetrators of violations against women" (USAID 2009a, 4–5). The commission itself then added the requirement of an information bank cataloging incidents of violence against women and the need to process cases immediately (USAID 2009a, 4–5). While these were positive achievements, the law was not listed as a government priority at the beginning of parliament's second session in August 2009, remaining in committee discussions for the length of the session. By December 2009, the bill had still not been passed, after controversial committee debates and even a threatened boycott on the part of male MPs (USAID 2009b, 7).

There are a number of reasons for this delay, not the least of which is the way in which parliamentary commissions function. As mentioned, there are eighteen commissions divided by theme, and bills are discussed in commissions before moving to the plenary. Bills are also often sent back to the commissions for revision. Problematically, however, MPs' attendance at commission meetings is often minimal, and in the Women, Civil Society, and Human Rights Commission in particular, there has been long-standing conflict between the leader and other members, generating legislative inertia. Of greater concern, however, is that some male MPs have threatened to boycott the discussions. While their reasons may be varied, the effect is potentially debilitating. Boycotting issues in general (for example, reserved seats for the Kuchi population in elections) has happened on a number of occasions and has prevented some legislation from progressing at all.

Security

In the five years since the parliamentary term began, the security environment in Afghanistan has deteriorated dramatically. Even in the early days, however, parliamentarians were concerned about speaking their minds in parliament because of the potential repercussions that might affect their personal safety and that of their families, as the following male MP for a province in southwestern Afghanistan explained: "In order to be safe, I do not talk about 80 percent of the realities in my province because of the lack of security in Afghanistan. I am sure also that 80 percent of MPs in parliament do the same thing; they do not want to say everything because they feel that they will be in danger" (interview). This was not the case with all MPs at the time, but some of those who ventured to speak about "realities" were isolated by colleagues and had difficulty garnering support.

One particularly outspoken MP for Farah province, Malalai Joya, spoke in interviews about female colleagues passing her covert notes of appreciation when greeting her, because of her prominent stance against warlords who had committed gross human rights abuses holding parliamentary seats, but refusing to voice their support publicly for fear of being targeted by violent opposition groups orchestrated by the warlords in question (interview, 2007). Joya was often interviewed by Afghan and international media and was seen as a prominent women's rights activist—although in essence, her speeches were more often about the need to exclude warlord MPs from parliament. Before being ousted from parliament herself on the grounds of offending these personalities, she was forced to move house regularly and employ armed protection as a response to continual threats to her well-being. These threats were not merely articulated against MPs who gave inflammatory or radical speeches, however. Others, both male and female, with far less controversial views were receiving "night letters" and having family members intimidated, kidnapped, or even killed in 2007. At the time of this writing, ten MPs in total have lost their lives to insurgent attacks (American Free Press 2009).

Insecurity has had a cumulatively damaging effect on the issues that MPs are able and willing to raise in parliament. Concern for family located in insecure areas is often enough, understandably, to prevent parliamentarians from speaking out on controversial issues. Women's gender interests—often aligned with Western, "un-Islamic" values (Larson 2009b, 12)—fit into this category easily, as shown by the reaction to a female MP who spoke out against the now infamous Shiite Personal Status Law. The MP was threatened by a male MP carrying a firearm *inside* the parliament building. This law was particularly controversial because of its apparent condoning of (among other things) marital rape in family law applying to the Shia minority in Afghanistan. Promoted by influential conservative Shia MPs in mid-2008, it caught international media attention following Karzai's ratification of the law in early 2009, at which point it had already been passed by parliament. Female MPs were not unified in their condemnation of the law. Some were categorically against it, but others from the Sunni majority considered it an issue for Shias and not something about which they could comment. Others were opposed more generally to international intervention in Afghan religious affairs. The law was submitted to the Ministry of Justice and published in July 2009, becoming legally enforceable at that point (Oates 2009, xii). Democratic political parties voicing concern about this law also demonstrated the restrictions brought about by insecurity, in releasing a statement against the law but circulating it only to members of the international community (interview, party leader, April 2009).

The Rise of Social Conservatism and Its Political Implications

Related to the issue of security is the rise (or resurrection) of a certain conservative element in social politics at the national level. The term *conservative* in this context refers to a movement that promotes things such as removing women from the workforce and the unquestioned authority of men over women. The rise of conservatism has been particularly notable over the last two years, with the introduction of bills such as the Shiite Personal Status Law (Oates 2009) and the Law on Social Behavior (USAID 2008a, 4).

These laws are at different stages of the legislative process. As mentioned, the Shiite Personal Status Law passed parliament in early 2009 (Oates 2009, xii). The Law on Social Behavior, by contrast, has been on the parliamentary agenda for more than a year at the time of this writing but has yet to pass. According to the APAP parliamentary newsletter for November 16, 2008, "The draft law includes a code for properly wearing a Hijab, and prohibitions on: pigeon flying; men and women sharing the same room at weddings; unrelated men and women speaking with each other in public; long hair on men; loud music at weddings; shops selling revealing clothing; and materials considered offensive to Islam, etc." (USAID 2008b, 3). Both laws impose strict controls over how individuals and families conduct their daily lives.

Relatedly, interviews with both male and female MPs in 2007 predicted the potential for conservative backlash against women's empowerment, should this be seen to happen too quickly. Many referred to reactions against Amanullah Khan's reform policies promoting women's empowerment in the 1920s, or the Mujahideen's reassertion of conservative values following the Soviet occupation. Both Amanullah and the Soviets instigated immediate, radical, and top-down changes, which were met with considerable and violent opposition (Kandiyoti 2005, 3). As one male MP from Ghazni explained, "When a country has a history of marginalizing women, then we have to work at this in a calculated way. Then we will cover more ground in a shorter time. We should not have a knee-jerk reaction" (interview). The desire for gradual and strategic change, so as not to provoke backlash, was repeated in interviews with MPs from diverse political stances, demonstrating a marked support for the gradual revision of women's role in Afghan society, but with frequent reminders that the process should be slow and cumulative.

Interestingly, however, while the introduction of sixty-eight reserved seats for women in parliament was a radical change in Afghanistan's political landscape and was a talking point for many during the first elections in 2005, research conducted in 2009 suggests that it is has become less controversial over time. In a study on perceptions of democracy and democratization, respondents referred to the role of women in society extensively, associating women's behavior with "democracy" and Western values—but it referred specifically to the kinds of behavior considered acceptable for women *within* the public sphere (such as the wearing of hijab), rather than concern about their presence in the first place (Larson 2009b, 12). Although this study was relatively limited and should not be generalized for the country as a whole, it provides a snapshot of public opinion, which, in the context of confidential interviews, at least, does not seem to oppose reserved seats for women. It seems that reserved seats have normalized women's public presence, something that represents a significant shift, reminiscent of the acceptance of women in public roles under the Soviet regime in the 1980s. Of course, the opinions disclosed in private are far removed from the dominant discourse in the public sphere, where voicing any view that could be labeled "liberal" and thus "pro-West" is becoming increasingly uncommon. Furthermore, as indicated above, conservative elements continue to seek to restrict women's presence in parliament by enforcing a limit on the sixty-eight reserved seats.

International Intervention

Immediately following the Bonn process, international intervention in its various forms was largely welcomed by Afghans as a means to move forward. Since this time, however, expectations for economic development and security have not been met, and growing anger and frustration have been directed to "the international community"—a category usually not subdivided—for increased civilian casualties, the influx of Western culture, and interference in general.

A good example is the international reaction to the Shiite Personal Status Law. Particular articles of the law, such as those dictating women's conjugal duties within marriage, provoked international outcry. However, while many female MPs were concerned about the content of the law, they were more concerned about the way the international community responded (interviews, female MPs, April 2009). While some donor country governments justified intervention on the grounds of protecting the "democracy" they had helped establish, many Afghans viewed these actions as Western meddling in sovereign Afghan and Muslim affairs.

This is relevant when considering the potential effects of reserved seats for women in Afghanistan. As highlighted above, there is a fine line between the promotion of women's gender interests and an international, Western agenda—even if in reality, *Afghan* women's gender interests are actually quite removed from those of women in other contexts. Changing attitudes toward Western intervention in Afghanistan could also mean changing attitudes toward women's rights and could potentially further restrict female MPs' ability to promote these, should they want to.

A key aspect of the reserved seats system in the Afghan parliament is the way in which it was proposed as part of the internationally driven Bonn process. This is not to say that it was unwanted by Afghans—many women and men activists supported the measure at the time of its introduction. From an international perspective, however, as part and parcel of the state-building machinery established during Bonn, the system has remained in the realm of technical, as opposed to political, interventions. In general, international actors have been reluctant to acknowledge the highly political nature of their involvement in Afghanistan. Instead, there is a stated preference for "technical assistance," seen, for example, in decisions to promote the development of civil society over political parties. This approach, in denying the political nature of women's considerable presence in the public sphere, seems to see female MPs as the beneficiaries of innovative Western intervention instead of viewing them as political actors in their own right.

Finally, as conservative elements gain more control in governance institutions such as parliament, the incentive to emphasize the more conservative aspects of one's political identity as a woman becomes greater—threats to security are lessened, and opportunities for patronage are increased. This is not to deny Afghan female MPs their commitment to representing women's gender interests necessarily, but it is to warn against assumptions that (a) they will automatically promote these interests because they are women; (b) they have an agreed, collective definition of these interests which also coincides with Western perspectives; and (c) as women, they are less inclined than men to follow paths of patronage and politicking to attain power and influence.

CONCLUSION

Women's influence in Afghanistan's parliament remains limited, in spite of their considerable presence. Their propensity to represent women's gender interests cannot be assumed on account of their gender, and collective mobilization that does occur is limited by institutional and contextual factors. Nevertheless, it is clear that the introduction of a reserved seats system has opened a new and considerable political space for women within the public arena. Never before has there been systematic inclusion of women in the legislature. This is no small achievement, and the fact that this space appears to be increasingly accepted by the Afghan public is also clearly positive. With women's presence constitutionally guaranteed, at least for the time being, it appears that the focus must now shift to how to make more effective use of this space, especially in the second post-2001 parliament elected in 2010.

Of course, this is easier said than done. On one level, certain technical changes within parliament and to the electoral system could make significant improvements to the efficiency of procedures. Without a fundamental shift in the security environment and a correspondingly open arena in which MPs are able to speak freely without fear of repercussions, however, these technical measures will have limited effect.

Finally, while in many ways Afghanistan remains a unique case for analysis given its very particular political history and its turbulent relationship with women's rights, there are nonetheless two key lessons that can be applied more generally to understanding the impact of reserved seats or quotas on substantive representation. First, the means of representation are fundamental, and in a highly divided society, collective action is imperative. Second, the relationship between means and outcomes is not fixed, and even if collective action is undertaken consistently and thoroughly, there may be factors internal to legislative procedures or stemming from the broader sociopolitical context that ultimately determine the fate of efforts to represent women's gender interests substantively. Thus, the impact of quotas in increasingly unstable contexts such as Afghanistan may have little to do with the merits of the quota mechanism itself and may depend to a far greater degree on the complex and shifting nature of the context in question.

NOTES

1. Franceschet and Piscopo (2008) utilize a similar framework, distinguishing between process and outcome, where process is the means through which women can influence legislative agendas, and outcome is the successful enactment of legislation promoting women's gender interests.
2. This chapter is based on findings from qualitative research undertaken between 2006 and 2009 for the AREU. Data gathered in 2006–07 was published in Wordsworth (2007).

3. In the upper house (Meshrano Jirga), two-thirds of the 102 seats are indirectly elected through provincial councils, and one-third are appointed by the president. Of the appointed seats, 50 percent (seventeen) are reserved for women. In the provincial councils, candidates are elected through direct public elections, and one-quarter of these (124 out of 420 seats across the country) are reserved for women (AREU 2009, 70–72).

4. In interviews, women and men frequently related the perception that (other) female MPs were being told how to vote by parties, but no individual related having experienced this himself or herself, as might be expected.

5. This statement is made based on parliamentary observations over three years. It is clear that the value of votes in plenary sessions is not lost on male or female MPs and that the practice of exchanging these votes for material payoffs is becoming increasingly common.

REFERENCES

American Free Press. 2009. Bomb Kills Anti-Taliban Afghan MP. March 19, 2009. http://www.google.com/hostednews/afp/article/ALeqM5hO2HcsxNJhJ4wZU3vAZhWWm-REgXA (accessed September 3, 2009).

AREU (Afghanistan Research and Evaluation Unit). 2009. *The A–Z Guide to Afghanistan Assistance,* 7th ed. Kabul: AREU.

Brunet, Ariane, and Isabelle Solon Helal. 2003. Seizing an Opportunity: Afghan Women and the Constitution-Making Process. Rights & Democracy, Montreal. http://www.dd-rd.ca/site/publications/index.php?id=1360&page=3&subsection=catalogue (accessed December 12, 2009).

Coburn, Noah, and Anna Larson. 2009. *Voting Together: Why Afghanistan's 2009 Elections Were (and Were Not) a Disaster.* Kabul: AREU.

Dahlerup, Drude. 2009. Women in Arab Parliaments: Can Gender Quotas Contribute to Democratization? *Al Raida* 126–127 (Summer/Fall): 28–38.

Franceschet, Susan, and Jennifer M. Piscopo. 2008. Gender Quotas and Women's Substantive Representation: Lessons from Argentina. *Politics & Gender* 4 (3): 393–425.

Giustozzi, Antonio, and Noor Ullah. 2006. "Tribes" and Warlords in Southern Afghanistan, 1980–2005. Working Paper series 2, 7. Crisis States Research Center, London School of Economics and Political Science, London.

Goetz, Anne-Marie. 2002. No Shortcuts to Power: Constraints on Women's Political Effectiveness in Uganda. *Journal of Modern African Studies* 40 (4): 549–575.

Government of Afghanistan. 2004. Constitution of Afghanistan. Printed in *The A to Z Guide to Afghanistan Assistance* (unofficial translation), 84–113. Kabul: AREU.

———. 2010. Decree: President of the Islamic Republic of Afghanistan, Promulgation of the Electoral Law, February 18. Available at Electoral Complaints Commission (ECC), Kabul. http://www.ecc.org.af/en/images/stories/pdf/Electoral%20law%202010%20UN%20Feb%20(E)%20unoff.pdf (accessed April 25, 2011).

Kandiyoti, Deniz. 2005. The Politics of Gender and Reconstruction in Afghanistan. UNRISD Special Events Paper 4. Geneva: UNRISD. www.unrisd.org (accessed December 27, 2005).

———. 2007. Political Fiction Meets Gender Myth: Postconflict Reconstruction, 'Democratization,' and Women's Rights. In Andrea Cornwall, Elizabeth Harrison, and Ann Whitehead, eds., *Feminisms in Development: Contradictions, Contestations, and Challenges,* 191–200. London: Zed.

Larson, Anna. 2008. *A Mandate to Mainstream: Promoting Gender Equality in Afghanistan.* Kabul: AREU.

———. 2009a. *Afghanistan's New Democratic Parties: A Means to Organise Democratisation?* Kabul: AREU.

———. 2009b. *Toward an Afghan Democracy: Exploring Perceptions of Democratisation in Afghanistan*. Kabul: AREU.

———. 2010. *The Wolesi Jirga in Flux, 2010: Elections and Instability 1*. Kabul: AREU.

Liddell, James. 2009. Gender Quotas in Clientelist Systems: The Case of Morocco's National List. *Al Raida* 126–127 (Summer/Fall): 79–86.

Oates, Lauryn. 2009. *A Closer Look: The Policy and Law-making Process behind the Shiite Personal Status Law*. Kabul: AREU.

Phillips, Anne. 1995. *The Politics of Presence: The Political Representation of Gender, Ethnicity and Race*. Oxford: Clarendon Press.

Reynolds, Andrew, Lucy Jones, and Andrew Wilder. 2005. *A Guide to Parliamentary Elections in Afghanistan*. Kabul: AREU.

Roy, Olivier. 2003. Afghanistan: Internal Politics and Socio-Economic Dynamics and Groupings. WRITENET Paper No. 14. CNRS/UNHCR, Paris. http://www.unhcr.org/refworld/pdfid/3e9ae5535.pdf (accessed October 12, 2009).

Ruttig, Thomas. 2006. *Islamists, Leftists and a Void in the Center: Afghanistan's Political Parties and Where They Come From (1902–2006)*. Kabul: Konrad Adenauer Stiftung. http://www.kas.de/wf/doc/kas_9674-1522-2-30.pdf?061129052553 (accessed August 8, 2008).

Tinker, Irene. 2004. Quotas for Women in Elected Legislatures: Do They Really Empower Women? *Women's Studies International Forum* 27: 531–546.

USAID, Afghanistan Parliamentary Assistance Project (APAP). 2008a. *Legislative Newsletter*. Vol. 1 (16), August 24. http://www.sunyaf.org/newsletter/2008/APAP%20Newsletter%2024%20August%2008.pdf (accessed September 1, 2008).

———. 2008b. *Legislative Newsletter*. Vol. 1 (25), November 16. http://www.sunyaf.org/newsletter/2008/APAP%20Newsletter%2016%20%20November%2008.pdf.

———. 2009a. *Legislative Newsletter*. Vol. 2 (30), October 26. http://www.sunyaf.org/newsletter/2009/APAP%20Legislative%20Newsletter%2026%20October%202009.pdf (accessed October 28, 2009).

———. 2009b. *Legislative Newsletter*. Vol. 2 (37), December 15. http://www.cid.suny.edu/APAP_Newsletter/2009/APAP_Newsletter_December.15.09.pdf.

Wilder, Andrew. 2005. *A House Divided: Analysing the 2005 Afghan Elections*. Kabul: AREU.

Wordsworth, Anna. 2006. The Politics of Patronage: An Exploration of Women's Acquisition of Power in Afghanistan. Case Study: Legislative Elections in Balkh Province, 2005. Unpublished master's thesis.

———. 2007. *A Matter of Interests: Gender and the Politics of Presence in Afghanistan's Wolesi Jirga*. Kabul: AREU.

PART THREE
SYMBOLIC
REPRESENTATION

Symbolic representation captures how legislators' presence shapes the beliefs and attitudes held by elites and mass publics. In this sense, quota policies can directly affect the symbolic representation of women in several ways. Some advocates suggest that women's inclusion will heighten citizens' perception that their political system is fair, progressive, and legitimate. Others hold that women's greater presence in office will enhance female citizens' feelings of equality, sense of empowerment, and willingness to participate in civic and political life. Quota proponents thus anticipate that women's greater access to elected office will have far-reaching effects, ranging from increasing citizen engagement to enhancing democratic legitimacy.

The chapters in this section raise several theoretical and methodological points with respect to analyzing the impact of quotas on symbolic representation. First, studies must define the *audience*, that is, the subset of the population among which beliefs and attitudes are changing. The authors variously conceive of symbolic effects as occurring among political elites, female constituents, and the polity as a whole. They suggest, further, that symbolic effects may vary among these audiences and also by sex within these audiences; for instance, male political elites may feel resentful at losing control over candidate nominations, while female aspirants may feel more empowered to seek office. Second, these chapters highlight the importance of understanding the *mechanism* through which opinion change occurs. Quotas' ability to enhance symbolic representation depends on such contextual features as the legitimacy of quota policies and the degree of democratization within the political system. Third, the authors show that symbolic representation can also include *negative* impacts, such as greater resistance to gender role change and increased skepticism about democratic procedures. Overall, the chapters ask what it is about women's presence that influences beliefs and attitudes and whether these effects vary by context or over time.

Taken together, the chapters in this section show that among the three facets of political representation analyzed in this book, symbolic representation is the most far-reaching in terms of its potentially diverse manifestations in multiple audiences. Quotas complicate these already complex dynamics, adding considerations about inclusion and fairness to the formation of citizens' beliefs about gender, elections, and politics. Moreover, attitudinal and behavioral shifts may be first-order, resulting directly from the adoption of the quota policy, or they may be second-order, deriving from and building on initial reactions to quota implementation and quota women's profiles, behavior, and accomplishments. Finally, the complex processes underlying belief formation in mass publics challenge analysts to develop rigorous and innovative research designs. Without specific survey or interview questions that focus research subjects on the quota intervention, studies will be limited in their ability to draw causal connections between the presence of quotas and the beliefs of citizens. Attitudinal and cultural change is broad and complicated, and the political empowerment of women—and its manufacture through quotas—makes up only one part of the puzzle.

10 Paradoxes in the Meaning of Quotas in Belgium

Petra Meier

Gender quotas have raised high expectations over time. Proponents hoped they would lead to an improvement in the gender balance and ultimately an equal number of men and women in politics, thereby mirroring their respective proportions in the population. An improvement in the gender balance would also, in the long run, lead to more than equality in numbers. Greater numerical equality would involve a redefinition of the political space to make its founding concepts, norms, values, rules, practices, and processes more gender-sensitive and, in that respect, neutral.

Gender quotas did indeed improve the gender balance in some cases. In this respect, the changes over the last two decades in the Inter-Parliamentary Union's world ranking of parliaments with the highest percentage of women are telling.[1] However, gender quotas improved the gender balance more in some cases than in others, depending on the rules established, the extent to which they were implemented, and the degree to which they fit with the electoral system to maximize their impact. Also, gender quotas did not necessarily change anything except numbers. In this chapter, I argue that gender quotas constitute a paradox: they simultaneously reflect the high expectations of a gender-equal political space and the merely "symbolic" achievements of such measures in many respects.

The focus of the chapter is on what gender quotas could signify for the symbolic representation of women in the Belgian case, where statutory gender quotas were adopted in 1994 and 2002. After providing some background information on this case in the next section, I develop the argument that gender quotas are signifiers of the political representation of women and that, thereby, they can contribute to the symbolic representation of women. In the two sections after that, I look into two empirical examples: a study of the opinions of male and female politicians on gender quotas and a study on the implications of gender quotas for party rules and practices. In both cases, I analyze to what extent the political elite has adopted and internalized the equality norms underlying the gender quota laws.

In the conclusion, I explore why gender quotas, contrary to the expectations they raise, are sometimes mere "symbolic" measures in the struggle for gender equality in politics and do not further the symbolic representation of women. I argue that gender quotas focus on numbers, not on the larger setting of what makes the political arena a male domain. When the equality norms underlying gender quotas are not internalized by political actors, gender quotas do not contribute to the symbolic representation of women; that is, they provoke no cultural or attitudinal changes and simply constitute a symbolic change in terms of women's presence. This chapter shows the need to pay more attention to symbolic representation, next to descriptive and substantive representation, to come to a better understanding of its causes, dynamics, and consequences, in order to achieve full equality in matters of political representation.

GENDER QUOTAS AND THE BELGIAN POLITICAL CONTEXT

Belgium is a long-established parliamentary monarchy. Elections are based on a proportional open-list system, whereby voters can—but need not—cast multiple preferential votes. Since 2003, preferential votes count for 50 percent in the allocation of seats to candidates. Electoral lists are therefore "half open," as the order in which candidates appear on the list does not completely determine who is elected. Yet a candidate's list position influences his or her chances of getting elected, because positions higher on the list take advantage of the list votes, in which voters choose the party and not an individual candidate.

Belgium was the first European country to apply a gender quota law to lists of candidates at a national level. This pioneering step was in sharp contrast with the traditionally weak position of women in Belgian politics. Female politicians were few in number and lacked access to top positions. Therefore, the women's movements of the 1970s, but especially the political women's organizations, lobbied for more women in political decision making and for gender quotas as tools to reach this aim.

The first gender quota law was adopted in 1994, after a long and arduous government formation process. It stipulated that electoral lists must not include more than two-thirds of candidates of the same sex. In the event of noncompliance, public authorities in charge of receiving parties' lists of candidates would not accept the lists for election. This singular law affected all levels of elections. In 2002, several gender quota laws needed to be adopted, because electoral matters were then devolved to different levels of government when the regions were placed in charge of organizing local elections.[2] All of the 2002 gender quota laws nonetheless impose more or less the same regulations. They compel parties to put forward an equal number of male and female candidates. Furthermore, candidates of the same sex may not occupy the top two positions on a list. Noncompliance again results in a rejection of the list by the public authorities. The 2002 gender quota laws were a reaction to the persisting feminist criticism that the 1994 gender quota law did not impose equality among male and female candidates, nor did it contain placement mandates (Meier 2004).

While the number of women in politics started to rise in the mid-1990s, this increase cannot simply be attributed to the gender quota laws. As legal instruments, the laws had no effect. The 1994 gender quota laws did not impose any placement mandates at all, and the placement mandates included in the 2002 laws did not have much impact. The reason for this weak impact resides in the fact that, parallel with the new gender quota laws, the impact of the list vote was divided by two in order to increase the impact of the preferential vote. In combination with the strategic placing of well-known candidates toward the bottom of the lists, the traditionally safe seats at the top of electoral lists lost their safe character. The fact that the number of women nonetheless increased since the middle of the 1990s was, at least partially, the result of a simultaneous increase in district—and party—magnitude. More female representatives can be found in assemblies where party magnitude increased over time or where it has traditionally been high (Meier 2008a; Sliwa, Meier, and Thijssen 2009).

GENDER QUOTAS AND THEIR IMPLICATIONS FOR THE SYMBOLIC REPRESENTATION OF WOMEN

Gender quotas are technical tools to improve the gender balance in politics; yet they also *signify* the goals associated with this gender balance. Quotas reflect both the high expectations of a gender-equal political space and the merely symbolic results of gender quotas in many respects. For instance, gender quotas stand for the optimism that measures, which are at the outset mainly technical fixes, can contribute to changing norms, values, and attitudes. Quotas signify the renegotiation of the public sphere, through the way in which they reflect the emancipation and empowerment of women. But gender quotas also stand for the unilaterally gendered character of the public space, its male connotations, norms, habits, rules, and processes. Gender quotas also emphasize the lack of equality between men and women as citizens and politicians. They not only do so by underlining the need for extra measures to make women participate in politics on an equal footing with men but can also signify the lack of equality by imposing only a small number of women. The achievement, then, is symbolic and not substantive.

Theorists have suggested that through signifying women's inclusion, gender quotas can contribute to the symbolic representation of women. In Pitkin's seminal work on the concept of representation, descriptive and symbolic representation are both conceived of as representatives "standing for" absent principles (Pitkin 1967, 60–111). While in the former case, representation is achieved by mirroring the composition of society, in the latter case, representation is accomplished through the use of symbols. Women can be important symbols in politics; think of Marianne, the female symbol of France's postrevolutionary republic. And important political symbols are to a large extent gendered; think of the male connotations of state power, such as the army, and the contradiction in the image of the Spanish minister of defense, Carmen Chacón, inspecting her troops while in an advanced stage of her pregnancy.

Although symbols are of utmost importance in politics, given that the political space and its processes, activities, language, public policies, and the communication around them are full of symbols, Pitkin's symbolic representation has received little attention. In the literature on gender and politics, the importance of symbols and of symbolic representation is to be found in studies on how nations or states symbolize women and how symbols use, reproduce, and produce images of women (Tolz and Booth 2005; Yuval-Davis 1997). With respect to the symbolic effects of political representation, however, the issue has been largely neglected, especially when it comes to the study of gender quotas.

The question, then, is what expectations are signified by gender quotas and how the meanings associated with quotas then contribute to the symbolic representation of women, that is, actual attitudinal changes. I approach this question by looking into three arguments for gender quotas, which were developed in the 1980s and 1990s, when gender quotas were an important issue of academic and political debate (Arioli 1996; Arioli 1997; Degauquier 1994; Kittilson 2005; Lister 1997; Meier 2001; Phillips 1995; Sawer 2000; Squires 1996; Voet 1998; Young 2000).

A first argument in favor of gender quotas is what the Anglophone literature calls the justice argument and what is known as the democracy argument in the Francophone literature. Given our contemporary inclusive definition of democracy, it is unfair that women, making up half of the population, are structurally underrepresented in decision making. This argument presumes that there are no differences intrinsically related to men's and women's willingness to participate in politics. Opinions differ on whether the underrepresentation of women is a result of badly functioning democratic institutions or of failing normative foundations of contemporary democracies. In the French literature, this latter argument was mainly developed within the plea for parity democracy (Meier 2001). The argument further runs that women would have long ago participated in politics in greater numbers if no discriminatory mechanisms existed. In this respect, the justice or democracy argument directly appeals to measures meant to improve women's access to positions of political decision making.[3]

Gender quotas, then, contribute to the recognition of women as citizens and as politicians on an equal footing with men. Even more, gender quotas signify that gender is a decisive constituting entity of social relations and positions characterizing society. They reinforce the symbolic representation of women by reformulating the concept of citizenship, adding a female face to the previously male one, or, put differently, by replacing the male connotation of citizenship with a more diverse vision. Also, gender quotas imply the recognition of the role that women as citizens can and should play in politics. They enhance the symbolic representation of women in that they contribute to the reformulation of this role by making it a role that can be taken on by women and by men. The initial male connotation of this role is thus broadened or replaced.

A second argument in favor of gender quotas is the issue of representing what are generally called the interests and needs or perspectives of women, based either on a gendered division of roles and tasks or on a more essentialist definition of the sexes. The argument holds that women have specific interests, needs, perspectives, and thus requests, partly because of biological characteristics but especially because of the societal gendered division of roles and tasks. The argument does not necessarily mean that only women can defend women's issues or that women need to defend women's issues. Rather, the presence of an important number of women in politics increases the chance that their experiences get considered and that the gendered character of interests and needs gets respected, which brings us close to Phillips's (1995) "politics of presence." Gender quotas, then, underline the fact that female citizens are as entitled as male citizens to having representatives act as their agents. Gender quotas contribute to the symbolic representation of women in that they broaden the perspective of whom representatives, and politicians more broadly speaking, should represent and to whom they should be responsive.

The third argument for gender quotas builds on the first two. It runs that more participation from women in politics will lead to a qualitative change of politics and policies (Degauquier 1994; Lister 1997; Phillips 1995; Sawer 2000; Squires 1996; Voet 1998). Processes of political decision making, and hence public policies, will better reflect the diversity characterizing society. This comes close to the argument of substantive representation but focuses less on outcomes that benefit groups and more on policies' reflection of diversity (Meier 2001). If public policies better take into account the diverse needs and interests present in society, this would improve the legitimacy of democratic institutions and of the polity. Finally, a better gender balance in politics would also diminish the masculine mode of political behavior and would provide for female role models.

Gender quotas, then, underline that the public space and its normative foundations, structures, processes, and outcomes are not neutral. By questioning the traditional assumption of the neutrality of the public space, gender quotas might, in the long run, contribute to turning it into a space reflecting and considering the diversity characterizing society. Gender quotas also underline the need for gender equality not to be stripped of any reference to the social context but to be embedded in this reality. Gender equality should thereby not only be transposed into formal rules but also internalized by norms and practices.

In the next two sections, I analyze whether and to what extent the Belgian gender quota laws have enhanced the symbolic representation of women. I first examine how male and female politicians think about women's position in Belgian politics and the need and efficiency of gender quotas in that context. Then I look into the extent to which the gender quota laws had an effect on Belgian parties' recruitment and selection rules and practices.

In both examples, and contrary to the other chapters in this section, the focus is on elites or elite structures as the audience, as opposed to the public and its attitudes toward gender quotas. The reason is that the political elite, both political parties and individual politicians, are most directly affected by and concerned with gender quotas. They have to implement the measures and experience their impact. A transformation of the gender equality norms underlying quotas into party rules and practices, or an internalization of these values by individual politicians, thus most directly contributes to the symbolic representation of women.

The focus of both examples is mainly on how gender quotas contribute to the symbolic representation of women by challenging attitudes about the maleness of the public space and by underlining the need for the equality of men and women as citizens and politicians. Also, while the quota laws have been lobbied for by the women's movement and by some of the female political elite, they have ultimately been imposed by the government, although in accordance with the party leaders of the governing coalition. It is therefore interesting to understand how the political elite as a whole receives such measures.

The first case is based on survey research conducted among a broad selection of Flemish representatives across the various federal and regional assemblies of the country.[4] The questionnaire included a broad set of questions on the acceptance of gender quotas, their legitimacy, their effectiveness, and the explanations for women's underrepresentation in politics. While the initial impetus for the project was not to study women's symbolic representation (Meier 2008b), these data do provide information on the extent to which gender quotas contribute to the symbolic representation of women. Positions on the legitimacy or effectiveness of gender quotas or on the causes of women's underrepresentation in politics reveal information about the extent to which the equality norms underlying gender quotas have been internalized.

The second case is based on an analysis of the statutes of the ten major Belgian political parties,[5] information that was complemented with semistructured interviews with different profiles of members of each party (for details, see Meier et al. 2006). The question was what impact the gender quota laws had on the formal rules and informal practices of the Belgian political parties when it came to their recruitment and selection policies, both for elected mandates (members of parliament and local councilors) and for the offices elected within the party itself (party president, party secretary, and head of local or regional party section). The interest is, again, in the internalization of the equality norms underlying the gender quota laws.

BELGIAN POLITICIANS ON GENDER QUOTAS

Many more female politicians (88 percent) are in favor of gender quotas than their male colleagues (34 percent). Also, while women do not call into question the legitimacy of gender quotas, men consider that they clash with a number of basic principles of the Belgian political system. The majority of women (80 percent) do not agree that gender quotas would harm democratic principles or tamper with the foundations of the Belgian constitutional state. On the contrary, the majority of women (64 percent) think that the democratic system functions badly and that gender quotas correct this bias. Among women, gender quotas are considered to be legitimate because they promote equality and justice (70 percent). A majority of women also think that gender quotas fit into the prevailing conceptualization of political representation and do not clash with the principles underlying a fair, democratic electoral process (74 percent). Men believe precisely the opposite. To them, gender quotas are unacceptable because they undermine the basic principles of the Belgian democratic order (51 percent), that is, they undermine the principle of non-discrimination (48 percent). Nor are men convinced that gender quotas would promote equality or justice (59 percent and 67 percent, respectively). This fits with men's conviction that gender quotas would not correct the poor functioning of democracy (65 percent). Furthermore, men consider that gender quotas do not fit into the dominant conceptualization of representation in Belgium (51 percent).

While men and women were divided on the acceptance of gender quotas and their legitimacy, they were less separated in their perceptions of the effectiveness of these measures. A majority of both women (92 percent) and men (79 percent) share the opinion that gender quotas give women easier access to political office and to positions of power. However, the perception of gender quotas as an effective tool does not necessarily involve the attachment of a positive value to this effectiveness. While 74 percent of the women think that gender quotas are not redundant, 63 percent of the men think the opposite—that women would make their way in politics without such measures. Furthermore, a majority of men think that gender quotas have a negative effect on the credibility of women candidates (53 percent, as compared with 20 percent of women). The fact that both sexes acknowledge the redistributive character of gender quotas, facilitating women's access to political office, does not prevent them from perceiving this effectiveness differently. Women frame quotas' success in positive terms, as a correction of incorrectly functioning selection mechanisms. Men frame the effectiveness of gender quotas in negative terms, as an interference with selection mechanisms that already functioned properly.

Finally, men and women differ again in their perception of the causes of women's underrepresentation in politics. The main difference lies in the fact that men locate the explanation for women's underrepresentation at the level of the individual woman, while women locate the causes at a structural level, for example, in the way in which political parties operate. While 64 percent of the female politicians believe they receive fewer chances in politics than men, 73 percent of the men do not agree on this point. To a lesser extent, women also think that political parties prefer men, because party leaders assume that women are less suited for politics than men. While 40 percent of the women are convinced that such discrimination occurs, 79 percent of the men doubt that there are structural barriers to women's participation.

Neither women nor men think that women lack the experience and training required for politics. Eighty-eight percent of women and 91 percent of men consider women to have sufficient qualifications in this regard. Likewise, 71 percent of men believe that women have the contacts necessary to make their way in politics. Yet on this point, women differ, with 58 percent of them believing that they lack the contacts necessary for pursuing a political career. Men and women also differ in their perception of whether women sufficiently defend their ambition to become elected. While 46 percent of the men consider that women fight sufficiently hard to realize their political ambitions, 58 percent of the women believe that this is not the case.

Table 10.1 Differences between male and female politicians on gender quotas

	Disagree		Agree		Neutral	
	M	W	M	W	M	W
Quotas are legitimate because they lead to more justice.	67%	8%	16%	70%	17%	22%
Quotas are unacceptable because they undermine our democratic principles.	28%	80%	51%	4%	21%	16%
Quotas are acceptable because they promote equality.	59%	10%	22%	70%	19%	20%
Quotas are acceptable because they correct the poor functioning of our democracy.	65%	20%	12%	64%	23%	16%
Quotas are legitimate because they fit in with our perception of political representation.	51%	10%	22%	74%	27%	16%
Quotas are unacceptable because they undermine the principle of nondiscrimination.	32%	72%	48%	10%	20%	18%
Quotas are redundant because women also make their way without them.	10%	74%	63%	10%	27%	16%
Quotas have a negative effect on the credibility of women as competent candidates.	22%	56%	53%	20%	25%	24%
Quotas help women to gain a place in politics.	6%	6%	79%	92%	15%	2%
Women get fewer chances in politics than men.	73%	24%	10%	64%	17%	12%
Parties prefer men because they consider women to be less suited to politics.	79%	32%	6%	40%	15%	28%
Women lack important contacts.	71%	30%	6%	58%	23%	12%
Women do not fight strongly enough for their ambition to be elected.	46%	24%	38%	58%	16%	18%
Women are less interested in political office than men.	32%	38%	53%	36%	15%	26%
Women lack suitable experience and training.	91%	88%	2%	6%	7%	6%

However, while men's perceptions of women's adequate preparation and ambition lead 53 percent of them to believe that women are less interested in a political mandate than themselves, women are more divided on this point. Thirty-eight percent of women do not agree that they would be less interested in a political mandate than men, while 36 percent share the male viewpoint of equal interest.

Although the data do not reveal anything about the evolution of men's and women's perceptions, they show that both sexes think very differently about women's political opportunities and about gender quotas. These differences in response patterns of female and male politicians reveal a relatively coherent female perception, and a relatively coherent male perception, of women's position in politics, its causes, and its potential remedies. As has been argued elsewhere (Meier 2008b), this difference in perception might correlate with men's and women's different experiences during their political careers.

Considering these findings, the adoption and implementation of the Belgian gender quota laws did not contribute much to the symbolic representation of women, neither with respect to challenging the maleness of the public space nor with respect to reframing ideas about citizens and politicians. The absence of a broad consensus on the problematic nature of women's underrepresentation in politics prevents gender quotas from contributing to the symbolic representation of women.

Although formally the goal of gender equality was put at center stage, this was not how the issue was perceived among male politicians. The impetus for the Belgian government to adopt the gender quota laws was the aim to enhance the equality of men and women; the 2002 gender quota laws also corrected for the lack of equality contained in the 1994 law (Meier 2004). The 1994 law was of a symbolic nature, in that it required only 33 percent of women candidates on the list and no more than 25 percent in an initial phase. In that respect, it did not so much improve gender equality as reflect its absence. The 2002 gender quota laws did better than their predecessor in this respect and formally contributed to the symbolic representation of women. They underlined the equality of the sexes and thereby put the issue of gender equality at center stage. The 50 percent gender quotas contribute to the symbolic representation of women, putting men and women, at least when it comes to numbers, on an equal footing.

However, the deeper meanings of equality associated with gender quota laws have been neither perceived nor internalized among male Belgian politicians. Instead of seeing them as a measure underlining the centrality of the issue of gender equality, men perceived the gender quota laws as a measure distorting equality. The discussion of gender quotas in the political arena, and their adoption, might be thought to require the reframing of concepts such as citizenship, representation, and equality in such a way as to make the lack of gender equality in politics become defined as a problem and gender quotas as an acceptable means to solve it. However, the adoption and implementation of gender quotas seems by definition not to involve all of these changes. Many of the male politicians responding to the questionnaire did not see the need to reconsider the concept of citizenship and thereby to enhance women's symbolic representation. Nor did they see the need to reconsider the position and role of the representative and women's access to this role.

Unlike what Jennie Burnet (chapter 12 in this volume) reports for the Rwandan case, the gender quota laws in Belgium have not altered ideas about the roles of both sexes in the public or private sphere. The Rwandan and the Belgian cases are very different in that they are not examining quotas' effects on the same audiences, and they take place in countries with different political and institutional contexts and different gendered social positions and roles. Nonetheless, as a consequence of the adoption of gender quotas, neither did many male respondents interrogate the eventually unilaterally gendered character of the political space, which is all the more interesting since the female respondents did report such a bias in the political space. Finally, neither did men see the need to reconsider the normative underpinnings of the political space. They did not internalize the norms underlying the gender quota laws. All of this is not surprising given that the quota laws provoked a lot of resistance among the party leaders, notwithstanding the fact that they had been negotiated with the party leaders of the leading coalition and not simply imposed from above. There was no broad consensus on the necessity or even desirability of a quota law. This limits the extent to which gender quotas can contribute to the symbolic representation of women.

BELGIAN POLITICAL PARTIES AND GENDER QUOTAS

Several parties had already applied their own gender quotas before the 1994 quota law was voted. Parties also adopted similar measures in the years following the implementation of the 1994 genderquota law (Meier 2004). Given the fact that these rules did not exceed the legal requirements imposed from 2002 onward, most of them disappeared from later party statutes. None of the Belgian political parties' statutes contains measures that reach beyond the statutory gender quotas from 2002. For instance, parties do not extend the zipper principle to the entire list of candidates. However, most left-wing parties and some parties from the center copied the stipulations of the 2002 gender quota laws into their party statutes. This copying of the legal stipulations does not have an added value for the composition of lists of candidates, but it has a symbolic value in that parties herewith underline their support for these principles. It also enhances how quotas symbolize women as citizens and politicians, since it formally puts the equality of men and women more at center stage within parties.

All parties also underlined that the 2002 gender quota laws increased the importance of sex as a criterion in the recruitment and selection of candidates for elected office. Party officials reported a change in mentality regarding the share of male and female candidates. Parties with fewer women candidates now actively recruit them. However, sex is not the only criterion. Parties speak of a "sound mix" of candidates, including, in addition to an equal number of male and female candidates, a balance of juniors and seniors, of candidates with foreign backgrounds and candidates with Belgian roots, or, more traditionally, of various geographical regions or various subgroups or clans within the party. New candidates need to have a profile that is complementary to that of the existing ones. Women's current advantage is therefore short-lived; the specific interest in female candidates will disappear once there are more female incumbents. But even if the interest in female candidates diminishes in the future, this should not hamper the symbolic representation of women, since this lack of interest would signify that an equal number of men and women candidates has been attained.

However, the increased attention to female candidates does not make parties question their recruitment and selection rules, practices, or criteria. Parties have difficulties defining a good candidate, using criteria such as electoral potential, party affinity, knowledge, and expertise in specific policy matters but also mentioning attitudes such as perseverance and, especially, that candidates must be driven by an interest in politics. Interviewees, also female but mainly male, who were relatively new in the party or in politics or who were mainly involved with the internal functioning of the party (i.e., party spokespersons), report no gender bias in the recruitment and selection practices and criteria. However, respondents who have been involved in recruiting and selecting candidates are more open to the idea that these processes might be gender-biased.

But most political parties nonetheless do not seek the reasons for the smaller share of women in politics within themselves. They do not see themselves as gatekeepers in this respect. However, parties also define politics as being a "tough sector," which requires a high degree of availability and flexibility. Parties share the opinion that women face disadvantages in this sector because of the prevailing gendered division of care work. An argument regularly invoked during the interviews is the fact that women are less present at meetings and that they are not always willing to put the necessary time and energy into politics. Some go so far as to link this to the fact that women are less interested in politics than men and that they seem to be less driven by the will to invest in politics. Parties do not neglect that there are expectations regarding the qualities of candidates, and they do not ignore that men on the whole meet them more often, but they do not think that there is a gender bias in these criteria. There is nothing wrong with the requirements and expectations on behalf of the political sector; they are inherent to it.

In sum, the gender quota laws led to an increase in the number of female candidates and made political parties consider sex an important criterion for selecting candidates, but quotas did not lead to a questioning or revising of the existing procedures, rules, and practices when it comes to recruiting and selecting candidates for elected office. Although the gender quota laws did not oblige parties to put such procedures, rules, and practices into question, they could have sparked these changes, showing that parties internalize the norms underlying gender quotas. Yet this was not the case; the gender quota laws did not enhance the symbolic representation of women.

The formal adoption and implementation of the gender quota laws led neither to a reflection on the existing practices nor to a consideration of the extent to which institutions, structures, norms, and processes might not be gender-neutral. The formal embracing of the principle of gender equality in the wake of the 2002 gender quota laws and the copying, in some cases, of the legal requirements into the party statutes were not a consequence of the will to change existing practices. Similar to the conclusion drawn in the previous section, the adoption of the principle of gender equality does not necessarily imply that there is a consensus on the fact that something has been wrong in the past and needs to be remedied. This absence of a match between the adoption of formal principles and the practices they target hollows out the symbolic representation that underlies the formal enshrinement of principles of equality.

A similar conclusion can be drawn when looking at the party rules and practices governing the recruitment of candidates for elected office within their own structures, such as the head of a local party section, the party president, and members of the party bureau. Although the gender quota laws did not require parties to change such rules, the underlying idea is that gender quota laws might have an impact on them since more women within the party would increase the pool of potential female candidates for party office.

Party statutes deal extensively with the composition of party organs and mandates, and we indeed find two types of gender quotas. First, in the period after the adoption of the first or second gender quota laws, most parties created the function of vice presidents, with the stipulation that men and women must share party leadership. This finding is surprising, in that party leadership positions are very powerful in Belgian politics. It would have been less of a surprise to find gender quotas at a lower level in the party hierarchy rather than at the center of power. In a couple of parties, women are indeed still weakly represented at the party top, being, for instance, one of four vice presidents, while the president is also a man.

However, over the last couple of years, a growing number of Belgian parties have been led by women. In 2011, four major parties have had women as presidents. The French Christian Democrats have been led by a woman for the last decade. Other parties with female presidents are the French and Dutch Greens[6] and the Dutch Social Democrats (for a brief period in 2009–2010, the Dutch Christian Democrats were also led by a woman, but she stepped down after the disastrous results of her party during the 2010 federal elections). All of these parties were in power during at least part of their female presidency. Although there need not be a causal relationship between the gender quota laws and parties changing their rules regarding party leadership, the latter increases the symbolic representation of women. The issue of gender equality is, at least in some parties, made central to the parties' internal organization. Further, a couple of parties seem to put this principle into practice. Although the parties might not consciously be meeting the goals of gender equality, the prevalence of female presidents does indicate some change in leaders' attitudes with respect to the position of women in politics.

However, this change in mentality does not account for other offices elected within the party. With the exception of the Dutch Radical Right Populists, all parties' statutes contain a declaration of intent regarding gender balance or parity when it comes to offices elected within the party. While most parties have named parity as an overall goal for quite some time, the concrete gender quotas or target figures tend to be more modest. When concrete percentages are mentioned at all, parties impose gender quotas varying between 20 percent and 33 percent of women for offices elected within the party.

Also, party statutes have not changed much in this respect over the last two decades. With some exceptions, parties' self-imposed gender quotas that were adopted before the national quota laws did not change much afterward. The Dutch Christian Democrats and the French Social Democrats increased their internal gender quotas from 20 percent in the middle of the 1980s to 33 percent in 2005.[7] The Dutch Social Democrats extended their 25-percent gender quotas to all executive functions within the party.[8] All in all, these are minor changes. The Liberal parties made an opposite move. Both the Dutch and the French Liberals deleted all gender quotas from their statutes once the gender quota laws were adopted, notwithstanding the fact that the latter do not directly concern posts elected within the party. Other parties tempered the gender quotas for functions within the party. The party statutes of the Dutch Regionalists N-VA stipulate that the gender quotas apply only if there are enough female candidates for the functions to which these gender quotas apply.[9] And the French Social Democrats make the future of their gender quotas depend on an evaluation of these measures after a five-year period, without being more precise about what this evaluation entails.

So, while parties enhanced the symbolic representation of women when it comes to the position of party leader, this development did not extend to the many other functions elected within the party. Also, not all parties established gender parity at the top. This makes the current case very similar to the one revealed in the survey of party elites; the gender quota laws did not contribute much to enhance the symbolic representation of women, for parties have not internalized the equality norms underlying the gender quota laws and have not changed their behavior accordingly. Again, the reason for this might partly be sought in the fact that the quota laws were not initiated by the parties themselves. Nonetheless, all of this limits the extent to which gender quotas can contribute to the symbolic representation of women.

CONCLUSION

In this chapter, I explored how gender quotas can enhance the symbolic representation of women but found that, at least in the Belgian case, the 1994 and 2002 gender quota laws did not bring about large attitudinal and behavioral changes among political elites. This is all the more interesting since the Belgian gender quota laws enacted in 2002 improved the *formal* representation of women, symbolizing women's equality and citizenship by imposing an equal number of men and women candidates on all electoral lists. While the former 1994 gender quota law signified the inequality of men and women, by accepting the underrepresentation of women on lists of candidates and within politics, the 2002 laws stand for equality. They place the goal of gender equality at center stage and translate it into concrete policy measures, thereby enhancing, formally speaking, the symbolic representation of women.

Looking more deeply into Belgian politics, however, reveals that this formal enhancement of the symbolic representation of women in politics has few far-reaching effects on attitudes and beliefs. Efforts to improve women's symbolic representation are actually hollowed out, because the equality norms underlying the gender quota laws are not being internalized by the political elite. Neither among male politicians nor within political parties was there much impetus, in the wake of the 1994 and 2002 gender quota laws, to revise the concepts of citizenship; the concept of the politician, its role, and women's access to it; the processes, rules, and practices of recruiting and selecting candidates, both within the parties and for elected office; or, more broadly speaking, the normative foundations of the political process and system. The absence of the internalization by the political elite of the equality norms underlying the gender quota laws means that the achievements of the latter are symbolic and not substantive and that they fail to contribute to the symbolic representation of women.

The current research looked into data regarding the political elite as the audience, and it might be that there are differences between elite and mass opinions on these matters. It remains to be seen if the public is more inclined than the political elite to adopt the equality norms underlying the gender quota laws, and the public might sense the symbolic representation of women. However, contrary to what Pär Zetterberg (chapter 11 in this volume) suggests for the Mexican case, the quota policies themselves might not be contributing to the symbolic representation of women. In Belgium, the quota debates were mainly held within the political arena and within the women's movement, and they did not stir any discussion in the media or in the broader arenas of citizen involvement. It is therefore unlikely that the symbolic representation of women in Belgium, let alone an increase of it, stems from the quota laws.

How is it that gender quotas, standing for such high expectations with regard to a gender-equal political space, signify, at least in the Belgian case, merely symbolic achievements? An explanation that holds at least for the Belgian case—but probably also beyond it—resides in the fact that gender quotas only focus on numbers, not on the larger context of politics and not on its underlying normative foundations, processes, rules, and practices. A change in numbers might entail a change in these norms, processes, rules, and practices, similar to the argument that more women in politics will enhance the substantive representation of women. But this might require time, and there is no guarantee that such a change will occur. Indeed, the adoption and implementation of gender quota laws do not necessarily imply a broad consensus on the existence of gender inequality, on this being a political problem, and on this problem requiring political action. The Belgian case, then, points at the limits of legal strategies. The issue at stake is not the acceptance of quotas as such but the acceptance that the underlying problem—women's exclusion—is indeed troublesome and that gender quotas are a means to solve it. A focus on numbers might not suffice for triggering such changes in beliefs. If gender quotas are to contribute to the symbolic representation of women, they need to be accompanied by measures focusing on the normative foundations of the political space, and its processes, rules, and practices, in order eventually to break down traditional associations between men and the public sphere and to develop broader meanings of women's presence in politics.

NOTES

1. See http://www.ipu.org.
2. Law of May 24, 1994, to promote a balanced distribution of men and women on electoral lists, *Belgisch Staatsblad*, July 1, 1994; law of June 17, 2002, to guarantee an equal representation of men and women on the electoral lists for the European Parliament, *Belgisch Staatsblad*, August 28, 2002; law of July 18, 2002, to guarantee an equal representation of men and women on the electoral lists for the federal Parliament and for the Council of the German-speaking Community, *Belgisch Staatsblad*, August 28, 2002; special law of July 18, 2002, to guarantee an equal representation of men and women on the electoral lists for the Council of the

Walloon Region, the Flemish Council, and the Council of the Brussels Capital Region, *Belgisch Staatsblad*, September 13, 2002; law of December 13, 2002, containing various changes of the electoral legislation, *Belgisch Staatsblad*, January 10, 2003.

3. It should be added, though, that most advocates of parity democracy make a sharp distinction between gender quotas and the principle of parity democracy. The latter stands for full gender equality, while the former are argued to contain benchmarking fallacies for women by turning a request for a minimum number of women into the maximum being admitted (Meier 2001) and for reducing the problem to one of numbers (Meier et al. 2005). However, concrete measures for achieving parity democracy in elected politics come close to gender quotas.

4. These were the federal Senate and House of Representatives, the Flemish Parliament, and the Parliament of the Brussels Capital Region.

5. These were, at the time of the research project in 2005–2006, the Dutch and French Christian Democrats (CD&V and CDH), Social Democrats (SP.A and PS), Liberals (VLD and MR), Greens (Groen! and ECOLO), and the Dutch Radical Right Populists (VB) and Regionalists (N-VA).

6. In the case of ECOLO, it is a shared position.

7. CD&V statutes 2005, art. 42.1.2; PS statutes 2005, art. 7.1.

8. SP.A statutes 1995, art. 57.

9. N-VA statutes 2004, art. 2.0.3.

REFERENCES

Arioli, Kathrin, ed. 1996. *Quoten und Gleichstellung von Frau und Mann*. Basel: Helbing & Lichtenhahn.

———. 1997. *Frauenförderung durch Quoten*. Basel: Helbing & Lichtenhahn.

Degauquier, Catherine. 1994. Retour sur les Arguments Fondant la Demande d'une Représentation Accrue des Femmes en Politique. *Res Publica* 36 (2): 119–127.

Kittilson, Miki Caul. 2005. In Support of Gender Quotas: Setting New Standards, Bringing Visible Gains. *Politics & Gender* 1 (4): 638–645.

Lister, Ruth. 1997. *Citizenship: Feminist Perspectives*. London: Macmillan.

Meier, Petra. 2001. On the Theoretical Acknowledgement of Diversity in Representation. *Res Publica* 43 (4): 551–570.

———. 2004. The Mutual Contagion Effect of Legal and Party Quotas: A Belgian Perspective. *Party Politics* 10 (3): 583–600.

———. 2008a. Belgium: The Collateral Damage of Electoral System Design. In Manon Tremblay, ed., *Women and Legislative Representation: Electoral Systems, Political Parties and Sex Quotas*, 137–147. New York: Palgrave Macmillan.

———. 2008b. A Gender Gap Not Closed by Quotas: The Renegotiation of the Public Sphere. *International Feminist Journal of Politics* 10 (3): 329–347.

Meier, Petra, Emanuela Lombardo, Maria Bustelo, and Maro Pantelidou Maloutas. 2005. Gender Mainstreaming and the Bench Marking Fallacy of Women in Political Decision-Making. *Greek Review of Social Research* 117: 35–62.

Meier, Petra, Benoît Rihoux, Silvia Erzeel, Anouk Lloren, and Virginie Van Ingelgom. 2006. *Partis Belges et Égalité de Sexe: Une Évolution Lente mais Sûre?* Brussels: Institute for the Equality of Women and Men.

Phillips, Anne. 1995. *The Politics of Presence*. Oxford: Clarendon Press.

Pitkin, Hanna Fenichel. 1967. *The Concept of Representation*. Berkeley: University of California Press.

Sawer, Marian. 2000. Parliamentary Representation of Women: From Discourses of Justice to Strategies of Accountability. *International Political Science Review* 21 (4): 361–380.

Sliwa, Sandra, Petra Meier, and Peter Thijssen. 2009. *Een Nuchtere Kijk op Quota Is Niet Noodzakelijk Ontnuchterend*. Brussels: Institute for the Equality of Women and Men.

Squires, Judith. 1996. Quotas for Women: Fair Representation? *Parliamentary Affairs* 49 (1): 71–88.

Tolz, Vera, and Stephenie Booth, eds. 2005. *Nation and Gender in Contemporary Europe*. Manchester, U.K.: Manchester University Press.

Voet, Rian. 1998. *Feminism and Citizenship*. London: Sage.

Young, Iris Marion. 2000. *Inclusion and Democracy*. Oxford: Oxford University Press.

Yuval-Davis, Nira. 1997. *Gender & Nation*. London: Sage.

11 Political Engagement and Democratic Legitimacy in Mexico

Pär Zetterberg

In 1996, Mexico became one of the first Latin American countries to include legislative quotas in its federal electoral code. Since then, the quota law has been revised twice, in 2002 and 2008, to make it more powerful. The current regulations mandate that the political parties field no more than 60 percent of candidates of the same sex on their candidate lists. Parties failing to comply are denied the right to register for the elections. The rather strict quota provisions apply, with some limitations, to both facets of the mixed electoral system: proportional and majority seats (Baldez 2007).[1] Further, at the subnational level, some states have chosen to include quotas in their electoral codes. Others, however, have chosen not to do so.

Whereas the impacts of Mexican quota regulations on women's numerical representation have been documented (i.e., Reynoso and D'Angelo 2006), the more far-reaching consequences of the law are largely shrouded in mystery (but see Zetterberg 2008). Yet these positive action measures are often believed to alter traditional views of politics among the electorate and signal greater inclusiveness in the political system. Such possible effects of quotas are important for the long-term work involved with eliminating gender inequalities in politics and society. This chapter pays attention to the possible broader societal consequences of quota policies, in terms of the political values of the mass public. It is particularly important to analyze such broader implications of quotas in a recently democratized country such as Mexico, where politics have traditionally been considered a male domain and where the end of seventy-one years of one-party dominance in 2000 has not eliminated problems of the past. Clientelist practices in processes of candidate selection, along with allegations of political corruption and electoral fraud, have created mistrust among citizens toward politicians and have made large shares of the population reluctant to enter the world of politics.

This chapter aims at analyzing the possible effects of quotas on the Mexican electorate's political attitudes, in two respects: first, in terms of women's political engagement and second, in terms of the perceived legitimacy of democratic institutions. I pay attention to what scholars have depicted as one specific facet of representation: symbolic representation (Sawer 2000). I operationalize symbolic representation by focusing on three political attitudes: political interest (in order to test political engagement) and attitudes toward the legislature and political parties (in order to test perceptions of democratic institutions' legitimacy). The three attitudes do not cover the full range of quotas' effects on the political values of mass publics; however, they illustrate key features of the concept of symbolic representation. Moreover, a practical motive for choosing these indicators concerns the relative ease with which large-scale data on these attitudes are collected, making them suitable for empirical scrutiny.

By performing an over-time analysis (from 1995 to 2005) at the federal level, along with a within-country comparison (with data from 2005) at the state level, I test two hypotheses. Effectively implemented quota policies, defined as quotas that generate a numerical increase in the number of female legislators, will increase (1) women's political engagement and (2) the perceived legitimacy of democratic institutions among the electorate. To preview my results, the empirical analysis gives no general support to the hypotheses, with one exception: the federal analysis provides tentative support to the claim that quotas spur women's political engagement. I suggest at least three reasons for why quota provisions in Mexico have had generally limited effects on symbolic representation. First, the undemocratic legacy of Mexican politics and the continued use of informal practices to select candidates might enhance citizens' mistrust not only of the old (male) political elite but also of the new (female) representatives. Second, citizens might still lack information about the law, particularly the fact that it has contributed to an increase in the number of women in legislative bodies. Finally, any positive effects of quotas on mass publics might be first visible among those already politically engaged, that is, among already organized women. If that is the case, it is likely to take a longer time for quotas to have beneficial effects on citizens' attitudes about politics.

The chapter proceeds as follows. First, I give a brief historical background to quota legislation in Mexico and include a short review of the numerical effectiveness of the policies. Second, I define and operationalize the concept of symbolic representation and spell out the hypotheses that are being tested in the chapter. Here I also present my motivation for testing these hypotheses in the case of Mexico. Next, I perform the analysis, which is presented in two parts: a descriptive over-time analysis at the federal level, followed by a cross-sectional regression analysis at the state level.

The first quota provision in Mexico was voluntarily adopted by one of the opposition parties: the Democratic Revolution Party (PRD). In 1993, PRD included in its party statutes a 30 percent quota for committees and candidate lists (Bruhn 2003). Three years later, the hegemonic party for almost seventy years, the Institutional Revolution Party (PRI), approved a recommendation to field no more than 70 percent of candidates of the same sex on its candidate lists. In the same year, 1996, the PRI-dominated congress wrote this measure—again as a recommendation—into law (Baldez 2004).

The quota regulations of 1996 were not effectively implemented. The major political parties—the PRI, the PRD, and the National Action Party (PAN)—adhered to the provisions in a minimalist way. As a result, there was a slight decrease in the number of women elected after the 2000 cycle, from 17.4 percent to 16.8 percent in the lower house (Baldez 2004). The unsuccessful quota law prompted female legislators to redouble their efforts to turn the recommendations into enforceable quota provisions, and in 2002, new quota rules were included in the federal electoral law. The quota regulations forced the political parties to nominate at least 30 percent women and no more than 70 percent women to both proportional and majority seats; parties failing to comply would be denied the right to register. Moreover, the law stipulated that at least one of the top three candidates to proportional seats was to be a woman (Baldez 2007).

At the state level, a few states adopted rather strict quota rules in the 1990s, that is, before the 2002 revision of the federal quota law. The state of Chihuahua was a pioneer in this respect, adopting quotas in 1994 and revising the rules in 1997. During the following six years, another sixteen of thirty-one states, in addition to the Federal District of Mexico City,[2] introduced enforceable quotas into their electoral code (Reynoso and D'Angelo 2006). After 2005, which is the final year included in this analysis, an additional eleven states have adopted enforceable quotas into their electoral code (Zetterberg 2011).[3]

Previous research has scrutinized the reasons for adopting gender quotas in Mexico. Bruhn (2003) argues that the first quotas, within the PRD, "did not result from a powerful reformer nor from grassroots pressure, but from aggressive activism among second-tier leaders" (Bruhn 2003, 110). Women from the PRI had linkages to female leaders in the PRD and copied their strategies to push for quota provisions in their own party. Thus, the first quota law, in 1996, was mainly brought about by elite women, rather than by a broad-based grassroots movement of women activists. The quota law of 2002 was also mainly an elite project, with a cross-partisan network of female legislators serving as protagonist. Their ultimate aim with the reform was to undo traditional gender roles in society; thus, the elite network expected broader societal consequences of the law. The fact that women in the legislature were united brought public attention to the law, which raised the costs of opposing quota legislation. Moreover, political parties feared the negative electoral consequences of opposing the law. A final factor was the role of the judiciary. Quota law opponents took the issue to the courts, claiming that gender quotas were unconstitutional. Yet the Supreme Court's decision to declare quotas constitutional undermined the opposition to quotas (Baldez 2004).

The numerical effects of the 2002 quota law have largely been positive, although the law's language and subsequent interpretation by the Federal Electoral Institute (Instituto Federal Electoral, IFE) may have limited the increase in the number of female legislators by imposing a ceiling rather than a floor (Baldez 2007). In the 2003 election, there was a 7 percent increase, marking the entrance of 23 percent women into the Chamber of Deputies as an all-time high. There was neither an increase nor a decrease in the subsequent election in 2006. After a 2008 statutory revision raised the quota from 30 percent to 40 percent, the number of female legislators increased to approximately 30 percent in the 2009 election. Likewise, at the state level, the introduction of enforceable quotas has generally had beneficial impacts on the number of women in the legislature. A longitudinal analysis has shown that quota policies represent the most important explanatory factor in increasing the number of women in the state legislatures (Reynoso and D'Angelo 2006).

Whereas the roots of Mexican quota policies, in addition to their numerical impacts, have been rather comprehensively documented, the possible attitudinal impacts on the Mexican electorate are, to my knowledge, unknown. However, in the normative and political debate on quotas' implementation in Mexico, these measures have been held to provide women with new political role models, and they may also send a cue to female constituents that women can pursue political careers (Zetterberg 2009). Empirical support in another Latin American context has been found in Brazil, where the quota reform has encouraged politically engaged women to act collectively (Sacchet 2008). On the other hand, a cross-national analysis of the effects of quotas on mass publics in Latin America gives no support to such propositions (Zetterberg 2009).

SYMBOLIC REPRESENTATION: DEFINITION, HYPOTHESES, AND OPERATIONALIZATION

The theoretical focus of this chapter is on the contested concept of symbolic representation. In short, this facet of representation deals with the representative's possibility of being a symbol and, more specifically, on that symbol's power to "evoke feelings or attitudes" among the represented (Pitkin 1967, 97). A representative's presence might affect the self-image of constituents or their perceived status in society (Goodin 1977).

In the literature on gender and politics, it has been argued that there are certain benefits that only women representatives could bring to female constituents. Female politicians stand as symbols, or political role models, for other women (Phillips 1995). They show women citizens that men are not the only ones who may play an active role in public life. Therefore, scholars have claimed that an increased number of visible female players in the electoral arena will generate more positive attitudes toward politics among women and spur their propensity to engage in political activities (Wolbrecht and Campbell 2007). Thus, the mere presence of female legislators is suggested to have a positive impact on women's political engagement (Sawer 2000).

Sawer's definition of symbolic representation includes also a second characteristic: the legitimacy of democratic institutions (2000). A more gender equal legislative body has been held to increase the perceived legitimacy of elected bodies (Schwindt-Bayer and Mishler 2005). The argument suggests that such trends could be observed not only among female constituents but also among the entire electorate. Thus, I suggest that specific quota policies, by generating a larger number of women in legislative bodies, increase the legitimacy of the key institutions of representative democracy.

From this discussion, I formulate two hypotheses:

Hypothesis One: Effectively implemented quota policies (i.e., those in which quotas generate a numerical increase in the number of female legislators) increase women's political engagement.

Hypothesis Two: Effectively implemented quota policies increase the electorate's perceived legitimacy of democratic institutions.

At least two comments should be made in relation to the hypotheses. First, the symbolic representation perspective, as interpreted here, implies a specific causal mechanism for both hypotheses: an increased number of female legislators who can provide mass publics with new political role models.[4] It should be noted, however, that this approach makes it difficult to separate the impact of quotas from the impact of a general increase in female legislators. To the extent that it is possible, I will try to separate the two effects in the statistical analysis.

Second, although hypothesis one tests theories suggesting that quotas increase only female constituents' political engagement, the empirical examination also includes any effects on male citizens. It becomes an empirical question of whether quotas have an impact on either—or both—of the two sexes. For instance, it is perfectly conceivable that men are similarly persuaded by quotas' demonstration of fairness, thus becoming more willing to participate themselves. Conversely, men could become more resentful of women's expanded opportunities, as Jennie Burnet (chapter 12 in this volume) shows for the Rwandan case. Such negative attitudes toward quotas could generate two contradictory reactions: either an increase in men's activism, and thus an increase in political involvement, or the creation of men's disengagement and apathy (see Hirschman 1970). By including men in the analysis, these propositions are also tested.

Mexico represents a suitable case for testing these hypotheses. First, by selecting a country that has had quotas for quite some time and that has revised the quota law to make it more effective, it becomes possible to follow long-term developments and distinguish between the effects of different quota rules. As some quota provisions have proven to be largely successful in terms of numerical achievements, it is relevant to examine if these quota rules have generated more far-reaching consequences for Mexican society, as they have in Rwanda (chapter 12 in this volume) and elsewhere. Second, feminist activists and feminists within the subnational bureaucracy have suggested that quotas do provide Mexican women with new political role models and increase their political engagement; thus, there is anecdotal evidence for at least hypothesis one in the Mexican context. In addition, the different electoral codes at the state level make Mexico an ideal case for a specific within-country comparison. Intracountry analyses have the advantage of holding constant institutions such as party systems and, to a greater extent than in cross-national analyses, political culture and other cultural or historical factors. A within-country comparison is further justified for empirical reasons. It has been hypothesized that symbolic effects of quotas are more likely at subnational levels of government, because of the potentially closer ties between representatives and the represented at more local levels in society (Zetterberg 2009).

Thus, I perform an over-time analysis at the federal level in addition to a cross-sectional state-level analysis. The two analyses should, on the one hand, be seen as complementary approaches that reveal a more comprehensive picture of the relationship between quotas and symbolic representation in the Mexican context. On the other hand, by analyzing the impact of both federal and state-level quotas, it is possible to address the question of whether the level of government matters for quota impact on mass publics.

The first hypothesis, on political engagement, is analyzed by examining the level of political interest among male and female citizens. This indicator is imperfect, as it does not capture all of the ways in which a person could be politically engaged. For instance, it does not cover manifest political behavior (for example, voting). However, changes in political interest are likely to precede changes in actual political behavior; in that sense, it could be an adequate indicator for an early assessment of a relatively recent electoral reform such as gender quotas. In other words, if there is a relationship between quotas and political engagement, we would expect a positive effect on political interest.

The second hypothesis, on the legitimacy of democratic institutions, is captured by analyzing citizens' attitudes toward the main political arena of representative democracy: the parliament, as well as the main actors in legislative politics, the political parties. Since the effects of legislative quotas on symbolic representation relate to the functioning of one specific democratic institution—the parliament—the idea is to focus specifically on this institution and the players involved in its elections. Thus, attitudes toward the executive are not included in the analysis. Unfortunately, the data set used for the state-level analysis does not include questions about citizens' attitudes toward the subnational legislatures. Therefore, I restrict the focus of the state-level analysis to attitudes toward the political parties.

THE FEDERAL LEVEL: POLITICAL INTEREST, TRUST, AND QUOTA POLICIES

The over-time analysis at the federal level uses data from the Latinobarómetro.[5] This survey asks questions about politics and society of approximately one thousand respondents in each of many Latin American countries, including Mexico. The political engagement aspect of symbolic representation—political interest—is measured by the question "How interested are you in politics?" to which respondents may answer "very," "fairly," "a little," and "not at all interested." The second aspect of symbolic representation—the perceived legitimacy of democratic institutions—is captured with two questions. Trust in political parties is measured by the question "How much confidence do you have in the political parties?" and trust in parliament is measured by the question "How much confidence do you have in the congress/parliament?" To both of these questions, respondents may answer "a lot," "some," "a little," or "no confidence."

To estimate the possible impact of quota policies on the two aspects of symbolic representation, it would be preferable to have panel data that also include questions about the quota policies. Such questions could specifically gauge respondents' familiarity with and opinion of the law, making it possible to link certain political attitudes to the adoption of quotas. Similar surveys were implemented by Jennie Burnet (chapter 12 in this volume) in Rwanda and Petra Meier (chapter 10) in Belgium. In Mexico, however, the Latinobarómetro data set does not include questions about quotas, nor are the same respondents interviewed in different rounds of the survey. Therefore, I use an alternative approach. The approach uses descriptive statistics measuring respondents' level of political interest, confidence in political parties, and confidence in the legislature, at two points in time: before and after the adoption of a federal quota policy.

Consequently, I use data from three rounds of the Latinobarómetro survey: 1995, 2000, and 2005. In 1995, there were no quotas in the federal electoral code. By 2000, the first, rather toothless quota law was four years old; thus, the data allow for a comparison between a situation in which there were no quotas and a situation in which quota recommendations were in place. By 2005, the new quota law had been effectively implemented in the 2003 election, and women's increased presence in the legislature had been evident for about two years.

Hypothesis one is given preliminary support if there is an increased level of political interest among women but not among men, mainly between 2000 and 2005, that is, during the period in which the revised quota law was enforced. Tentative support to hypothesis two, on the other hand, is given if there is an increased level of trust in parliament and in the political parties among both sexes, especially between 2000 and 2005. Note that I use the words *preliminary* and *tentative* in relation to the support that the analysis may generate. The nature of the data (e.g., no panel data) restricts the drawing of definitive conclusions from the analysis.

Figure 11.1 summarizes the findings of the descriptive analysis. In line with hypothesis one, women's political interest increases over time, which narrows the gender gap in men's and women's level of political interest. In 1995, there was a statistically significant gender gap: 28 percent of the women were very or fairly interested in politics; the corresponding share of male respondents was 37 percent. During a five-year period, there was a generally large increase in political interest among men (49 percent) and women (41 percent); however, a significant gender gap persisted. In contrast, between 2000 and 2005, there was no increase in political interest among men, while the increase among women continued. This resulted in a closed gender gap by 2005: 49 percent of the Mexican women claimed that they were very or fairly

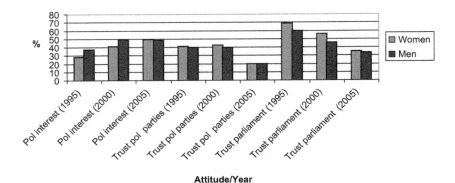

Attitude/Year

FIGURE 11.1 Political attitudes in Mexico, by attitude, year, and gender.
Sources: Latinobarómetro 1995, Latinobarómetro 2000, Latinobarómetro 2005.

interested in politics, whereas 48 percent of the men expressed similar opinions, with no statistically significant difference.

As for the legitimacy of democratic institutions, there is no support for the hypothesis that quotas enhance citizens' positive valuations of politics. Rather, there was a dramatic decrease in Mexicans' confidence in political parties between 2000 and 2005. For both men and women, approximately 40 percent expressed a lot of or some confidence in the political parties in 2000, compared with only 20 percent in 2005. There are no statistically significant differences between men and women, either before or after quota adoption. Citizens' trust in parliament shows a similar decrease over time. Both men and women had almost half as much confidence in the legislature in 2005 (approximately 30 percent) than in 1995 (60 percent to 70 percent). Women are slightly more trusting than men, especially in 2000, and this is a statistically significant difference; however, the gap was almost closed in 2005.

As a result, the analysis gives mixed findings. The results suggest a positive relationship between quotas and symbolic representation in one respect only: quotas are positively associated with women's political engagement. This goes against the findings of previous research on Latin America (Zetterberg 2009). The finding points to the possibility that quotas might be positively related to some political attitudes and not others. For instance, the quotas may boost women's political self-esteem, without necessarily increasing their trust in, and inclination to engage in, the main institutions of representative democracy.

However, a positive relationship between quotas and women's political interest does not necessarily imply a causal relationship between the two factors. Other features of Mexican society might account both for quotas' adoption and for changes in women's political interest (see Zetterberg 2009). For instance, Mexico's socioeconomic development has positively increased over the last few decades, and the living conditions for citizens are, on average, significantly better today than they were thirty years ago (United Nations Development Program 2008). As a result, citizens should be better educated and have greater political skills than previous generations; such changes are likely to spur their political engagement (see, for example, Norris 2002). Women's increased political interest and demands for quota policies might both be related to women's ability to benefit from enhanced socioeconomic development. As a consequence, there is not necessarily a positive causal relationship between quota policies and women's political interest.

The present study, with the data at its disposal, is not able to control accurately for such propositions. However, a rough comparison with a control case—Chile—offers no different result from those presented here. Chile is among those countries in Latin America that have experienced the largest socioeconomic expansion, and the number of women in parliament (the lower house) has increased from 10.8 percent in 1997 to 15.0 percent in 2005; however, it has not included any quota provisions in its electoral code. A closed gender gap in political interest in the Chilean case would then suggest that the positive relationship between quotas and women's increased political interest in Mexico is spurious. However, descriptive statistics not presented here from the Latinobarómetro surveys reveal no closed gender gap in Chile. After an increase in political interest between 1995 and 2000, there is a large drop between 2000 and 2005, for both men and women. At all three points in time, Chilean men are significantly more politically interested than Chilean women, whereas in Mexico, with the quota present, women become as politically interested as men.

To conclude, the results of the analysis lend preliminary support to the idea that quota legislation is positively associated with women's political interest. For beliefs in the legitimacy in democratic institutions, however, I find no such support. Yet, as indicated above, it is necessary to be cautious when drawing conclusions. It is not possible to use advanced statistical analysis, which includes important control factors, in the federal-level analysis.

THE STATE LEVEL: NO CAUSAL RELATIONSHIP BETWEEN QUOTAS AND POLITICAL ATTITUDES

The analysis of quotas' effects in the states uses a different data set, namely, the Mexico 2006 Panel Study (Lawson et al. 2007). This survey occurred during Mexico's 2005–2006 general election campaign, asking questions about the campaign of approximately 2,400 individuals across the country. There are different waves of the survey, covering different stages of the campaign, and the same individuals are asked to answer the questions each time. Here, I use the first wave, conducted in October 2005, which has the largest number of respondents.

Among the questions about political attitudes and values, I analyze two questions that capture the concept of symbolic representation. For the political-engagement aspect, the survey asked, "How much interest do you have in politics?" with respondents choosing either "a lot," "some," "a little," or "none." This question is almost identical to the question posed at the federal level in the Latinobarómetro.

For the legitimacy issue, the question about political parties is rather different from those of other surveys, such as the Latinobarómetro.[6] Usually, questions are asked about the confidence that citizens have in the political parties. The Mexico 2006 Panel Study, on the other hand, asks respondents for their opinion about institutions. The political-party question was phrased as follows: "On a scale from zero to ten, where zero means you have a very negative opinion and ten means you have a very positive opinion, what is your opinion of the PRI/the PAN/the PRD?" (three separate questions). This wording might not fully capture whether the respondent perceives that political parties are legitimate actors in a representative democracy. Rather, the questions target an individual's ideological attachment to a specific political party and his or her willingness to vote for that party. However, by summing the values of each question and creating an index (ranging from zero to thirty), I can obtain an estimate of the general attitudes that citizens have toward political parties. If a respondent has generally positive opinions about all three political parties, then he or she probably thinks that the main political actors are doing a fairly good job. In other words, he or she should express a fairly large amount of confidence in key representative institutions.

To examine the relationship between quotas and symbolic representation at the state level empirically, I first use descriptive statistics for the sixteen states plus the Federal District that are included in the survey and for which there is information for both men and women.[7] In order for hypothesis one to receive preliminary support, the average level of political interest *among women* should be higher in the states that have adopted strong quota laws than in states that have not adopted such policies. Hypothesis two, on the other hand, is tentatively supported if opinions about the political parties are more positive among *both* men and women in the states that have adopted forceful quota laws than in states that have not adopted such policies.

Table 11.1 shows average levels for both political interest and opinion about political parties, separating men and women, in addition to states that, by 2005, had introduced quotas and those that had not.[8] In line with hypothesis one, the analysis shows that the level of political interest among women is on average higher in the states with legislative quotas than in other states. Thirty-six percent of the women living in a state with gender quotas claimed that they had "a lot" or "some" interest in politics, whereas 21 percent of those in other states expressed similar attitudes. The difference is statistically significant. As for the opinions about political parties, there are no differences between women living in states having and not having gender quotas. Women who live in a state without strict quota laws have slightly more positive attitudes toward the political parties than others (16.26 versus 15.68, on a thirty-graded scale); however, the difference is not statistically significant.

These results resemble the findings at the federal level. Based on descriptive statistics, quotas appear to be positively associated with women's political engagement but not with citizens' perception of the legitimacy of political institutions. Interestingly, however, the state level analysis shows—in contrast with the findings at the federal level—that men's political interest is also positively related to quota policies. Forty percent of the men living in a state with gender quotas claimed that they had a lot or some interest in politics, whereas 25 percent of those in other states had at least some political interest. This difference is statistically significant. Regarding opinions about political parties, there are no such differences.

Given the limitations of purely descriptive analyses, the same problem is highlighted here as at the federal level: it is not possible to know from the analysis if quotas and political interest are causally related or if the relationship is spurious. However, a state-level approach is better equipped to deal with the problem. The differences in quota legislation across states make it possible to control for some state-specific

Table 11.1 State means for men's and women's political interest and opinions about political parties, separating between states that by 2005 had adopted and not adopted legislative quotas

State	Political interest (0–1)			Opinion about parties (0–30)		
	Men	Women	Diff.	Men	Women	Diff.
With quotas						
Chihuahua	0.30 (0.47)	0.10 (0.31)	+0.20	16.26 (5.90)	18.65 (4.09)	−2.39
Federal District (DF)	0.47 (0.5)	0.50 (0.50)	−0.03	14.19 (6.04)	14.09 (5.68)	+0.10
Guerrero	0.40 (0.55)	0.33 (0.47)	+0.07	16.80 (4.44)	16.13 (5.32)	+0.67
Jalisco	0.38 (0.49)	0.36 (0.49)	+0.02	17.65 (5.82)	17.84 (6.27)	−0.18
Mexico State	0.31 (0.47)	0.26 (0.44)	+0.05	15.80 (6.07)	15.38 (6.32)	+0.42
Oaxaca	0.23 (0. 42)	0.18 (0.39)	+0.05	16.74 (6.54)	14.40 (6.84)	+2.34
Puebla	0.39 (0.49)	0.17 (0.39)	+0.22	15.47 (4.73)	14.68 (6.18)	+0.79
San Luís P.	0. 32 (0. 48)	0.35 (0.49)	−0.03	20.11 (6.00)	15.21 (6.32)	+4.90
Sonora	0. 32 (0. 47)	0.26 (0.45)	+0.06	18.18 (6.24)	18.47 (5.50)	−0.29
Tamaulipas	0. 54 (0. 51)	0.40 (0.50)	+0.14	19.89 (6.09)	17.85 (6.18)	+2.14
Average with quotas	0.40 (0.49)	0.36 (0.48)		15.80 (6.22)	15.25 (6.05)	
Without quotas						
Chiapas	0.26 (0.44)	0.14 (0.35)	+0.12	17.18 (5.73)	16.53 (7.29)	+0.65
Guanajuato	0.14 (0.36)	0.31 (0.47)	−0.17	13.90 (6.69)	14.89 (6.73)	−0.98
Hidalgo	0.15 (0.37)	0.20 (0.41)	−0.05	18.81 (5.39)	16.50 (4.65)	+2.31
Michoacán	0.20 (0.40)	0.15 (0.37)	+0.05	16.00 (6.18)	16.85 (5.71)	−0.85
Nayarit	0.46 (0.52)	0.14 (0.38)	+0.32	17.62 (4.37)	19.29 (4.46)	−1.67
Nuevo León	0. 25 (0.44)	0.25 (0.44)	0	15.33 (4.89)	17.92 (6.46)	0
Veracruz	0.35 (0.49)	0.28 (0.45)	+0.07	16.00 (4.17)	15.32 (5.80)	+0.68
Average without quotas	0.25 (0.43)	0.21 (0.41)		16.63 (5.80)	16.01 (6.31)	
Diff. quotas and non-quotas	+0.15**	+0.15**		−0.83	−0.76	
All	0.37 (0.48)	0.33 (0.47)		15.99 (6.14)	15.43 (6.12)	
n	1067	904		996	823	

Source: Lawson et al. 2007

Only states that had adopted legislative quotas *and* had implemented them in elections by 2005 are labeled "With quotas."

* = diff. sign. at < 0.05;

** = diff. sign. at < 0.01

characteristics of the political, cultural, and/or economic environment that might account both for why quotas were adopted in the first place and for differences in citizens' political interest.[9] I therefore perform an additional analysis exclusively on political interest in order to gain a more complete picture of the relationship. The limited number of states restricts the control factors to three: a human development index (HDI), gender equality attitudes, and the number of women in parliament.[10]

The first two factors take the level of socioeconomic modernization into account (Inglehart and Norris 2003), for better living conditions, such as access to education and wages, may lead to more politically engaged individuals. In this scenario, both political interest and demands for quota policies might be the result of socioeconomic progress. To control for this possibility, I use the United Nations Development Program's (UNDP) Human Development Index for each of the Mexican states (United Nations Development Program 2006).[11] Socioeconomic development has also been held to generate a cultural shift among the population, who will pay greater attention to nonmaterial issues such as gender equality. To control for this alternative possibility, I use aggregate data from the Mexican Election Panel Study of 2000 (Lawson et al. 2000) to control for the possibility that women's-rights issues are more prioritized in some states than in others. This variable accounts for both quota adoption and differences in political interest.[12]

The last characteristic—the number of women in parliament—controls for the possibility that differences in women's political interest are the result not of quota policies but of women's overall political inclusion. Remember that interparty coalitions of female legislators have been crucial for introducing quotas in Mexico (Baldez 2004). Therefore, I control for the number of female state legislators in 1997, which was before the adoption of quotas at the state level (Reynoso and D'Angelo 2006). In addition to these factors, I use "lagged" aggregate data of political interest (mean values) to control for the possibilities of a reversed causal order (Lawson et al. 2000). In other words, there is a possibility that high levels of political interest do not result from quota policies but actually generate the reform itself.

Table 11.2 shows that when state characteristics are taken into account, gender quotas are no longer positively associated with political interest.[13] The overall presence of women in the legislature is also not significantly related to political interest. The lack of relationship between quotas and political interest implies that the relationship that was visible in the descriptive analysis (table 11.1) was spurious. This means that other factors, such as socioeconomic development, which is positively related with political interest, are likely to account both for why quotas were adopted in the first place and for differences in political interest among individuals in different Mexican states. The findings hold for both men and women. In fact, for women, there is a statistically significant *negative* relationship between quotas and political interest. The size of the relationship, however, is substantially small: living under a quota regime is associated with a 3.4 percent-lower level of political interest than not living under such a regime.

The regression analysis signals the methodological importance of having rigorous controls for other explanatory factors when attempting to draw conclusions about the effects of quotas on symbolic representation. The lack of a positive relationship

Table 11.2 Relationship between gender quotas (state-level) and political interest, by gender (multivariate analysis)

	Men	Women
	Political interest (0–3)	Political interest (0–3)
Gender quota law	0.282 (0.149)	−0.103* (0.039)
Human development (HDI)	2.204** (0.642)	3.209** (0.427)
Gender role attitudes (state-level; lagged)	−1.427 (1.047)	0.296 (0.466)
Women in state legislature (lagged)	¹	0.668 (0.459)
Political interest (state-level; lagged)	−0.332 (0.214)	0.589** (0.071)
Adjusted R² (n)	0.040 (1086)	0.079 (917)

Source: Lawson et al. 2007.

Unstandardized OLS regression coefficients; robust standard error in brackets. Checked by VIF statistics to be free of multicollinearity problems. Only respondents from different states are treated as independent from one another (to take auto-correlation problems into account). Missing = list-wise deletion.

¹Variable excluded from the analysis because of multicollinearity problems.

* = sign. at < 0.05;

** = sign. at < 0.01.

also places the results of the federal-level analysis in a new light. Given the similarities between the federal- and state-level analyses in the bivariate case, there are potentially some country-level characteristics missing in the analysis that partly account for why Mexico adopted quota policies, and revised them, and for the differences in political interest. For instance, the analysis is unable to control for the level of democracy in Mexico, specifically, the seventy-year PRI hegemony that ended in 2000 (after the Latinobarómetro survey was conducted) and accelerated the country's democratic transition.[14] Thus, the findings of the federal quota law should—again—be treated cautiously.

CONCLUSION: NO GENERAL IMPACT OF QUOTAS ON WOMEN'S SYMBOLIC REPRESENTATION

This chapter has examined the possible broader societal consequences of quota policies in Mexico by scrutinizing the issue of symbolic representation. Here, this concept has been operationalized as two key political attitudes among the electorate: political engagement and the perceived legitimacy of democratic institutions. The findings suggest no general relationship between quotas and women's symbolic representation, neither at the federal level nor at the state level. However, there is one exception from the general pattern. The federal-level analysis provides tentative support for the idea that quotas are positively associated with women's political interest. Exceptions notwithstanding, the conclusions from this study generally confirm previous large-scale research on the topic (Zetterberg 2009), which find that quotas produce no generalizable impact on citizens' political attitudes. However, they go against the results from qualitative case studies (Kudva 2003; Sacchet 2008), which have found that quotas generally boost women's political organization and involvement.

I suggest at least three reasons to explain why an increased numerical representation has not been accompanied by increased symbolic representation, a finding also reported by Petra Meier's study of Belgium (chapter 10 in this volume). First, in Mexico, clientelist practices, allegations of political corruption and electoral fraud, and informal candidate-selection procedures continue to play a role in politics, even after quotas were adopted and even after the end of one-party rule (see, e.g., Bruhn 2003). Thus, Mexican democracy retains its authoritarian features. In such an informal setting, party gatekeepers are unlikely to select women with strong popular support, a conclusion also drawn by Jennie Burnet (chapter 12 in this volume) in the Rwandan case. The authoritarian features of Mexican politics might make citizens disappointed in and mistrusting of politicians and reluctant to engage in politics. Second, female citizens might simply lack information about the law. Mexican political parties generally do a poor job of disseminating information about the quota policies. If women lack information about the law, then they might be unfamiliar with the increase in the number of women represented in the legislature.

Finally, it is likely that any impact of quotas on the attitudes and behavior of female citizens is first evident among those already politically engaged. For instance, quotas have been suggested to strengthen mobilization among organized women (Sacchet 2008). Thus, it is possible that political efficacy is increased among women who work for women's rights and for gender equality. Quotas could thereby stimulate women's activity at the meso level, within civil society organizations and political parties. This scenario is especially likely in a Mexican context, where federal quotas were mainly brought about by elite women within the political parties, rather than by a broad-based grassroots movement of women activists. It thus might take several decades for quota policies to have an impact on ordinary citizens' beliefs about politics. If this is the case, then we should use a longer time span when assessing the impacts of quotas on the electorate, a point also acknowledged by Petra Meier (chapter 10 in this volume) in the Belgian case.

The analysis highlights some theoretical and methodological challenges related to the analysis of quotas and symbolic representation. Theoretically, the analysis challenges the idea that subnational quotas have more positive impacts on female constituents' political beliefs than do national quotas. It might not necessarily be the local nature of the ties between the representative and the represented that potentially matter but how female representatives are portrayed and how much attention they are given in the public debate. Alternatively, the politicians themselves may be irrelevant for the possible relationship between quota policies and mass publics: perhaps the debate before quota adoption, and its possible impact on how women (and men) are portrayed in society, is of greater relevance. In other words, the quota policies themselves might send certain signals to the constituents or to groups of constituents (see also Zetterberg 2009). As further studies are being carried out, these propositions should be taken into consideration.

Methodologically, this study has pointed at the challenges in gaining reliable information in order to assess properly the symbolic impacts of quotas. At the level of the electorate, large-scale survey data are perhaps the most suitable source of information, as they are able to control for alternative explanations. However, the lack of experimental designs, such as those used by Lori Beaman, Alexandra Cirone, and Rohini Pande (chapter 13 in this volume) for studying India, generates uncertainties about the reliability of the conclusions drawn from statistical analyses. The character of the problem is slightly different at other levels of analysis, such as the meso level. In these analyses, interviews with leaderships and organizational data are likely to be fruitful sources of information, as demonstrated by Burnet's focus groups in Rwanda and Meier's surveys of party elites in Belgium. However, relying on the narrative of individuals has a drawback. As Burnet mentions, individuals have difficulties in distinguishing the impact of gender quotas from other policy changes. Thus, it is difficult to single out the specific role of quota policies in relation to other movements within society.

As a consequence, future analysts of the symbolic impacts of quotas should be careful about the methods and measurements they use. Given the complexity of this research endeavor, multimethod approaches are likely to be a good way forward. These research designs will help gain a more comprehensive understanding of the relationship between electoral quotas and women's symbolic representation.

NOTE

1. Forty percent of the 500 seats to the lower house, the Chamber of Deputies, are proportionally elected, while the remaining 300 seats are elected in single-member districts.
2. The Federal District of Mexico City has its own legislature.
3. Those states having "recommendations" in their electoral codes not to have more than a certain percentage of the same sex on their candidate lists are *not* included in this group, as these do not *require* the political parties to change their procedures for candidate selection.
4. Elsewhere, I have suggested that this is not the only possible way in which quotas might have an impact on constituents (Zetterberg 2009).
5. Latinobarómetro is a survey carried out every year since 1995. It represents the opinions, attitudes, behavior, and values of eighteen countries in Latin America, representing approximately 400 million people from the Rio Grande to the Antarctic. In the survey for 1995, there were 9,040 individuals in the sample, and the margin of error was between 2.8 percent and 4.0 percent. In 2000, there were 18,038 individuals in the sample, and the error of margin was between 2.8 percent and 5.0 percent. In 2005, there were 20,222 individuals in the sample, and the margin of error was between 2.4 percent and 3.1 percent. The Latinobarómetro survey is carried out by Corporación Latinobarómetro, a private, noncommercial corporation with its head office in Santiago, Chile (www.latinobarometro.org).
6. Again, there is no question about trust in the legislature in the Mexico 2006 Panel Study.
7. The Mexico 2006 Panel Study does not cover the states Baja California Sur and Quintana Roo. The other twenty-nine states are covered by the survey. However, in

thirteen states, there are only male or female respondents; thus, there is not information for both genders. Therefore, I exclude these states from the analyses and concentrate on the Federal District of Mexico City and on the remaining sixteen states: Chiapas, Chihuahua, Guanajuato, Guerrero, Hidalgo, Jalisco, Mexico State, Michoacán, Nayarit, Nuevo León, Oaxaca, Puebla, San Luís Potosí, Sonora, Tamaulipas, and Veracruz.

8. Again, those states that have mere recommendations in their electoral code are characterized as "nonquota states" in this analysis.

9. Here I use a contextual model, in which the analytic task is to examine the possible impact of an external factor (at the state level) on an individual's internal political attitudes (see also Huckfeldt and Sprague 1993). For closer details on the statistical model and on the problems related to such an approach, see Zetterberg 2009.

10. Ideally, I should control for more state characteristics. However, with more control factors at the state level, the risk for so-called multicollinearity problem increases. In other words, there is a risk for close relationships among explanatory factors, which makes the regression coefficients unstable (Gujarati 2003). To some extent, this limitation is counterbalanced by analyzing states in a single country. Thereby it is possible already at the outset to control roughly for factors such as the level of democracy, the electoral and party ystem, and so on.

11. Ideally, I would use HDI data from a time period before quota adoption, rather than from 2005 (see also Zetterberg 2009). However, there are few reasons to expect that the internal ranking in human-development levels will change substantially in a ten-year period.

12. More precisely, respondents are asked to mention the three policy areas that they think are the most urgent to deal with for the next president. "Women's rights" is one of fifteen policy areas. The values are aggregated to state averages (see Zetterberg 2009).

13. No significant differences in results were found when I ran models that included common sociodemographic factors at the individual level: education and age (see Lawless 2004).

14. However, there are circumstances speaking against the proposition that regime changes account for both the introduction of a revised quota law and changes in political interest. First, there are few theoretical reasons for expecting that men and women are differently affected by political regime change. Second, the new ruling party, the PAN, was an opponent of quota policies.

REFERENCES

Baldez, Lisa. 2004. Elected Bodies: The Gender Quota Law for Legislative Candidates in Mexico. *Legislative Studies Quarterly* 29 (2): 231–258.

———. 2007. Primaries vs. Quotas: Gender and Candidate Nominations in Mexico, 2003. *Latin American Politics and Society* 49 (3): 69–96.

Bruhn, Kathleen. 2003. Whores and Lesbians: Political Activism, Party Strategies, and Gender Quotas in Mexico. *Electoral Studies* 22 (1): 101–119.

Goodin, Robert E. 1977. Convention Quotas and Communal Representation. *British Journal of Political Science* 7 (2): 255–261.

Gujarati, Damodar N. 2003. *Basic Econometrics*. Boston: McGraw-Hill.

Hirschman, Albert O. 1970. *Exit, Voice, and Loyalty: Responses to Decline in Firms, Organizations, and States*. Cambridge, Mass.: Harvard University Press.

Huckfeldt, Robert, and John Sprague. 1993. Citizens, Contexts, and Politics. In Ada W. Finifter, ed., *Political Science: The State of the Discipline II*, 281–303. Washington, D.C.: American Political Science Association.

Inglehart, Ronald, and Pippa Norris. 2003. *Rising Tide: Gender Equality and Cultural Change around the World*. Cambridge, U.K.: Cambridge University Press.

Kudva, Neema. 2003. Engineering Elections: The Experiences of Women in Panchayati Raj in Karnataka, India. *International Journal of Politics, Culture and Society* 16 (3): 445–463.

Lawless, Jennifer L. 2004. Politics of Presence? Congresswomen and Symbolic Representation. *Political Research Quarterly* 57 (1): 81–99.

Lawson, Chappell, Andy Baker, Kathleen Bruhn, Roderic Camp, Wayne Cornelius, Jorge Domínguez, Kenneth Greene, Joseph Klesner, Beatriz Magaloni, James McCann, Alejandro Moreno, Alejandro Poiré, and David Shirk. 2007. The Mexico 2006 Panel Study. Wave 1. http://web.mit.edu/polisci/research/mexico06 (accessed June 23, 2009).

Lawson, Chappell, Miguel Basañez, Rodrigo Camp, Wayne Cornelius, Jorge Domínguez, Federico Estévez, Joseph Klesner, Beatriz Magaloni, James McCann, Alejandro Moreno, Pablo Paras, and Alejandro Poiré. 2000. Mexican Election Panel Study, 2000. http://web. mit.edu/polisci/people/faculty/chappell-lawson.shtml#linkResearch (accessed June 23, 2009).

Norris, Pippa. 2002. *Democratic Phoenix: Reinventing Political Activism*. Cambridge, U.K.: Cambridge University Press.

Phillips, Anne. 1995. *The Politics of Presence*. Oxford and New York: Clarendon Press.

Pitkin, Hanna. 1967. *The Concept of Representation*. Berkeley: University of California Press.

Reynoso, Diego, and Natalia D'Angelo. 2006. Las Leyes de Cuota y Su Impacto en la Elección de Mujeres en México. *Política y Gobierno* 13 (2): 279–313.

Sacchet, Teresa. 2008. Beyond Numbers: The Impact of Gender Quotas in Latin America. *International Feminist Journal of Politics* 10 (3): 369–386.

Sawer, Marian. 2000. Parliamentary Representation of Women: From Discourses of Justice to Strategies of Accountability. *International Political Science Review* 21 (4): 361–380.

Schwindt-Bayer, Leslie, and William Mishler. 2005. An Integrated Model of Women's Representation. *Journal of Politics* 67 (2): 407–428.

United Nations Development Program. 2006. *Indicadores de Desarrollo Humano y Género en México*. Mexico City: United Nations Development Program.

———. 2008. *Human Development Report 2007/2008: Human Development Index Trends*. http://hdrstats.undp.org/indicators/14.html (accessed August 19, 2009).

Wolbrecht, Christina, and David E. Campbell. 2007. Leading by Example: Female Members of Parliament as Political Role Models. *American Journal of Political Science* 51 (4): 921–939.

Zetterberg, Pär. 2008. The Downside of Gender Quotas? Institutional Constraints on Women in Mexican State Legislatures. *Parliamentary Affairs* 61 (3): 442–460.

———. 2009. Do Gender Quotas Foster Women's Political Engagement? Lessons from Latin America. *Political Research Quarterly* 62 (4): 715–730.

———. 2011. The Diffusion of Sub-national Gender Quotas in Mexico and Their Impacts. In Adriana M. Piatti-Crocker, ed., *Diffusion of Gender Quotas in Latin America and Beyond: Advances and Setbacks in the Last Two Decades*, 53–69. New York: Peter Lang.

12 Women's Empowerment and Cultural Change in Rwanda

Jennie Burnet

Ntankokokazi ibika hari isake. (Hens do not crow where there is a cock.)
—Rwandan proverb

Urugo ruvuze umugore ruvuga umuhoro. (At home, when the wife speaks, out comes the knife.)
—Rwandan proverb

Since 1999, the Rwandan government has pursued three kinds of quotas for women: reserved seats, party quotas, and legislative quotas. Reserved seats and legislative quotas were instituted by the 2003 constitution. Party quotas have been pursued by all political parties since at least 1999, although a precise date is hard to determine, since party quotas were not implemented by statute but rather were a strategy used by parties to gain more seats in the parliament and the executive branch.

Elsewhere I have explored the dramatic increase in women's participation in public life, their representation in government, and their practical effects on policy (Burnet 2008a). In this chapter, I examine the impact of gender quotas on the symbolic representation of women and girls in Rwandan society. My main purpose is to understand the cultural meanings of national, local, and party gender quotas in the Rwandan political system. I assess these cultural meanings by examining women's (and some men's) perceptions of women, in addition to their perceptions of women's roles in politics and society. I also consider changing cultural practices vis-à-vis gender roles. These data were gathered over twenty-four months of ethnographic research conducted between 1997 and 2009 and also through monitoring of the legal statutes and policy changes in Rwanda and ongoing literature reviews.

In Rwanda, legislative gender quotas have thrust women into the public spotlight in unprecedented ways. Significant changes in gender roles and ideologies and in the representation of women in both government and civil society preceded the 1994 genocide. Nonetheless, the Rwandan Patriotic Front (RPF)[1] and its women-friendly policies, in combination with international aid that has focused on increasing women's economic autonomy and supporting women's community-based organizations, have dramatically sped up these processes, resulting in a gender revolution. While female Rwandans have embraced this revolution and become entrepreneurs in every facet of society, many Rwandans, male and female, lay the blame for the perceived disintegration of marriage as an institution on this "upheaval" of gender roles (interviews, 2009).

The Rwandan case is relevant to scholarly and practical debates about gender quotas and representation because the country is so frequently cited as a success story in terms of the impact of quotas. Since legislative elections in 2008, the Rwandan parliament became the first and only national legislative body in the world to be majority female. Yet increased representation of women has not led to a greater statutory protection of women's rights, since parliament originates very little legislation. Given that Rwanda scores very low in terms of democracy measures, increased representation of women in government has not necessarily led to a more democratic political terrain.

Nonetheless, this case study finds that gender quotas have generated impacts far beyond the political sphere. The top-down policies that brought large numbers of women into government improved women's career and economic opportunities, thereby improving social mobility among women. Because quotas apply to national, regional, and local levels, their impact has been broad and deep. Additionally, the RPF's women-friendly policies overturned the colonial and postcolonial patriarchal gender paradigm, whereby husbands worked and made important decisions while wives managed the domestic sphere and remained financially dependent on men. Yet urban, elite women have reaped the greatest benefits from these changes, thanks to increased access to salaried jobs, including lucrative positions in the national legislature and ministries, and greater purchasing power (for items such as automobiles, clothing, and domestic service), whereas rural peasant women in elected positions in local government have seen their workload increase and their economic security undermined.

Another key finding of this case study is that citizens do not distinguish between the impact of gender quotas and many other policy changes and laws that have improved the status of women in Rwandan society more broadly. When asked about the impact of the gender quotas, respondents did not make explicit, causal links between the increased representation of women in all branches of government at the national, regional, and local levels, on the one hand, and new women-friendly legislation or policies or changed relationships between citizens and the state, on the other. Rather, they viewed the quotas as part of this broader set of reforms implemented by the RPF-led government. Given that policy decisions and their implementation flow top-down and that members of parliament are not perceived as representing constituents' interests or concerns, it is no surprise that citizens link the gender quota policy and women in office to a broader set of commitments to equality. These government policies have had a diffuse and widespread impact on citizens' daily lives, particularly in terms of women's choices and opportunities.

QUOTAS AND THE POLITICAL CONTEXT OF RWANDA

Today Rwanda is most known for the 1994 genocide, in which an estimated eight hundred thousand Tutsi and moderate Hutu civilians lost their lives, and for the subsequent renaissance in Rwandan society, guided by the RPF's Paul Kagame, initially as vice president and later as president. The genocide and civil war (1990–1994) and their aftermaths resulted in rapid change within society, especially in terms of gender roles. Today the national parliament has a greater percentage of women, 54 percent, than any other national legislative body in the world. Women have been granted full and independent economic rights, both in law and in practice, and given legal right to inheritance.

Since 1999, the government has simultaneously pursued all three types of quotas: reserved seats, party quotas, and legislative quotas. These policies can be attributed primarily to the RPF but also to increasing demands made by women's civil society organizations. Since its origins as a rebel army, the RPF has mainstreamed women in its own infrastructure and in the government (Burnet 2008a, 363). Many of the RPF policies and approaches have been modeled after those of the Museveni and the National Resistance Movement in Uganda (Burnet 2008a, 367). Powley (2005, 159) sees the RPF's approach to gender as a result of Tutsi exiles' experiences of discrimination. Based on statements from RPF leaders, such as Rose Kabuye and John Mutamba, the RPF embraced notions of gender equality in the hopes of improving society.[2]

Since at least 1998, other political parties have promoted women to cabinet-level appointments and actively recruited female candidates, including them on party lists and putting them forward as candidates in general elections for nonreserved seats. For instance, the 2001 local-level elections witnessed the selection of female candidates for reserved seats at the cell, sector, and district levels. The 2003 constitution simultaneously created reserved seats for women in the Chamber of Deputies and provided legislative quotas reserving 30 percent of positions in all decision-making bodies for women (see article 9, number 3). As a result of these policies, Rwanda elected the first female-majority national legislative chamber in 2008 when females secured 56.25 percent of the seats in the Chamber of Deputies.[3] As Meier (chapter 10 in this volume) finds in the Belgian case, the rising number of women in Rwandan politics cannot be attributed to gender quotas alone; in Rwanda, many women have won seats not reserved by the quota system.

After the genocide, Rwanda went through a nine year transition period. The RPF portrayed this period as a power-sharing arrangement with the other political parties recognized in the 1993 Arusha Peace Accords, with the exception of parties that were banned because of their role in the genocide. Most international and national observers, however, viewed this transition period as a consensual dictatorship whereby most Rwandans accepted authoritarian RPF rule as a necessity. The transition ended in 2003, when a new constitution was accepted and presidential and parliamentary elections took place. The 2003 constitution created a presidential system with a national parliament and a prime minister who performs many of the duties of a vice president. Most seats in both houses of parliament are elected through direct elections, but eight senators are appointed by the president and another four by the Forum of Political Organizations, an umbrella organization that all political parties must join by constitutional mandate. The Rwandan political system is nominally multiparty, but in practice, it is a single-party system, with the RPF functioning as a state party.

Rwanda ranks very low on most democracy measures because the RPF orchestrates elections, suppresses the independent media, and retains control over most civil society organizations.[4] While the parliament is majority female, most of these women are card-carrying members of the RPF or its coalition partners. In addition, women elected to reserved seats are nominated, or at least vetted, by the RPF via the Forum of Political Organizations. Thus, most of these women owe allegiance to the RPF rather than to the constituencies who elected them.

OPERATIONALIZATION, METHODS, AND DATA COLLECTION

Several scholars have argued that women's increased presence in government sends important signals to female citizens, leading them to become more politically involved or to feel more politically efficacious (Atkeson 2003; Atkeson and Carrillo 2007; High-Pippert and Comer 1998). Yet others have found that the election of women appears to have weak effects on trends in women's political engagement (Karp and Banducci 2008). In Rwanda, the impact of quotas on women's political engagement, defined as participation in elections, is difficult to assess, because voting is required in practice although not by law. Participation in elections is recorded on citizens' voter-registration cards and, since 2009, on the electronic chip embedded in the new national identity cards. Local officials question citizens who do not vote and may assess fines or withhold government services, such as issuing birth certificates or other documents.

Measuring the impact of quotas on female citizens' political involvement or feelings of political efficacy is equally difficult, because the country is not democratic, and citizens—and even legislators—have little capacity to influence policy. Although the political system is representative in name, in that parliamentarians are said to "represent" specific geographic regions, this connection does not exist in practice, because most members of parliament do not reside, and in some cases may never have resided, in the communities they were elected to represent. Moreover, elections are staged events with predetermined outcomes, and members of parliament have little or no incentive to represent their constituents' interests. In addition, almost all legislation originates in the executive branch, so members of parliament rarely generate or even shape legislation. In fact, they are strongly incentivized to follow the policies dictated by the executive so that they remain in good stead with the RPF and retain their seats in parliament, which come with generous salaries, stipends, significant social prestige, and many other tangible and intangible benefits.

What is measurable in the Rwandan case is how the dramatic increase of women in the public sphere raised "awareness of what women can achieve and legitimate[d] women as political actors, unraveling at least to some degree previously accepted gender roles," as Franceschet, Krook, and Piscopo (chapter 1 in this volume) describe symbolic representation. In conversations with a wide variety of Rwandans, in group interviews with grassroots women's organizations, and in individual interviews with leaders of women's civil society organizations conducted in May and June 2009, most respondents agreed that the gender quotas and the high profile of women in the political system have encouraged women to take leading roles in other areas of Rwandan society.

This chapter draws on ethnographic research conducted in urban and rural Rwanda between 1997 and 2009, including more than a hundred formal interviews with the leaders and members of women's civil society organizations, several hundred ethnographic interviews with ordinary citizens in rural and urban Rwanda, and monitoring of legal statutes and policy changes in Rwanda and ongoing literature reviews. In-depth ethnographic research constitutes a holistic approach, often summarized as "participant observation," and has widespread acceptance within anthropology; the approach consists of intensive, mixed-methods research, often with a focus on qualitative data.[5] Data collected as part of my ongoing ethnographic research in Rwanda have included indirect and direct observation of behavior and elicitation techniques, including ethnographic interviews, unstructured and semistructured individual interviews, and semistructured group interviews.[6] In the highly politicized context of postgenocide Rwanda, ethnographic interviews have proven to be "the only realistic tool available for gathering information," as Bernard and Ryan (2010, 28) explain. While ethnographic interviews might appear to be informal conversations, they are instead intentional interactions on the part of the ethnographer, who elicits information on issues of interest through the use of simple questions, such as "What do you think about X?" or by asking follow-up questions when informants spontaneously bring up an issue of interest to the ethnographer.

To investigate the cultural implications of the gender quota policies, I conducted individual and group interviews with male and female citizens, members of grassroots women's organizations, members of government, former members of government, and women leaders of civil society organizations during a five-week field trip in 2009. This intentional sample was selected in order to assess the broader impacts of gender quotas on Rwandan society and perceptions of women. Except where noted, I conducted all interviews myself, in either Kinyarwanda, French, or English. Interviews in Kinyarwanda were conducted with a Rwandan interpreter. Questions about the impact of gender quotas were integrated into semistructured interviews that covered several other topics. First, a basic question on the impact of gender quotas was asked: "What changes in Rwandan society or your daily life have resulted from the government's gender quota policy?" Then several probing questions were used to elicit additional information, such as "Anything else?"; "You mentioned many positive changes—have there been any negative changes?"; and "You mentioned several negative changes—have there been any positive changes?"

All interviewees refused to be recorded with a digital audio recorder, so interview "transcripts" were re-created based on detailed, handwritten notes taken by the author and the research assistant.[7] The transcripts and field notes were then hand-coded for major themes that emerged during the interviews. Additional themes were generated during the production of interview transcripts and during subsequent readings of transcripts and field notes. A code book was compiled for data analysis (see Bernard and Ryan 2010). Finally, the 2009 data were compared with earlier data gathered in previous field trips to Rwanda, including previous interview transcripts, field notes, and documentary evidence.[8] Examples of the last include Rwandan newspaper and magazine articles, online articles and discussions on Rwandan Web sites, and ongoing monitoring of the domestic and international news agencies such as Rwandan's government newspapers, the BBC, and AllAfrica.com.

In the 2009 group interviews, most respondents were female, but some men were also interviewed on the subject.[9] Throughout this chapter, I indicate the sex of interviewees and usually the region where the interview was conducted, but names and other identifying information have been withheld according to confidentiality protocols. Given the composition of my sample, I am primarily relating the effects of women's attitudes and of men's attitudes as perceived by women.

WINNING THE RACE: POSITIVE PERCEPTIONS OF GENDER QUOTAS AND THEIR IMPACT

In 2009, when asked whether broader cultural changes had been provoked by gender quotas, women responded with a decisive yes. Respondents consistently reported that women have become "entrepreneurs" in every arena, including politics; that they have attained greater access to education; that they feel more free to assert their authority in the household and to speak out in public; and that they have gained respect.

Women as Entrepreneurs in Every Arena

The majority-female legislature and greater representation of women at all levels of the government have made a dramatic impact on Rwandan society generally. In response to a question about the impact of gender quotas in the Rwandan political system, one female interviewee said: "You see that women have become true entrepreneurs in every arena. Most of the cars on the road today in Kigali are driven proudly by women. They [women] have raced ahead and seized every opportunity. They have gone back to school to get their degrees. They have started businesses. They have joined the Party [the RPF] and gotten government posts" (interview, Kigali, June 2009). Women have surged ahead in all domains in the wake of the 2003 Constitution which created legislative gender quotas.

While the majority-female legislature has been an important symbolic victory for Rwandan women, of greater impact has been women's increased engagement in local-level governance structures. Many women serve as local-level (cell, sector, or district) elected officials in posts not reserved for women. Their acceptance by local communities represents a dramatic change in public attitudes toward women. Increased participation of women at the local level has helped to legitimize women as political agents in the popular imagination of rural people. When asked whether women were capable of leading and wielding power as well as men, one woman from North province responded, "Better than the men, even. A woman knows what she should do and when she should do it," implying that men can easily be distracted from their mission by recreational pursuits such as beer or women.

Chattopadhyay and Duflo (2004, 1428) found that female citizens in India were twice as likely to communicate with local elected officials if there was a female elected official occupying a seat reserved for women. My findings in Rwanda suggest a similar effect. Several women interviewed in 2009 noted that the gender quota policies had given women an advantage over men in regard to problem solving. As one woman stated in a focus group with a women's cooperative in a rural community in North province, "A woman can easily approach her female friend who is an authority. This authority understands her well and can help her with her problems. That's where the men have found problems" (focus group, May 2009). Thus, female community members hope that a female local authority can understand problems from their perspective and give assistance in their capacity as government officials. Yet this respondent also noted that men feel that they have lost out, because they no longer have the advantage of approaching local authorities informally, such as at a local bar, to discuss their problems and seek solutions. Furthermore, as I discuss in detail below, not all interviewees indicated that female local authorities were any different from the men in terms of their accessibility or helpfulness.

Greater Access to Education

Many interviewees in 2009 cited girls' increased access to education as a benefit of the increased representation of women in governance. National campaigns to promote universal education, along with newfound career opportunities for educated women, have convinced many rural families that educating girls is a worthwhile investment. A female interviewee noted that "girls attend school in large numbers in Rwanda today, not like in the past, when they were kept at home to cook, clean, take care of younger children, and work in the fields" (interview, rural community, North province, May 2009). Although the campaign for universal education cannot be directly tied to actions of women in government or to women elected under quotas, in the minds of average citizens, particularly rural farmers, increased education of girl children is connected to gender quotas because these initiatives are perceived as part of government policy initiatives to improve the status of women.

Speaking Out in Public

In a 2009 focus group with women in North province, one respondent said, "Women [now] dare to speak up at public meetings. . . . There is a Kinyarwanda proverb that says, *Ntankokokazi ibika hari isake* ['Hens do not crow where there is a rooster']." She went on to explain how this proverb no longer accurately reflects realities on the ground. Over the past thirteen years, I have often heard this proverb used to express the notion that women should be silent in public and allow men to speak on behalf of the entire community. According to custom, husbands (or fathers or brothers) represented a household in meetings, and they voiced any concerns of the household on behalf of all household members, including their wives (or daughters or sisters). A wife could represent the household only if her husband was absent. Therefore, before the implementation of quotas in the 2003 constitution, women were unlikely to speak up at public meetings and were easily silenced by men who did not agree with opinions voiced by a woman.

The willingness of women to speak in public settings has grown dramatically since 2003. When I interviewed women members of a church-based organization in a rural community in southern Rwanda in 2001, they expressed reluctance to speak up at public meetings, although they were active participants in the life of their own organization. When I returned in 2007 and in 2009, the same women proudly recounted their vocal participation in local government and community meetings. Several of the association members served as *inyangamugayo* (judges) in the cell- and sector-level Gacaca courts that had adjudicated cases of genocide between 2003 and 2007.[10] In addition, the association members had conducted their own investigations, located witnesses, and advocated for the release of people falsely accused of genocide during the Gacaca process. All of these activities were somewhat risky given lingering tensions over the genocide (Burnet 2008b).

The women attributed their willingness to speak out to the broader impact of the national gender quota policy, specifically, its ability to generate positive attitudes among men and women about female citizens' competency. The large number of women in local government, coupled with the clear endorsement of women as political authorities by President Kagame, the RPF, and the central government, sent a clear message to rural citizens. Women must be accepted as legitimate political agents and local authorities.

Joint Decision Making about Domestic Resources

Rwandan women in colonial and postcolonial times lived beneath a legal regime that subordinated them to men by impeding women's economic autonomy. Many of the women-friendly policies implemented by the RPF-led government since 1994 have improved women's economic autonomy by restoring individual economic rights to married women. The transformation in women's economic independence accelerated rapidly starting in 1998, well before the implementation of the constitutional gender quota. Nonetheless, in interviews and focus groups conducted in 2009, the most frequently mentioned impacts of the Rwandan gender quota was the increase in men's and women's joint decision making about domestic resources and the increased autonomy of women as economic subjects. For instance, respondents offered the following reflections:

Before, the husband made decisions on his own. For example, a husband wanted to buy a field without his wife knowing it. He sold livestock as he wished without consulting his wife. But today, the men must try, and we discuss things together to see the advantages and disadvantages. And in making decisions about having children, we make them together. Except for some men who do not understand, this [policy] helps people to make decisions together. Before the state made this law, the men did as they wished. They brought many wives [married more than one woman at a time]. But now, that is no longer the case. (women's cooperative, city in North province)

There are men who sit down with their families, and they make their decisions together. A daughter who cultivated a field of cassava with her mother, and they made 60,000 RwF profit. When they showed the money to the father, they decided to buy a cow. The cow is there, and the husband is very happy, and he encourages his wife and daughter. (women's cooperative, rural community in South province)

Female interviewees, even those who classified their marriages as "good" before the 1994 genocide and civil war, noted a positive change in how spouses made decisions about family resources. They said that their husbands now recognized that wives sometimes had good ideas and that women were less likely to waste their money on alcohol or gambling.

Another key change that interviewees noted in 2009 was women's autonomy as economic agents, particularly their ability to become entrepreneurs. One woman explained how this change enhanced family life and marriage: "A wife can leave the house to go find money like men. In this way, there aren't any conflicts. Husband and wife, together, find a way to move the family forward" (rural community, North province, May 2009). Yet increased economic autonomy was not a benefit cited by all women. For instance, widows and other female heads of households emphasized how difficult it was to bear sole responsibility for the financial well-being of the family and the challenges of balancing work—whether managing a farm, a business, or a professional job—and domestic responsibilities.

"Women Have Found Respect"

Perhaps the most significant evidence of the impact of gender quotas on the symbolic representation of women in Rwandan governance was the repeated mention that the inclusion of women in governance has helped women "find respect" (*babona agaciro*). The word I have translated as "respect," *agaciro*, can also mean utility, value, importance, and (good) reputation (Jacob 1984, 188). In interviews and focus groups conducted in 2009, the term *agaciro* frequently appeared when women were commenting on the impact of quotas on relationships between men and women in the community or in the home.

In response to a follow-up question about the reduction in domestic violence in the region, one woman explained that husbands no longer hit their wives "because of awareness-raising campaigns and because men have realized the dignity of women [*agaciro k'umugore*]" (focus group, women's cooperative, rural community, North province, May 2009). This woman implicitly linked quotas to the government's awareness campaigns against domestic violence and explicitly linked the campaigns to men's changed attitudes. Another woman attributed changes in men's sexual practices to women gaining respect: "Women have found respect [*babonye agaciro*], the men no longer have many wives, almost not at all now" (women's cooperative, rural community, North province, May 2009). Respondents in this focus group went on to explain how women helped one another to oppose a husband who took a second wife, often by forcing him to leave.

One woman explained women's liberation as a fait accompli that a few stubborn men had yet to recognize and internalize. She noted, "There are still those men who do not want to accept the authority of women, who don't know that women have found respect [*yahawe agaciro*]" (women's cooperative, South province, May 2009). Almost universally, urban and rural women voiced pride about the change in the status of women in Rwandan society. One rural woman marveled, "Even the population obeys these female authorities. It's a step forward for us [women]" (focus group, women's cooperative, rural community, North province, May 2009).

Yet class distinctions emerged in these responses. Urban women and rural elite women tended to focus on the spreading of "modern" ideas about the equality of the sexes to less educated Rwandans. Peasant women, on the other hand, tended to talk more about the recognition of women's innate dignity by both men and women but by men especially. These class distinctions are important, since urban and rural elite women have benefited from gender quotas in material ways more than peasant women. As I discuss in detail later, peasant women have found their unpaid service in local governance structures to be an added burden that takes away from their productive time in the fields and in the household. By contrast, urban and rural elite women who work for a salary, whether in government, in civil society organizations, or in a profession; who run a business; or who support a husband's career have used their unpaid government service as a means to accrue social capital.

In sum, when responding to questions about the broader impacts of the gender quota policy on Rwandan society, respondents did not explicitly cite women's increased representation as the impetus for gender role change. Rather, they linked the gender quota policies to a broader set of equality reforms implemented by the RPF-led government. These reforms, as a whole, have changed perceptions about, and the activities involved in, women's roles. Given that policy implementation is top-down and given that members of parliament are not perceived as representing constituents, it is no surprise that citizens link gender quotas to broad government initiatives that increased women's public presence.

WHO ARE THE LOSERS? THE DOWNSIDES OF GREATER EQUALITY

While most interviewees mentioned positive changes in Rwandan society resulting from quotas and the empowerment of women more generally, several also mentioned unexpected downsides. After all, if women win greater opportunities and autonomy, then some group must lose. While I never asked a direct question about men's perceptions of these changes to avoid generating biased responses, several respondents spontaneously stated that men, or at least some men, felt as if they had lost their chances for wealth and mobility because of women's advancement. Three key themes emerged in the interviews: anger from brothers over the extension of inheritance rights to women, withdrawal of men from politics, and increased marital discord.

Angry Brothers

When asked about social changes related to the gender quotas, many female respondents noted that the 1998 inheritance law had increased friction between women and their brothers. Again, this answer demonstrates how respondents perceived quotas as part of those policies that protected women's rights and extended equality to women. For instance, interviewees offered the following statements:

Our brothers have never been happy because they are obliged to divide the property of our parents with us. It's a total negative for the men. (focus group, rural community, North province, May 2009)

Allowing women to inherit is good, but we now have conflicts with our brothers. They [the government] say that we should inherit property from both our in-laws and our own lineage as well. They [our brothers] have found that they are the losers. (interview, city in North province, May 2009)

According to custom, fathers and brothers are those who traditionally intervene when women find themselves in difficult or violent marriages, offering land—and thus livelihood—in the event of a failed marriage or early widowhood. Thus, increased friction with their male siblings puts women, especially peasant women, in a more fragile position.

Male Withdrawal from Politics

Before the 1994 genocide, politics, whether at the national, regional, or local level, was largely monopolized by men. Although a few prominent women stood out, including Agathe Uwilingiyimana, the prime minister in April 1994 and one of the first politicians killed in the genocide, men dominated the political arena. With the rise of women in Rwandan politics since the late 1990s, many men have turned away from politics as a career because "women are the winners," meaning that women are metaphorically the winners because of their access to better opportunities, and they are literally the winners because they "win" most of the elections in which they run (interviews, 2009).[11] Given that the outcomes of most elections in Rwanda are predetermined, some men present their candidacy while knowing in advance that the position will go to a woman.

Furthermore, quotas have influenced civil society organizations to favor female candidates over males with similar qualifications. This corrective to past gender biases has catapulted women ahead, but men feel left out. As a result of this perceived exclusion from government and civil society organizations (the primary employers in the Rwandan economy), many men prefer to focus their energies on private business endeavors. Other men face long-term unemployment, leading to crises of self-identity.

Explaining this withdrawal from politics is a general "psychological complex" among men that it is "not even worth it to try" because the "good positions" always go to women (interviews, 2009). As one elite woman from Kigali noted, "it's as if men have a complex nowadays" (interview, Kigali, June 2009). She went on to explain that more women than men return to school to seek degrees necessary for the constantly rising employment standards and that it seems as if some Rwandan men "don't even try."

Marital Discord

Rural and urban respondents cited increased marital discord as a consequence of the quotas and improved status of women. Rural respondents attributed the increased discord to men's ignorance about women's dignity and rights, whereas urban respondents attributed it to women taking on male behaviors and attitudes. For instance, women's greater economic autonomy has led them to enjoy individual freedoms, such as socializing after work, that had previously been reserved for men.

Many women interviewed, particularly married women, indicated that many husbands are frustrated about their wives' participation in governance.

Author: How have people here received these changes?
Woman: Positive for the women, negative for the men. Men have never been able to understand sudden changes. They are not at all happy that women are progressing. *Urugo ruvuze umugore ruvuga umuhoro* ["At home, when the wife speaks, out comes the knife"]. (focus group, rural community, North province, May 2009)

Here the respondent uses the Rwandan proverb to explain the transformation in women's agency and willingness to speak for themselves. This proverb captures how a vocal wife in the home means that there is little peace or harmony in the family.

Rwandan custom calls for a wife's submission to her husband and his decisions, although in practice, most wives who characterize their marriages as "good" state that husbands consult with wives when making important decisions. Nonetheless, when husband and wife do not agree, the husband's decision prevails. One consequence of women's empowerment is that some wives are less willing to silence themselves when they think their husbands are making unwise decisions. While I cannot use the data I have gathered to estimate how widespread this phenomenon is, it was frequently mentioned as a contributing factor to marital discord. Of greater consequence to marital discord, however, are the competing responsibilities to household and community that women in elected positions must negotiate.

Many rural women interviewed in 2009, whether they thought gender roles in Rwanda had changed "a lot" or "not at all" as a result of quotas, said that the gender revolution in Rwanda had increased domestic conflict for some families. Two primary reasons for increased conflict were offered: (1) husbands who had not come to recognize the "dignity of women" and (2) husbands who were frustrated by the lack of benefits to the domestic unit from wives' service as local officials: "For those [men] who do not understand [the gender equality laws], there are always conflicts in the family, always fights, because the men say, 'When has there ever been a wife who makes decisions for the household?' If these conflicts persist, then there is a divorce. . . . It does not happen all that often, but even so, this type of story is not unheard of" (women's cooperative, city, North province, May 2009).

In particular, rural married women elected to cell-, sector-, or district-level administrative positions often found themselves unable to explain to their husbands "what good" was coming of their work as government officials. Local-level officials do not receive a salary or a stipend, and they must spend a great deal of time exercising their duties and participating in meetings or training. As one woman from North province stated:

We never thought that things would be like this. A wife leaves her family for trainings, for communal labor, for meetings, and then a week has gone by. No time to work at home or to go to the fields. The husband who is there thinks you are going to come with something for the family [i.e., money or other tangible benefit]. You see, there is nothing but trouble and conflicts in the family. When you think about leaving this position, something that is not at all easy to do, you are accused of having the [genocidal] ideology.[12] We have found that it's not anything more than exploitation, creating poverty in our families. . . . We are going to die. (interview, North province, May 2009)

Many wives noted that their husbands were angry or frustrated that they were absent from the home and the fields with "nothing to show for it." In the past, men who served in local-level positions reaped many social benefits, such as increased prestige in the community, increased networking opportunities, and small "gifts" in the form of beer, crops, or money given by citizens in gratitude for duties rendered. Women local officials are not gaining these benefits as a result of perceived gender differences and vigorous anticorruption campaigns and prosecutions by the Rwandan government.

Despite lamenting the lack of tangible benefits, men do little to make their wives' workload more productive. Husbands often refuse to assist wives with their work in the fields, at home, or in their role as local officials. Most rural women cannot afford to hire workers to help with the numerous duties that fall on a wife's shoulders: cooking, cleaning, caring for children, and fetching water at home, and planting, weeding, and harvesting in the fields. Since local-level elected officials receive no compensation, rural women are left to their own devices to manage these competing responsibilities. While female local officials could justify their absence to their husbands if they were "bringing something home," the women arrive "empty-handed." Their husbands become angry because they believe that their wives are shirking their duties in the home.

Interviewees and focus group participants in urban areas also brought up increased marital discord as an unexpected outcome of quotas and other equality initiatives. Urban respondents attributed increased marital discord to women "behaving like men," referring to both positive and negative aspects of women's changed behavior. On the positive side, respondents cited women's increased assertiveness in decision making about the family and the family resources, in addition to women's increased educational attainment, which improves their ability to find lucrative employment. On the negative side, respondents cited several unexpected consequences of women's new economic autonomy, legal protections, and social opportunities. Because more wives have their own careers and thus sufficient means to lead an independent life, women are less likely to be "stuck" in unsatisfactory marriages. Strengthened legal protections have also made seeking divorce less risky for urban women. Yet respondents perceived a downside to this increased autonomy in the divorce rates.

Many urban respondents explained that the "promotion of women," referring not only to quotas but to the entire set of government initiatives to increase women's equality, has resulted in women spending more time outside the home. More women work outside the home and take night courses at the many new universities. Respondents concluded that because women spend more time outside the home, they have more contact with men other than their husbands. As a result, some women had begun to "behave like men" by taking lovers outside of marriage. Whereas in the past, the economic risks involved in divorce meant that many wives tolerated similar dalliances by their husbands, men are less constrained. Thus, according to the perceptions of many urban elites, gender quotas and policies promoting women's equality have destabilized the institution of marriage.

"NOTHING HAS CHANGED": GENDER, POWER AND DEMOCRATIC LEGITIMACY

A key measure of the impact of gender quotas on the symbolic representation of women is whether the way "citizens feel about government generally" has changed and whether the increased presence of women in governance has led citizens "to judge democratic institutions as more just and legitimate" (Franceschet, Krook, and Piscopo, chapter 1 in this volume). Although most respondents cited numerous social or cultural transformations resulting from the gender quota policies, several respondents stated explicitly that "nothing has changed" in terms of gender roles, political power, or the democratic legitimacy of the state in Rwanda.

Some rural women with low levels of formal education but high levels of engagement in community-based organizations insisted that gender roles in Rwandan society have not changed, mostly because women heads of households have always made decisions. As a woman from a rural community in South province explained, "Nothing has changed. A woman who is alone usually makes decisions by herself. She is used to doing everything for herself. Who is she going to ask for advice? We haven't noticed a change, because a woman who is by herself doesn't have a rival." In other words, widows and female heads of households have always exercised power in the family and in the community, enjoying status as household authorities and as symbolic men.

Another woman from a city in North province said that quotas "have changed nothing, really. Except to make things worse." She went on to characterize the inclusion of women in local governance structures as a form of exploitation. In her view, quotas have extended rural women's workload, in the service of maintaining the ruling RPF's hold on power, an issue I explore in more depth below. A female civil society organization leader and RPF party member likewise reported that rural women have found their increased role in local governance to be an added burden.

Many international organizations link the presence of women to better governance, a link often cited by Rwandan officials. However, the view from below is quite different. Peasants generally view female officials as "no better than men," in that female representatives face the same pressures to comply with directives from above and have the same human frailties and temptations to corruption. For instance, when asked whether female local officials required bribes, one woman replied, "Everyone must have that." She then illustrated her point with the following story: "One thing that happened to me, my husband was going to his parents' place to divide the fields among the brothers. I went in his place because he wasn't available. A mediator [*abunzi*], a woman, asked me directly for money by saying, 'Ma'am if you aren't able to give us money, your husband won't have a single field here.' I was obliged to give the money; I didn't have any other choice" (focus group, city in North province, May 2009).

Several other male and female respondents confirmed that female local officials were just as corrupt as the men. Also, when asked whether they found it easier to talk to a female rather than a male local official, most women stated that it was "no different." These results coincide with those of Zetterberg (chapter 11 in this volume), who found that the "undemocratic legacy of Mexican politics" led citizens to mistrust the "old (male) elite" and the new (female) representatives.

Moreover, the increased presence of women has not led Rwandan citizens to perceive the government as a more democratic institution. In numerous interviews, respondents insisted that women local-government representatives were just as inaccessible as male government representatives. Women parliamentarians were not viewed as representing either women's interests or the interests of the communities they were formally elected to represent.

The result of Rwanda's gender quota policies in the eyes of many Rwandans, especially well-educated urban elites in the capital of Kigali, is that quotas have solidified the RPF ruling party's hold on power. In the words of a former (male) senator and opposition party member, the only consequence of gender quotas is "to ensure RPF dominance." Because positions in the legislature and the ministries are well paid and come with many benefits, women who gain these positions through quotas in fact owe their loyalties to the RPF, which echoes the importance of patronage politics found in the Ugandan and Moroccan cases (O'Brien and Sater, respectively, chapters 4, and 5 in this volume). In Rwanda, no matter which party they are affiliated with, women toe the line in order to remain where they are. They rarely mobilize around women's issues and in some cases have voted for legislation that reduced legal protections for women or eliminated women-friendly policies.

CONCLUSION

A key question when measuring the impact of gender quotas on the symbolic representation of women is whether quotas have altered "gendered ideas about the public sphere, which have traditionally associated men with the realm of politics and women with the realm of home and the family" (Franceschet, Krook, and Piscopo, chapter 1 in this volume). In the Rwandan case, in contrast with the Belgium case (chapter 10 in this volume), gender quotas *have* made a significant impact on gendered ideas about the public sphere. RPF policies promoting women and women's rights and instituting legislative quotas have placed women at the forefront of public life. Women in both urban and rural political spaces have taken visible roles in local government, business, and civil society. These changes began before the institution of formal gender quotas in the 2003 constitution and date to the emergence of women's civil society organizations in the late 1980s and early 1990s (Burnet 2008a). However, gender quotas have accelerated these preexisting processes of change.

Because the Rwandan case is so frequently cited as a success story in terms of gender quotas, it is vital to assess broader transformations in Rwandan society accurately. While the Rwandan parliament is the first and only in the world to be majority female, this increased representation of women has brought little change to the legislative process, since most legislation originates in the executive branch. Furthermore, the increased representation has not led to a more democratic political terrain, as the executive branch still maintains tight control over civil society organizations and the media. As Zetterberg (chapter 11 in this volume) shows in the Mexico case, gender quotas are embedded in the broader political context and thus have little effect on women's political engagement or on the perceived legitimacy of democratic institutions among the electorate,

Yet the Rwandan case illustrates that gender quotas can have impacts beyond the political sphere. The RPF's top-down policies have improved women's economic and professional opportunities and increased their social mobility. The impact of gender quotas has been both broad and deep, since they apply to all levels of government, from the parliament all the way down to the "village" (*umudugudu*), the smallest administrative unit. A key symbolic impact of gender quotas has been the reversal of the colonial and postcolonial gender paradigm where men worked in the public sphere while women managed the domestic sphere and remained financially dependent on men. This symbolic reversal has benefited urban women more than rural women, because urban women have found increased access to salaried positions and greater purchasing power while rural women elected to local-government positions have faced increased workloads with no remuneration.

Another important finding of this case is that citizens do not distinguish between the impact of legislative gender quotas and the many other policy changes that have improved the status of women and girls (such as mandatory primary-school education). This factor may be a result of citizens' greater contact with local-level government officials than with parliamentarians, but it may also be attributable to another aspect of life in Rwanda today. The prevalence of generalized responses to specific questions about women and politics in my data signals an important reality of Rwandan life: criticism of the government (or of the RPF and President Kagame) and of policy or legislation is risky. By citing the broader benefits of an entire set of policies and laws that have improved the status of women in Rwandan society, respondents avoided making specific, and possibly critical, statements about those in power. In rare instances, respondents who trusted me and other listeners made frank (and critical) statements about some of the negative consequences of the gender quotas and their impact on symbolic representation of women.

Several lessons can be drawn from this case study. First, having more women in government does not necessarily lead to greater democracy or a more transparent and accessible government. Second, even when implemented as top-down policies originating in an authoritarian regime, gender quotas and equality policies more broadly can lead to significant cultural changes in attitudes toward and perceptions of women and their competence. Third, more women in government can lead to increased political, social, and economic agency among all female citizens, not only those women in government. Finally, women's increased autonomy can have unintended negative consequences, such as marital discord, rising divorce rates, and an increased workload for women who are already overburdened.

NOTES

1. The Rwandan Patriotic Front is the current ruling party in Rwanda. Founded in Uganda in the late 1980s, the RPF was a rebel movement that invaded Rwanda in 1990 with the intent of ending Juvénal Habyarimana's dictatorial rule. The RPF came to power in July 1994, when it ended the genocide by taking military control of the country.

2. For Rose Kabuye's comments, see the Hunt Alternatives Fund Web site, http://www.huntalternatives.org/pages/401_rose_kabuye.cfm. For John Mutamba's, see Powley 2005, 159.

3. See http://www.unifem.org/news_events/story_detail.php?StoryID=736.

4. For instance, Freedom House rated Rwanda as "not free" in its 2008 annual report, *Freedom in the World*.

5. See Bernard and Ryan (2010) for a detailed description of commonly used data collection techniques.

6. Indirect observation of behavior involves looking for what Bernard and Ryan call "behavior traces," meaning the material traces of human behavior that appear in physical objects, public speech acts, photographs, newspaper or magazine articles, Internet discussion boards, and publications, among other things (Bernard and Ryan 2010, 19–20).

7. Each person wrote a separate "transcript" of the interview based on individual notes, and then we reconciled our two versions, integrating the texts. Where we remembered things differently, we discussed our differences. Where we could not come to consensus, both versions were noted in the interview transcript considered in data analysis.

8. The research was conducted during a series of research trips. Data were gathered through group interviews, formal interviews, conversations, questionnaires, participant observation, and documentary research, among other means. The author traveled to Rwanda in 1997 (four months), 1998 (three months), 1999–2001 (twenty-four months), 2002 (two six-week trips), 2003 (two weeks), and 2007 (four weeks). The trips included different combinations of visits to Kigali, Kigali Rural, Butare, and Byumba prefectures and also to North, South, and West provinces. All field research was conducted under the auspices of the Institutional Review Boards of the University of Louisville or the University of North Carolina at Chapel Hill.

9. I did not gather demographic data on interviewees.

10. For more on the Gacaca courts, see Waldorf 2006, Wierzynska 2004, Oomen 2005, Human Rights Watch 2008, and Burnet 2008b.

11. As discussed above, most elections in Rwanda have a predetermined outcome, so women "winning" elections is not necessarily because they have the greatest support of the population.

12. "Having genocidal ideology" and "spreading divisionism" were criminalized in 2001 with the passage of Law No. 47/2001, "On Prevention, Suppression and Punishment of the Crime of Discrimination and Sectarianism."

REFERENCES

Atkeson, Lonna Rae. 2003. Not All Cues Are Created Equal: The Conditional Impact of Female Candidates on Political Engagement. *Journal of Politics* 65 (4): 1040–1061.

Atkeson, Lonna Rae, and Nancy Carrillo. 2007. More Is Better: The Influence of Collective Female Descriptive Representation on External Efficacy. *Politics & Gender* 3 (1): 79–101.

Bernard, H. Russell, and Gery Wayne Ryan. 2010. *Analyzing Qualitative Data: Systematic Approaches*. Thousand Oaks, Calif.: Sage.

Burnet, Jennie E. 2008a. Gender Balance and the Meanings of Women in Governance in Post-Genocide Rwanda. *African Affairs* 107 (428): 361–386.

———. 2008b. The Injustice of Local Justice: Truth, Reconciliation, and Revenge in Rwanda. *Genocide Studies and Prevention* 3 (2): 173–193.

Chattopadhyay, Raghabendra, and Esther Duflo. 2004. Women as Policy Makers: Evidence from a Randomized Policy Experiment in India. *Econometrica* 72 (5): 1409–1443.

High-Pippert, Angela, and John Comer. 1998. Female Empowerment: The Influence of Women Representing Women. *Women & Politics* 19 (4): 53–66.

Human Rights Watch. 2008. *Law and Reality: Progress in Judicial Reform in Rwanda*. New York: Human Rights Watch.

Jacob, Irenee. 1984. *Dictionnaire Rwandais-Francais*. Vol. 1 (A–H). Kigali: Imprimerie Scolaire.

Karp, Jeffrey A. and Susan A. Banducci. 2008. "When Politics Is Not Just a Man's Game: Women's Representation and Political Engagement." *Electoral Studies* 27 (1): 105–115.

Oomen, B. 2005. Donor-driven Justice and Its Discontents: The Case of Rwanda. *Development and Change* 36 (5): 887–910.

Powley, Elizabeth. 2005. "Rwanda: Women Hold Up Half the Parliament." In Julie Ballington and Azza Karam, eds., *Women in Parliament: Beyond Numbers*, rev. ed., 154–163. Stockholm: International Institute for Democracy and Electoral Assistance.

Waldorf, Lars. 2006. Mass Justice for Mass Atrocity: Rethinking Local Justice as Transitional Justice. *Temple Law Review* 79 (1): 1–87.

Wierzynska, A. 2004. Consolidating Democracy through "Transitional Justice": Rwanda's Gacaca Courts. *New York University Law Review* 79 (5): 1934–1969.

13 Politics as a Male Domain and Empowerment in India

Lori Beaman, Rohini Pande,
and Alexandra Cirone

India is the world's largest democracy, yet female presence in India's state and national legislatures has consistently remained less than 10 percent. In contrast, female representation in local village councils has risen dramatically in the last twenty years. A constitutional amendment instituted in 1993 both devolved significant powers to village councils and instituted a quota system that required that one-third of village council leader positions be reserved for women. While the mandatory nature of the quota system implied that it led to an immediate increase in descriptive representation, our work with coauthors demonstrates that it also increased substantive representation (Chattopadhyay and Duflo 2004; Beaman et al. 2009; Beaman et al. 2010).

In this chapter, we examine how quotas in Indian village councils have influenced symbolic representation for women. We consider a specific definition of symbolic representation: the extent to which the increased presence of women leaders, as a result of quotas, affects the perceptions and opinions of voters. We focus on whether exposure to more female politicians changes (negative) stereotypes held by voters about women's roles in politics specifically and in society generally. Our case study examines this by using survey and experimental data to measure voter attitudes toward female leaders.

We discuss findings from a large field survey conducted in the Indian state of West Bengal. Quotas, wherein 33 percent of village council leader positions are reserved for women, were introduced with the goal of both ensuring female participation and reducing voter bias against women as policy makers. The data from West Bengal has shown that exposure to female leaders caused villagers to update their implicit beliefs about women's ability to lead and made them more willing to vote for women (Beaman et al. 2009). In this chapter, we present new evidence that these changes were accompanied by limited changes in sexist attitudes in the population and use a sexism index that captures various dimensions of such attitudes. We use the West Bengal data to analyze whether sexism (as captured by a psychological index) and women's mobility (as measured through survey questions addressed to women) are altered after villagers are exposed to female council heads (called *pradhans*). Examples of our measures of women's mobility include a woman's ability to make decisions on household expenditures, the number of times women went outside the village in the last thirty days, and whether a woman could go unescorted to her parents' village. We find that negative stereotypes about women (as measured by "hostile sexism" measures) are reduced, but villagers' endorsement of traditional gender roles (captured by "benevolent sexism" measures) is not. Neither do we observe greater female empowerment in the domestic sphere.

We argue that the symbolic implications of quotas appear to be closely linked to substantive actions of female politicians. In the case of India, women leaders pursue different and sometimes more effective policies from those of men. Villagers respond by being more willing to elect women and reducing hostility toward women. However, this does not lead them to challenge social norms about women's roles or to give women more autonomy in the household (at least in the short-to-medium run). The evidence presented suggests that there may be little impact of quotas on women's symbolic representation in arenas that do not see direct substantive change. If correct, this may have significant implications for how we conceive of the relationship between quota policies and women's overall well-being. The next section provides an overview of the institutional background on India's political reservation system. We then describe the case study and methodology used, followed by the main findings.

RESERVATION IN INDIA

India granted women the right to vote at independence and has been home to several impressive female leaders, including former prime minister Indira Gandhi, current leader of the Congress Party Sonia Gandhi, and regional leaders such as Mayawati and Mamta Banerjee. However, the average share of women in national and state legislatures is low (less than 10 percent), and gender gaps persist in the education, health, and labor force (Hausmann, Tyson, and Zahidi 2010). There are also historically strong norms against women's participation in the public sphere, which can hinder women in their pursuit of public office and in their attempts to influence the formation of national laws. Political reservation is one tool that can be used to give women access to power structures and increase their role in policy decisions. At the moment, though, reservation based on sex is utilized only at the local level in India.

India is a constitutional democracy that operates with a bicameral parliament, consisting of the directly elected Lok Sabha (lower house) and the appointed Rajya Sabja (upper house). India uses the electoral system of first-past-the-post, with single-member districts; constituents vote for candidates rather than political parties. Yet there are few female parliamentarians: in 2009, only fifty-nine of the 545 seats in the Lok Sabha were held by women (11 percent). India's constitution guarantees universal suffrage in addition to equal treatment under the law regardless of caste, sex, religion, or race. In fact, the use of political reservation in India began in order to alleviate the stratified society created by the caste system, and in 1950, both scheduled castes and scheduled tribes were given reservation in the parliament and state legislatures and in civil-service jobs and university admittance.

While there are quotas in place at the national level that reserve seats for scheduled castes and tribes, there are no legislative quotas based on gender. However, India has made gender equality in politics a high priority by passing a historic bill in March 2010 that will reserve a third of all seats in both the national parliament and the state legislatures for women. This would triple the number of women in the Lok Sabha. However, this vote is an early step in the process to amend the constitution, and the bill must still be passed by the lower house and state legislatures. Regional caste-based parties oppose the bill, arguing potential unfairness to other underrepresented groups (Polgreen 2010a). Yet Beaman et al. (2010) provide evidence suggesting that the effect on such groups is largely absent in data from West Bengal.

So, how does the idea of mandated reservation based on sex fit into Indian politics? The institution of a reservation system is motivated by the expectation that such policy measures will have a positive effect on symbolic representation. This expectation is fairly recent, for reservation based on sex did not exist until 1993 and was instituted at the local level of village councils (*gram panchayats* or GPs). Mandated reservation coincided with the rise of political emphasis on local self-governance. The idea of self-governance has been an important motivation behind politics in India for the last half century. Mahatma Gandhi advocated a system of "Panchayati Raj," a decentralized form of self-governance in which each village was given responsibility for local affairs. The seventy-third constitutional amendment codified this concept—and the reservations system—in 1993. With the intention of "deepening democracy," the reform devolved administrative and development power responsibilities to the level of the *gram panchayats*. The GPs, each encompassing roughly ten thousand villagers, form the foundation of a three-tiered system of rural councils and serve as India's vehicle for the decentralized provision of public goods (including welfare programs and public works). GPs are also responsible for administering the large National Rural Employment Guarantee Act (NREGA), which guarantees one hundred days of employment for poor Indian households.

In addition to the reserved seats for women for the village council president seat, the *pradhan*, there are also reserved seats for council members. Specifically, 33 percent of such seats are reserved for women (including 33 percent of the seats also reserved for scheduled caste or scheduled tribe). Notably, these seats are still obtained using direct election. As a result, quotas increased the fraction of female village leaders from less than 5 percent in 1992 to roughly 40 percent by 2000. Today, there are more than 2 million elected female village leaders (Hunger Project 2009). In addition, research has shown that repeated exposure to women leaders increases the chances of women being elected in districts that experienced multiple cycles of reservation (Beaman et al. 2009).

The Indian quota system allocates reserved seats using random assignment, with each seat, on average, reserved for women once every three elections. This system creates a natural experiment and allows for the comparison of villages with female leaders as a result of quotas to villages without reservation. It has enabled several scholars to study empirically the effect of mandated reservation on a variety of outcomes, including policy preferences of women leaders, reelection patterns, and voter attitudes.

This information has painted a much clearer picture of women politicians in India after reservation. Women leaders have been shown to have different policy preferences from those of their male counterparts. Among village councilors in India, women are more likely to invest in goods preferred by women (Chattopadhyay and Duflo 2004). Duflo and Topalova (2004) find that women make better leaders in certain dimensions that are easy to observe, providing more public goods for their villages than men and goods of higher quality. Furthermore, Beaman et al. (2009) find that households reported giving fewer bribes and the number of measured public goods was greater in GPs reserved for women.

The body of evidence shows that the reservation system has led to an increase in substantive representation for women. A natural question follows: how do gender quotas in India affect the symbolic representation of women and the resulting public attitudes?

CASE STUDY AND METHODOLOGY

The case study in this chapter takes a particular approach to looking at the concept of symbolic representation. We ask how the increased presence of women leaders as a result of quotas affects the perceptions and opinions of voters.

Increasing the presence of women in politics using quotas can affect a number of outcomes, including constituents' attitudes toward both democratic institutions and minimum thresholds of representation. More significantly, reservation is a policy tool that also has the potential to erode any prior conceptions of politics as a male domain, essentially reframing the gendered nature of politics and weakening negative stereotypes concerning the performance of women leaders. Voters may be biased and view women as less experienced and less effective in the political arena, or they may hold preexisting attitudes that associate leadership with men. Such stereotypes can be a major hurdle for women seeking political involvement. The question of symbolic representation is especially salient in India, which is a society characterized by social stratification and strong norms against women's participation across the public sphere.

Many argue that quotas, by exposing voters to female leaders, can positively change public opinions about the presence and effectiveness of female politicians and thereby open a door for increased female participation. However, the symbolic effects associated with gender quotas are the most difficult to measure. Are voter attitudes shaped by a bias against the idea of a women leader or in response to the behavior of previous and ineffective women leaders? Once the mandated reservation is removed, are women not elected because they are less effective than male leaders, or do voters historically have more information on male leaders and therefore assume that male leaders are better? The specific choice of gender quotas as a policy option anticipates potential positive changes in symbolic representation. Therefore, it is more important than ever to disentangle the effects that affirmative-action policies may have on women's participation in politics and on voters' attitudes.

This case study begins to answer this question with findings from a large field survey conducted in the Indian state of West Bengal, which uses experimental and survey data to measure voter attitudes toward female leaders. We take advantage of the fact that GPs were randomly assigned a reservation policy: in both 1998 and 2003, one-third of leader positions in village councils have been reserved for women. This randomization created a natural experiment, which means that the difference in average outcomes between reserved and unreserved GPs reflects the causal impact of female leadership. We exploit this random variation to measure bias against female leaders directly and to observe how exposure to female leaders affects this bias. In this chapter, we summarize findings from completed research (Beaman et al. 2009) and also provide new results on how exposure to female leaders influenced sexism.

Our data come from villages in West Bengal affected by the reservation policy during the elections of 1998 and 2003. We conducted household surveys in 2006–2007 among villagers in 165 districts in Birbhum, with a total of 6,642 male and 6,568 female respondents. The survey asked respondents to evaluate their *pradhan* along several dimensions, including detailed questions about public-goods provision and villagers' satisfaction with the level of public-goods provision, and collected experimental data on villagers' evaluation of hypothetical leaders. These data document variation in voters' explicit opinions of their *pradhans* and look at whether these differences in voter opinion are paralleled by differences in implicit gender-biased voter beliefs.

Implicit Association Tests in the Case of West Bengal

How does one accurately measure voter beliefs? Especially in the case of gender politics, a voter could explicitly respond to survey questions involving women leaders in one way, while holding alternative beliefs that are acted on during voting. Voters may also have implicit beliefs that they are not fully aware of, unconscious attitudes that may also influence their voting behavior. In order to look at symbolic representation, one must analyze both the implicit and the explicit attitudes toward women leaders. An important contribution of Beaman et al. (2009) is the use of an instrument widely used in social psychology but seldom in politics: Implicit Association Tests (IATs). The study also incorporates experiments using speeches and vignettes about hypothetical leaders. These specific tools can help us clarify the attitudes and beliefs of voters who have been exposed to female leadership. As a result, this methodology can uniquely clarify the intangible effects of symbolic representation.

In a standard speech experiment, the subjects listen to previously recorded speeches that are identical except that the sex of the speaker is randomly varied for each participant. After listening, each subject is asked to evaluate the speech. In our study, villagers evaluated the effectiveness of hypothetical leaders by listening to one of six tape-recorded speeches (three per sex). The speech, while hypothetical, was adapted from an actual village meeting. In the speech, the village leader was responding to a villager complaint about a broken tube well by asking villagers to contribute money and support for local public goods. Respondents were randomly assigned one of the six recordings and were told that it was recorded during a village meeting in another district. After listening, the subject was asked his or her opinions of the politician's perceived performance and effectiveness along a number of dimensions, including whether the leader addressed villagers' concerns and whether he or she would succeed at mobilizing resources from villagers.

A vignette experiment gives the subject a scenario with multiple and competing options for a resolution and asks the subject either to make a choice or to evaluate a choice made at the conclusion of the scenario. In our study, each villager listened to a vignette describing a situation of resource scarcity in which the hypothetical *pradhan* chose to invest in either a drinking-water or an irrigation project. These two options were chosen because women (relative to men) invest more in drinking water and are more likely to cite drinking water (relative to irrigation) as an issue of concern. We randomized the leader's choice for each villager to ensure that the leader's decision was not systematically correlated with the leader's sex. In addition, we varied the sex of the leader. After listening to the vignette, the villager was asked to evaluate the leader's choice using similar questions to those in the speech experiment.

Finally, the Implicit Association Test (IAT) is based on the idea that subjects who strongly associate two concepts can more easily pair the same concepts in a computer-based rapid-categorization task. In cases where the subject population is illiterate, pictures or sounds can be used to represent the concepts being tested. When viewing the screen, the subject sees a sequence of stimuli (words or pictures) and uses a computer button to assign each stimulus to either side of the screen (each side representing one category). The time it takes to assign the stimuli to a category is recorded.

In our study, villagers were given two types of computer-based IATs. The first measured the strength of association between images of anonymous men or women and normative categories of good and bad, and the second measured how villagers associate gender with leadership and domestic tasks. For example, in the second IAT we conducted, the villager viewed two pictures (a setting and a person) on either side of the computer screen. In the "stereotypical" block, the male picture and the leadership setting (e.g., public speaking) were grouped together on one side of the screen, and the female picture and the domestic setting (e.g., taking rest) were on the other side of the screen. The "nonstereotypical" block was the reverse, pairing male pictures with domestic settings and female pictures with leadership settings.

We will now summarize the findings from the speech and vignette experiments and the IATs and also provide two new pieces of evidence. The first piece of evidence comes from a survey-based measure of sexism, the Ambivalent Sexism Index (ASI) (Glick and Fiske 1996). This index consists of a series of survey questions that seek to measure "hostile sexism" and "benevolent sexism" separately. Hostile sexism involves typical notions of prejudice. For example, a question used in West Bengal involved reading the sentence "A wife shouldn't contradict her husband in public" to respondents and then asking them to respond using a Likert scale from "strongly agree" to "strongly disagree." Benevolent sexism, on the other hand, involves attitudes that are sexist in that they stereotype women and view women as systematically different from men but are subjectively positive in feeling and tone. An example is the statement "Women, compared with men, tend to have a superior moral sensibility." Second, we examine respondent reports on female household members' decision-making powers within the household and their mobility outside the household.

The evidence, when taken together, allows us to examine directly one key facet of symbolic representation. We explore whether exposure to more female politicians changes (negative) stereotypes held by voters about women's roles in politics specifically and society generally. In this way, we can look at the true impact of quotas on public opinion.

MAIN FINDINGS

We start by summarizing our main findings from Beaman et al. (2009). Survey measures of villagers' stated (explicit) preferences demonstrate that even after reservation, villagers continue to have a stated preference for male leaders. However, when we probe their implicit attitudes, we observe significant changes. In villages that were never required to have a woman leader, we observe that respondents exhibit bias against women leaders in both the IAT that examines the association between leadership activities and sex and in how they rank the same speech delivered by a woman versus a man. In contrast, quota-induced exposure to women reduces both of these biases.

Villages that were never reserved for a female *pradhan* demonstrate that voters have implicit biases against female leaders when they have had limited to no exposure to female leaders. In the vignette and speech experiments, there is a significant bias among men in never-reserved villages; men rate the effectiveness of a hypothetical female *pradhan* far below that of a male *pradhan* (0.05 of a standard deviation below). This finding is echoed in the IAT measuring the association between domestic activities with women and leadership with men. Both men and women associate leadership activities with men in never-reserved GPs and are faster at linking women with domestic activities. However, we find that male villagers show no bias against women leaders in villages previously exposed to a female leader, as measured by the speech and vignette experiments. Moreover, the results are strongly significant: the coefficient on the interaction between female *pradhan* and ever-reserved is 0.09. The association between men and leadership is also weaker in villages that experienced a reserved *pradhan* seat.

These results are striking and suggest that reservation erases the bias against female leaders and, more significantly, this holds true across all reservation categories. Stereotyping and bias against women leaders disappear relatively quickly, within two years after reservation is introduced. Further, after being required to elect a woman, when presented with the same information on a leader's action, villagers judge male and female leaders as equally able. While the first women to be elected suffer from discrimination, we find that exposure leads to favorable updating among male villagers, meaning that the evaluation of female leaders improves between the first and second reservation cycles.

There is little evidence that female villagers changed their opinions of female leaders. The speech and vignette experiments find a smaller initial bias among women, but we cannot statistically reject the hypothesis of a similar bias across the sexes. This may be because women are less involved in local politics generally (which reduces their chances of interactions with or knowledge of the female leader, thereby making women less likely to react negatively to a woman in a position that challenges traditional roles). Given that men started with a worse opinion of women's leadership, it is intuitive that men are more likely than women to update their beliefs about women's ability to lead. In the domestic activities IAT, the effect of reservation actually works the other way: women exposed to a female *pradhan* for the first time in 2003 actually strengthen their association between women and domestic activities. This result is relatively weak, however, in a statistical sense.

Changes in Sexist Attitudes

In table 13.1, we examine whether changes in implicit preferences toward female leaders are paralleled by changes in sexism. The outcome variable of interest is the Ambivalent Sexism Index (ASI) and its two subcomponents: the Benevolent Sexism Index and the Hostile Sexism Index (please see the appendix for the full regression specification). The Hostile Sexism Index is the average of normalized responses to the following statements: (1) A man is never justified in hitting his wife. (2) Parents should maintain stricter control over their daughters than their sons. (3) For the most part, it is better to be a man than to be a woman. (4) It would be a good idea to elect a woman as the president of India. (5) A wife shouldn't contradict her husband in public. (6) Preschool children suffer if their mother works. The Benevolent Sexism Index includes the following: (1) In a disaster, women ought to be rescued before men. (2) Women should be cherished and protected by men. (3) Women, compared with men, tend to have a superior moral sensibility. (4) Men should be willing to sacrifice their own well-being in order to provide financially for the women in their lives. The ASI includes all ten questions.

The dependent variable in columns (1)–(3) of table 13.1 is the complete ASI with all ten questions; columns (4)–(6) show the Hostile Sexism Index, and the Benevolent Sexism Index is displayed in columns (7)–(9). Each column has two panels. Panel A examines the impact of having lived in a village that was reserved in at least one of the elections, 1998 or 2003 ("ever reserved"). The regression specification examines the difference between ever- and never-reserved GPs, where we introduce

Table 13.1 Ambivalent Sexism Index (ASI)

	ASI			Hostile Sexism Index			Benevolent Sexism Index		
	All	Male	Female	All	Male	Female	All	Male	Female
	(1)	(2)	(3)	(4)	(5)	(6)	(7)	(8)	(9)
				Panel A					
Ever reserved	-0.020	-0.016	-0.022	-0.035	-0.039	-0.031	0.004	0.019	-0.009
	(0.018)	(0.022)	(0.019)	(0.015)	(0.019)	(0.016)	(0.034)	(0.039)	(0.035)
				Panel B					
Only reserved 2003	-0.018	-0.019	-0.016	-0.030	-0.032	-0.028	0.000	0.001	0.001
	(0.021)	(0.025)	(0.022)	(0.018)	(0.023)	(0.019)	(0.042)	(0.048)	(0.045)
Reserved 1998 and 2003	0.001	-0.008	0.009	-0.012	-0.019	-0.006	0.020	0.009	0.033
	(0.029)	(0.033)	(0.032)	(0.025)	(0.029)	(0.028)	(0.051)	(0.057)	(0.053)
Only reserved 1998	-0.034	-0.018	-0.049	-0.056	-0.060	-0.050	-0.002	0.046	-0.047
	(0.025)	(0.030)	(0.026)	(0.022)	(0.028)	(0.022)	(0.045)	(0.053)	(0.045)

| Test: 2003 = both 1998 and 2003 = 1998 [p value] | 0.526 | 0.949 | 0.216 | 0.284 | 0.489 | 0.338 | 0.920 | 0.700 | 0.339 |
| n | 13,497 | 6,717 | 6,780 | 13,497 | 6,717 | 6,780 | 13,497 | 6,717 | 6,780 |

The Hostile Sexism Index is the average of normalized responses to the following questions: (1) A man is never justified in hitting his wife. (2) Parents should maintain stricter control over their daughters than their sons. (3) For the most part, it is better to be a man than to be a woman. (4) It would be a good idea to elect a woman as the president of India. (5) A wife shouldn't contradict her husband in public. (6) Preschool children suffer if their mother works. The Benevolent Sexism Index includes the following: (1) In a disaster, women ought to be rescued before men. (2) Women should be cherished and protected by men. (3) Women, compared with men, tend to have a superior moral sensibility. (4) Men should be willing to sacrifice their own well-being in order to provide financially for the women in their lives. The ASI includes all ten questions. See appendix, table 13.3, for more detail on the coding of the ten questions.

2. "Ever reserved" is an indicator for whether a GP was reserved for a female *Pradhan* in 1998, in 2003, or in both elections.

3. Additional control variables include (i) respondent-level variables: age, age squared, illiterate, < 5 years of schooling, 5–10 years of schooling; (ii) household-level variables: household size, SC, ST, OBC, landless, Muslim, wealth (quartile 1–4), interviewer female, interview round; (iii) village-level variables: total population, SC/ST share, sex ratio under age 6, percent literate, female literacy, percent of irrigated land, bus or train stop, *pucca* road to village, tube well, hand pump, well, community tap, number of schools, and number of health facilities.

4. Block fixed effects are included, and standard errors are clustered at the GP level.

several controls. These controls include respondent demographics such as age; 1991 village variables; indicator variables for block (an administrative unit larger than a GP); and indicators for investigator sex and survey year. In both panels, standard errors are adjusted to reflect the fact that all villagers in the same GP are exposed to the same "treatment": either a reserved or unreserved *pradhan* seat.

Columns (1)–(3) show that there is no impact of exposure to female leaders as a result of reservation on the complete ASI, the dependent variable. The complete ASI includes all ten questions, normalized by the never-reserved sample, meaning that the coefficients are expressed in terms of standard deviations. Column (1) includes both male and female respondents in a pooled regression, while columns (2) and (3) show each sex separately. In panel A, the coefficient is negative in all cases, indicating that exposure to a female *pradhan* at least once reduces measures of explicit bias against women, but the standard errors are so large that we cannot infer any statistical difference between ever-reserved and never-reserved GPs. Similarly, most of the point estimates for the disaggregated reservation variables ("only reserved 2003," "reserved 1998 and 2003," and "only reserved 1998") show no significant effect of reservation on sexism, as measured by the ASI.

Columns (4)–(6) focus on the components of the ASI that show hostile sexism. In panel A, we observe a significant decline in measured hostile sexism among villagers exposed to a female *pradhan* through a quota compared with villagers who were not. Looking at regressions of each question individually, the largest downward effect is on the statement "A wife shouldn't contradict her husband in public," where male villagers in ever-reserved GPs are less likely to respond that they agree or strongly agree. For female villagers, the strongest effect is for the statement "Preschool children suffer if their mother works," with female citizens in ever-reserved GPs less likely to agree or strongly agree. Panel B shows how these effects vary depending on whether the GP was reserved only once (either in 2003 or in 1998) or twice. For the pooled sample of men and women, both of the once-reserved GPs show a lower level of hostile sexism than never-reserved GPs but, surprisingly, GPs reserved twice are not significantly different from never-reserved GPs. The point estimate is negative, however, so this may be caused by noise in the data.

We look at how benevolent sexism is affected by the quota policy in columns (7)–(9). Similarly to the full index in columns (1)–(3), reservation did not have a significant impact on measures of benevolent sexism. This is true for male and female villagers and is supported in both panels A and B. Taken together, while there is some evidence that more hostile measures of sexism were affected by the reservation system, there is no evidence that explicit sexism toward women in general was reduced as a result of the reservation policy. A lower correlation between the two components of the Hostile Sexism Index has typically been observed among older respondents. Glick and Fiske (1996) have argued that these two components of the index move apart as respondents form opinions based on personal history. They argue that older men who have more satisfying relationships with women reduce hostile sexism but become more benevolently paternalistic. Consistent with this, our results would support the idea that respondents exposed to female leaders improved their perceptions of women as leaders, reducing hostile—but not benevolent—attitudes toward women.

In table 13.2, we turn to empowerment within the household. Many have suggested that changing roles for women outside the household may alter within-household dynamics (Jayal 2003). We therefore examine whether female respondents report changes in the role played by women within the household and their mobility outside the household. The regression structure is identical to those reported in table 13.1.

In column (1), the dependent variable is whether the female reports that no woman in the household has any say in household matters. This is the case in 25 percent of the households in the nonreserved (control) villages. We fail to observe any change in this variable in villages that were subject to a reservation quota. In columns (2)–(6), we consider measures of female mobility. First, we consider three measures of actual mobility. We examine the number of times the woman went outside the village in the last thirty days, the number of times she took a bus in the last thirty days, and the number of times she visited her parents in the last twelve months. The average for women in the nonreserved villages is low, almost always below one. Again, we observe no significant impact of reservation. In columns (5) and (6), we examine whether women report that they can travel unescorted, either to the parent's village or to the next village. Less than 20 percent of the women report that they can do so. Furthermore, exposure to female leaders (because of reservation) leaves women's mobility unchanged.

Taken together, the evidence in table 13.2 suggests that changes in beliefs about women in office do not extend to beliefs about women in the household. These findings are consistent with the fact that political reservation did not directly transform the opportunities available to women in the village.

However, there is reason to believe that such changes may occur in the long run. In ongoing work, we find that parents change their aspirations for teenage children and that teenage children also change their own aspirations, including their preferred age of marriage and whether they would like to work after marriage (Beaman et al. 2011). Thus, it may be the case that changes in individual behavior among the younger cohorts in the village will challenge social norms that restrict a woman's role within a household.

CONCLUSION

Gender quotas in politics have been implemented in more than a hundred countries, yet rigorous empirical evidence remains surprisingly limited regarding how increased female leadership has influenced policy outcomes and voter attitudes. Political reservation in India was, in effect, randomized across village councils. Thus, it is possible to test the causal impact of gender quotas by comparing villages with and without reserved seats.

In India, quotas through the *panchayat* system have had a significant effect in shaping local politics and have resulted in more than 2 million women assuming leadership positions. In addition, a bill extending the quota policy to parliament is being debated. A significant body of literature has shown that the introduction of gender quotas in India increased descriptive representation for women and also increased their substantive representation. In this chapter, we focused on whether exposure to more female politicians changes stereotypes held by voters about women's

Table 13.2 Women's mobility and decision-making, self-reports by women respondents

	No woman has decision-making power in any category of expenditure	No. of times woman went outside village in last 30 days	No. of times woman took bus in last 30 days	No. of times woman visited parents in last 12 months	Can go unescorted to last parents' village	Can go unescorted to next village	Average
	(1)	(2)	(3)	(4)	(5)	(6)	(7)
	Panel A						
Ever reserved	0.016	-0.033	-0.039	-0.143	0.007	0.009	-0.007
	(0.020)	(0.062)	(0.068)	(0.124)	(0.016)	(0.016)	(0.022)
	Panel B						
First reserved 2003	0.015	-0.066	-0.010	-0.015	0.004	-0.003	-0.011
	(0.024)	(0.090)	(0.094)	(0.176)	(0.022)	(0.021)	(0.031)
Reserved 1998 and 2003	-0.020	0.026	-0.085	-0.168	0.039	0.045	0.022
	(0.033)	(0.094)	(0.098)	(0.144)	(0.023)	(0.025)	(0.033)
Only reserved 1998	0.040	-0.039	-0.037	-0.257	-0.011	-0.002	-0.023
	(0.025)	(0.079)	(0.095)	(0.153)	(0.021)	(0.021)	(0.030)

Mean of unreserved	0.258	0.984	1.107	2.984	0.695	0.782	
	(0.438)	(2.198)	(2.476)	(3.805)	(0.461)	(0.413)	
Test: 2003 = both 1998 and 2003 = 1998 [p value]	0.176	0.745	0.829	0.376	0.194	0.173	0.518
n	6780	6759	6474	5298	5526	6780	6780

1. Additional control variables include (i) respondent-level variables: age, age squared, illiterate, < 5 years of schooling, 5–10 years of schooling; (ii) household-level variables: household size, SC, ST, OBC, landless, Muslim, wealth (quartile 1–4), interviewer female, interview round; (iii) village-level variables: total population, SC/ST share, sex ratio under age 6, percent literate, female literacy, percent of irrigated land, bus or train stop, *pucca* road to village, tube well, hand pump, well, community tap, number of schools, and number of health facilities.

2. Block fixed effects are included, and standard errors are clustered at the GP level.

3. Respondents are all women; this table only considers female reports.

roles in politics and in society more generally. Our case study used survey and experimental data to evaluate the role of quotas in influencing symbolic representation, defined as the opinions and attitudes of voters. As such concepts are often difficult to measure empirically, we utilized tools of social psychology to understand the causal impact of quota policies toward perceptions of women leaders.

The evidence we present strongly suggests that symbolic representation is closely related to substantive representation. Individuals change their attitudes about the effectiveness of female leaders when they are exposed to female leaders who deliver public goods. Interestingly, while voters change their willingness to vote for women and alter their implicit biases reasonably fast, their explicit attitudes (and therefore social norms) are much slower to change.

We also find that arenas where quotas have not led to substantive representation are those where there is only small or no change in attitudes. Here we focus on the household. Ten years after quotas were implemented, we still observe muted changes in the decision-making powers that women enjoy at home. Likewise, we see limited changes in the discrimination they face in terms of their ability to choose when to go where.

It is possible that changes in parents' aspirations for their girls and teenage girls' own aspirations will translate into labor market gains for women and that these, in turn, will influence social norms about the role of women. However, in the short to medium run, we would argue that it is unlikely that quotas will yield symbolic representation in areas where they are unable to ensure substantive representation. Our results also suggest that gender quotas in other arenas—such as labor markets and educational institutions—may be a more appropriate tool for achieving symbolic representation outside of politics.

APPENDIX

Regression Specification

The regression specification for the main results is:

$$y_{igj} = \beta_1 R_{g1} + \alpha_j + \varepsilon_{ig}$$

where y_{igj} is a dummy for whether the elected representative i in GP g and block j is a woman, R_{g1} is an indicator for whether the GP was reserved in 1998, and α_j denotes district dummies.

The panel B regression examines whether this effect varies across reservation categories and utilizes the same controls as listed above. The regression specification is:

$$y_{igj} = \beta_2 Rg_2 + \beta_{2and1} R_{g2and1} + \beta_1 R_{g1} + \alpha_j + \varepsilon_{ig}$$

R_{g1} and R_{g2} are indicator variables for the GP being reserved only in the first and second electoral cycle, respectively (i.e., only in 1998 and only in 2003). R_{g2and1} is an indicator for the GP being reserved twice (in 1998 and in 2003). Otherwise, the specification is identical to the previous regression. In both panels, standard errors are clustered at the GP level.

Table 13.3 Ambivalent Sexism Index, individual questions

	A man is never justified in hitting his wife	Parents should maintain stricter control over their daughters than their sons	For the most part, it is better to be a man than to be a woman.	It would be a good idea to elect a woman as the president of India.	A wife shouldn't contradict her husband in public.	Preschool children suffer if their mother works.	In a disaster, women ought to be rescued before men.	Women should be cherished and protected by men.	Women, compared with men, tend to have a superior moral sensibility.	Men should be willing to sacrifice their own well-being in order to provide financially for the women in their lives.
	(1)	(2)	(3)	(4)	(5)	(6)	(7)	(8)	(9)	(10)
					I. Males *Panel A*					
Ever reserved	-0.031	-0.024	0.010	-0.006	-0.117	-0.068	0.037	-0.006	0.031	0.016
	(0.055)	(0.052)	(0.049)	(0.051)	(0.060)	(0.053)	(0.041)	(0.065)	(0.044)	(0.049)
Panel B										
Only reserved 2003	0.003	-0.033	0.034	0.041	-0.121	-0.118	0.032	-0.083	0.048	0.006
	(0.069)	(0.065)	(0.062)	(0.060)	(0.067)	(0.062)	(0.054)	(0.076)	(0.056)	(0.060)
Reserved 1998 and 2003	0.050	-0.024	0.061	-0.028	-0.145	-0.028	0.041	0.001	-0.042	0.034
	(0.083)	(0.088)	(0.088)	(0.096)	(0.098)	(0.074)	(0.077)	(0.099)	(0.069)	(0.072)

(continued)

Table 13.3 (continued)

	A man is never justified in hitting his wife	Parents should maintain stricter control over their daughters than their sons	For the most part, it is better to be a man than to be a woman.	It would be a good idea to elect a woman as the president of India.	A wife shouldn't contradict her husband in public.	Preschool children suffer if their mother works.	In a disaster, women ought to be rescued before and protected by men.	Women should be cherished and protected by men.	Women, compared with men, tend to have a superior moral sensibility.	Men should be willing to sacrifice their own well-being in order to provide financially for the women in their lives.
	(1)	(2)	(3)	(4)	(5)	(6)	(7)	(8)	(9)	(10)
Only reserved 1998	-0.119	-0.015	-0.047	-0.039	-0.095	-0.046	0.039	0.067	0.063	0.013
	(0.073)	(0.068)	(0.066)	(0.063)	(0.088)	(0.079)	(0.052)	(0.088)	(0.055)	(0.069)
Test: 2003 = both 1998 and 2003 = 1998 [p value]	0.135	0.972	0.404	0.422	0.907	0.458	0.991	0.262	0.392	0.942
N	6,717	6,717	6,717	6,717	6,717	6,717	6,717	6,717	6,717	6,717
					II. Females Panel A					
Ever reserved	-0.007	-0.015	-0.051	-0.046	0.015	-0.082	0.020	-0.069	0.010	0.003
	(0.051)	(0.047)	(0.038)	(0.041)	(0.044)	(0.045)	(0.045)	(0.051)	(0.046)	(0.055)

Panel B

Only reserved 2003	0.034	-0.060	-0.054	-0.015	0.018	-0.091	0.038	-0.105	0.078	-0.006
	(0.067)	(0.054)	(0.046)	(0.054)	(0.054)	(0.061)	(0.054)	(0.073)	(0.058)	(0.065)
Reserved 1998 and 2003	0.050	0.061	0.014	-0.067	-0.016	-0.081	0.086	-0.119	0.050	0.115
	(0.082)	(0.087)	(0.055)	(0.081)	(0.076)	(0.067)	(0.070)	(0.073)	(0.073)	(0.075)
Only reserved 1998	-0.085	-0.020	-0.090	-0.064	0.031	-0.075	-0.042	0.000	-0.085	-0.063
	(0.062)	(0.055)	(0.054)	(0.047)	(0.056)	(0.060)	(0.063)	(0.059)	(0.059)	(0.075)
Test: 2003 = both 1998 and 2003 = 1998 [p value]	0.121	0.412	0.276	0.666	0.854	0.976	0.246	0.196	0.040	0.104
N	6,780	6,780	6,780	6,780	6,780	6,780	6,780	6,780	6,780	6,780

1. Dependent variables in all columns are originally on a scale of 1 to 5 from "strongly disagree" (1) to "strongly agree" (5). Questions 1 and 4 are recoded so that a value of (1) indicates "strongly agree" and (5) indicates "strongly disagree." Therefore, a higher value indicates a stronger bias against women. The variables are then normalized by the mean and standard deviation of the never-reserved sample.

2. All regressions include individual controls as defined in table 13.1, and standard errors are clustered by GP.

REFERENCES

BBC News Online. 2010. Indian Upper House Approves Women's Quota Bill. http://news.bbc.co.uk/2/hi/8557237.stm (accessed March 2011).

Beaman, Lori, Raghabendra Chattopadhyay, Esther Duflo, Rohini Pande, and Petia Topalova. 2009. Powerful Women: Can Exposure Reduce Bias? *Quarterly Journal of Economics* 124 (4): 1497–1540.

Beaman, Lori, Esther Duflo, Rohini Pande, and Petia Topalova. 2010. *India Policy Forum*, Vol. 7. Washington, D.C. and New Delhi: Brookings Institution Press and National Council of Applied Economic Research: Washington, D.C. and New Delhi.

Beaman, Lori, Raghabendra Chattopadhyay, Esther Duflo, Rohini Pande, and Petia Topalova. 2011. Learning to Aspire: The Impact of Gender Quotas on Teenager and Parent Aspirations. Mimeograph.

Chattopadhyay, Raghabendra, and Esther Duflo. 2004. Women as Policy Makers: Evidence from a Randomized Policy Experiment in India. *Econometrica* 72: 1409–1443.

Duflo, Esther, and Petia Topalova. 2004. Unappreciated Service: Performance, Perceptions, and Women Leaders in India. Mimeograph.

Glick, Peter, and Susan T. Fiske. 1996. The Ambivalent Sexism Inventory: Differentiating Hostile and Benevolent Sexism. *Journal of Personality and Social Psychology* 70 (3): 491–512.

Hausmann, Ricardo, Laura D. Tyson, and Saadia Zahidi. 2010. *The Global Gender Gap Report*. Geneva: World Economic Forum.

Hunger Project. 2009. Two Million Women Leaders and Counting: Indian Women Participate in Their Local Government. http://www.imow.org/wpp/stories/viewStory?storyId=100 (accessed: March 2011).

Jayal, Niraja Gopal. 2003. Locating Gender in the Governance Discourse. In Amrita Basu, Yasmin Tambiah, Niraja Gopal Jayal, and Marth Nussbaum, eds., *Essays on Gender and Governance*, 96–134. New Delhi: Impressive Communications.

Polgreen, Lydia. 2010a. Turnaround of India State Could Serve as a Model. *New York Times,* April 10.

———. 2010b. Uproar in India over Female Lawmaker Quota. *New York Times*, March 9.

CONCLUSION

14 Themes and Implications for Future Research on Gender Quotas

Susan Franceschet, Mona Lena Krook,
and Jennifer M. Piscopo

Gender quotas have been adopted around the world as a means to increase the numbers of women elected to political office. Yet as quotas are introduced, debates emerge about whether and how they affect—both positively and negatively—other political processes. The goal of this book has been to explore these effects in relation to trends in descriptive, substantive, and symbolic representation. To this end, the chapters have asked whether and how quotas shape the kinds of women elected; the form and content of policy making, particularly with respect to women's policy interests; and the broader political culture in terms of public attitudes and women's political engagement. The authors do not provide uniform answers but point to multiple meanings of representation that influence how these dynamics might be assessed.

The first set of chapters analyzes the impact of quotas on descriptive representation. Responding to claims often voiced in quota debates, they grapple with questions about which attributes of legislators matter when assessing qualities such as "merit" and whether legislators are sufficiently "representative" of their constituencies. In so doing, the cases reveal gendered underpinnings to how qualifications for elected office are defined. In particular, the authors note that female legislators often confront an impossible double bind: they are expected to be more representative of society and of women while also meeting the professional and educational criteria for selection established by male political elites. The chapters also reveal a disconnect between who "quota women" are perceived to be and who they actually are. While women elected via quotas are assumed to be less qualified than their male colleagues, they often have extensive political experience and equal or higher levels of education. A closer look thus exposes the implicit masculine bias in existing ideas about criteria for legislative office.

The next group of case studies examines the impact of quotas on women's substantive representation. They demonstrate that women's policy interests may be promoted by female legislators at different points in the policy-making process but also that substantive representation can occur at one stage and not others. The chapters further reveal the importance of context: not only do women's policy interests differ across countries, but political, institutional, and cultural factors can facilitate or obstruct elected women from promoting these concerns. Where democratic institutions are weak, women face particular difficulties that undermine the likelihood of substantive representation.

Therefore, the substantive representation cases suggest that the effects of quotas may be both direct and indirect. Quotas can immediately create mandates for women to promote gender issues or labels that delegitimize quota women and reduce their willingness and effectiveness in promoting women's rights. Yet these effects may change over time. Quotas may moreover reinforce a gendered division of labor in parliament whereby women work on less prestigious social issues, while men focus on policy areas traditionally deemed more important. Policy effects may also be subtle, as quotas interact with other features of the political environment to shape women's legislative behavior and its outcomes.

The final set of contributions analyzes the impact of quotas on symbolic representation. They highlight the importance of audience when examining whether quotas generate attitudinal, cultural, or behavioral shifts among citizens. Because quotas directly affect the nomination practices and recruitment policies that govern elite behavior, politicians may resist quotas, or view them more negatively than regular citizens. Likewise, men and women may experience these effects differently: quotas can raise resentment among men, who feel left behind, while simultaneously increasing women's empowerment in both the private and the public sphere. Quotas may also increase women's engagement while men's activity remains constant. Nonetheless, the assumption of a causal relationship between quota adoption and implementation, on the one hand, and attitudinal, cultural, or behavioral shifts, on the other, presumes that observers have knowledge of quota policies and attribute responsibility to these policies. As with other types of representation, both elites' and constituents' responses to quotas are embedded within the larger political context. As a result, quotas' meanings for citizens can often become lost within, or integrated into, generalized beliefs about politics itself.

As this volume is intended as a collective theory-building enterprise, the remainder of this concluding chapter revisits and connects the findings of the twelve case studies. The diversity of insights reflects the challenges inherent in studying quota impact and also in operationalizing and measuring complex concepts such as descriptive, substantive, and symbolic representation. Consequently, the chapters establish new theoretical directions for quota research, particularly with respect to the contextual features that must be taken into account when analyzing quota impact. Further, each author's focus on a single aspect of representation shows, perhaps paradoxically, that quotas' effects on one facet may emerge from, or depend on, their effects on another. The chapter concludes with thoughts on avenues for future research, emphasizing the need for cumulative and comparative studies of quota impact.

Studying the impact of gender quotas involves at least three major challenges. The first stems from the fact that existing research does not contain any uniform or standardized ways of operationalizing the concepts of descriptive, substantive, or symbolic representation. As a result, researchers independently make decisions about operationalization, indicators, and measurements. The second challenge concerns the lack of certain kinds of data, resulting in an often imperfect fit between concepts and measurement. These constraints, combined with the practical issues of time and resources, generate the third challenge, namely, the choice of methodology. Opting for qualitative versus quantitative research designs implies inevitable trade-offs between deep knowledge of individual cases and broad analysis of large-scale trends, both of which limit researchers' ability to draw generalizable conclusions. Individual authors' responses to these challenges explain some of the diverse findings reflected in this volume.

Operationalizing Women's Representation

Descriptive representation refers to who legislators are. Although this definition appears straightforward, it requires making choices about which attributes of legislators are the most relevant. Taking quota debates as their starting point, the authors of these chapters investigate whether the women elected through quotas were sufficiently "qualified" and "representative" of their constituencies. Rainbow Murray evaluates legislative competence by focusing on the backgrounds and levels of legislative activity of French legislators. Susan Franceschet and Jennifer M. Piscopo, in contrast, look in greater detail at the age, family status, education, and political experience of men and women in Argentina's congress. Diana Z. O'Brien combines elements of these two approaches by tracking the occupation, education, party identification, incumbency rate, previous experience, and interest in gender issues of legislators in Uganda. James Sater adopts a similar strategy, examining the education levels, political and familial ties, incomes, and views on cross-party collaboration among women in the Moroccan parliament.

Although differences across indicators mean that the results are not fully comparable, the chapters collectively point in similar directions. First, they demonstrate that "political experience" is a particularly complicated variable to capture. Researchers must decide which factors constitute political experience, which could be gauged by number of years in political office, history of grassroots activity, or coming from a political family, among other alternatives. Second, such an exercise exposes underlying assumptions about the normative value—whether positive, negative, or neutral—implicitly given to different factors; conflicting ideas of merit thus lead to uncertainty in how to interpret findings that women have different backgrounds from men. Differences might indicate that quota women are less competent or that women are newcomers who generate political renewal. They may also signal gendered power relations that have not afforded women the same opportunities as men. As Murray and Franceschet and Piscopo argue, gendered pathways to parliament may stem from inequalities in political access rather than women's lack of appropriate qualifications for office.

Operationalizing women's substantive representation raises similar challenges. Often understood in terms of policy making on behalf of women as a group, the contributions in this volume focus on distinct policy-making moments and differing definitions of the content of "women's policy interests." In their study of female MPs in the British Labour Party, Sarah Childs and Mona Lena Krook investigate whether being elected through quotas shapes women's perceptions of their representative mandate, using in-depth interviews with both quota and nonquota women to discern differences in perceived obligations to represent women substantively. In examining the Brazilian congress, Luis Felipe Miguel relies not on legislators' perceptions but on indicators of their actual activity. He examines bill initiation, committee work, debate participation, and political speeches, thus operationalizing women's substantive representation as the promotion of "soft" policy issues as opposed to "hard" policy issues and justifying the choice by conceptualizing soft issues as akin to an "ethics of care" or "maternal thinking."

Addressing party quotas in South Africa, Denise Walsh approaches women's substantive representation in terms of female legislators' responses to gender based violence, examining the initiatives taken—or not taken—and the outcomes. This approach permits close analysis of the environment shaping women's actions and their effects, but the single policy case study makes generalizations to other policy areas difficult. Anna Larson's study of reserved seats in Afghanistan similarly equates substantive representation with the promotion of women's gender interests. She measures the emergence of a gender based collective identity among women, which serves as a necessary condition for female legislators' actions on behalf of women. Consequently, the chapter by Childs and Krook and the chapter by Larson focus on the moments before the initiation of legislation, whereas Miguel and Walsh evaluate actions taken over the course of policy making. Despite these differences, the chapters reveal that female legislators can and will take policy actions to benefit women, provided that the institutional and political environments support their efforts.

The chapters exploring symbolic representation highlight quota impact in terms of attitudinal, behavioral, and cultural change. As noted in chapter 1, quotas are hypothesized to affect all aspects of citizens' beliefs, from trusting parliament as an institution to feeling more included and inclined to participate in politics. No study can systematically evaluate all of these possibilities, and the case studies in this volume analyze various "slices" of these dynamics. As a group, they capture a wide range of operational possibilities. Petra Meier, for instance, explores how political elites in Belgium feel about gender inequality after the introduction of quotas, seeking to discern whether these measures have transformed the gendered nature of the public sphere, and whether women and men react differently to these processes.

The other chapters, in contrast, focus on the opinions and behaviors of nonelites. In studying the impact of quota laws in Mexico, Pär Zetterberg explores whether citizens have gained more trust in democratic institutions or become more politically engaged. Jennie Burnet delves deeply into citizens' everyday lives, asking how reserved seats and legislative quotas in Rwanda have affected men's and women's community life, work outside the home, public meetings, and intimate relationships. Similarly, Lori Beaman, Rohini Pande, and Alexandra Cirone examine whether reserved seats in India have increased women's empowerment in the domestic sphere, although they also consider whether reservations lead villagers to assess women's leadership ability more positively. These varied research designs lead to diverse findings, although the chapters on symbolic representation are nonetheless linked. In all cases, quotas' symbolic effects were mitigated by elites' and citizens' reactions to broader political conditions, such as corruption in Mexico or state-building in Rwanda. The presence of these intervening variables adds urgency to researchers' need to delineate carefully which attitudinal, behavioral, or cultural changes are being studied—and how.

Data Availability and Research Methods

How representation is conceptualized affects the research methods and indicators chosen in each case. A particular problem confronted by many authors is how to distinguish quota from nonquota women. This challenge is mitigated somewhat in countries where quotas take the form of reserved seats and party quotas. In her case study of Uganda, O'Brien can differentiate between women elected to reserved versus open seats, which allows her to compare the attributes of quota women with those of both their male and female nonquota counterparts. Sater can likewise distinguish between women elected from the reserved list and those who were directly elected in Morocco. In the British case, as Childs and Krook note, the Labour Party quota is not responsible for the election of all female Labour MPs, but making a distinction is possible given that the policy applies to individual districts.

In countries with legislative quotas, in contrast, all female MPs become quota women, as the policy applies universally. Murray's methodology addresses this problem by studying trends over time. As the first substantial increase in women's numbers occurred in France in 2007, although the quota law was first passed in 2000, Murray compares nonquota women elected before 2007 to quota women elected thereafter. For Argentina, however, Franceschet and Piscopo are unable to distinguish between quota and nonquota women because data before the application of the 1991 law are not available. Further, there can be difficulties in separating quota and nonquota women even in some reserved seats systems. As Larson writes in the case of Afghanistan, this distinction has become blurred in practice, because women winning their seats outright in 2005 had their positions folded into the reserved seats. Likewise, Childs and Krook find that even while the all-women shortlists applied only to certain districts, all female Labour MPs are subject to the label of quota woman, although perceptions have changed to some extent over time. Consequently, measuring the impact of quotas can be a complicated task when it is not clear—or cannot easily be known—who is and is not a beneficiary of quota policies.

A second set of methodological questions arises in relation to data gathering and the choice to employ quantitative versus qualitative techniques. In Miguel's analysis, for example, the use of quantitative data provides an important means to detect sex differences in patterns of bill introduction, the proportion of a legislator's initiatives that are approved, participation in legislative committees, and the content of speeches in plenary sessions. Although these methods reveal that women are more likely to take up soft policy issues, they cannot indicate why. Conversely, the use of qualitative interview data to study women's legislative priorities in the chapters by Childs and Krook, Walsh, and Larson offers extensive insights into women's motivations for pursuing—or not pursuing—legislation on women's issues. Yet these chapters do not yield a systematic overview of legislative activity, leaving out, for instance, how men may seek to represent women substantively.

Trade-offs also emerge from the choice to build data sets from congressional archives or to conduct fieldwork, experiments, or surveys. Because there is detailed information on parliamentary websites in France and Uganda, Murray and O'Brien are able to gather extensive statistics on legislators' backgrounds and activities. Given the recent nature of quotas in these cases, the data are readily available. By contrast, Beaman, Pande, and Cirone use field experiments to evaluate Indian villagers' perceptions of female leaders, although such experiments might not reflect council leaders' actual policy records. For the Moroccan case, Sater created his own questionnaire for MPs, supplemented with materials from news reports. His analysis is constrained, however, because the survey was conducted only once, and not all subjects responded. The data for all chapters are therefore circumscribed, although the authors offer important insights about different aspects of quota impact.

Decisions to use primary versus secondary data and quantitative versus qualitative methods have similar implications in the chapters on symbolic representation. Meier designs her own surveys of elite attitudes in Belgium, while Zetterberg utilizes third-party surveys in Mexico. Drawing on preexisting and repeated surveys allows Zetterberg to distill important over-time trends in Mexican citizens' political engagement and perceptions of democratic legitimacy. However, the absence of questions about quotas means that he cannot reach conclusions about their causal impact. In contrast, Meier's original survey enables her to ask specific questions about quotas, permitting her to make causal assessments. Yet the one-time nature of her survey means that she cannot make conclusions about trends over time.

The other chapters rely more heavily on observations from fieldwork. Burnet employs focus groups to hear from ordinary women about how quotas in Rwanda have influenced their daily lives. The open-ended questions enable her to draw out extended responses on gender role change, revealing details about men's and women's relationships that might have been obscured in a survey. Nonetheless, focus-group results, like interviews, are less generalizable across the population. Using field experiments, Beaman, Pande, and Cirone have evidence of attitudinal change that is statistically robust, although its applicability to countries other than India will depend on conducting similar studies elsewhere. While the different methodologies chosen by contributors mean that the findings are not always directly comparable, each reveals important features of quotas' impact on elites' and citizens' beliefs.

EMERGING THEMES AND THEORETICAL IMPLICATIONS

Beyond signaling methodological challenges in studying quota impact, the pioneering research in this volume reveals common themes in quota regimes. These include the relationship between how quota policies are designed, approved, and implemented and how quotas shape representative processes. Many chapters also problematize notions of representation and constituency. The contributions reveal the importance of contextual features such as political and electoral institutions and the role of time and learning in shaping quota effects. Although not the central focus of each chapter, these insights signal new avenues for research into how the achievements of quota policies are perceived.

Quota Design, Adoption, and Implementation

Several chapters reveal important connections between how quotas are adopted and how processes of representation unfold. For example, Sater shows that the framework for selecting women to reserved seats in Morocco—via a series of competing party lists—reinforces dynamics of patronage, with consequences for the types of women who are elected. Similarly, Miguel's analysis implies that the initial design of quota policies matters for the pursuit of women's policy interests: because the Brazilian quota law lacks sanctions and includes loopholes, women have remained a very small minority of legislators, undermining opportunities for them to act for women as a group.

Other chapters highlight ramifications of quota campaigns themselves, indicating that policy effects may differ depending on whether quotas emerge from domestic mobilization versus external or elite imposition. Walsh notes that the party quota in South Africa originated in women's organizing, whereas Burnet describes quotas in Rwanda as top-down measures, implemented by government officials and disconnected from female activists' demands. Therefore, there is less expectation in Rwanda than in South Africa that quota women will, indeed, represent female constituents or change politics. Likewise, the elite-led nature of reform in Mexico—and thus the public's lack of familiarity with quota mechanisms—may explain why Zetterberg concludes that Mexican citizens' confidence in democratic institutions has not increased. The combination of activist and elite origins in Belgium, by contrast, may account for Meier's finding that female elites are more supportive of quotas than their male colleagues.

Finally, different quota designs contribute to assumptions that elected women have benefited—fairly or unfairly—from preferential treatment. As Childs and Krook show for the United Kingdom, even when party quotas apply only in some districts, label effects extend to all female MPs from the party. Likewise, reserved seats, as in Morocco, or legislative quotas, as in France, create climates of skepticism around female representatives' autonomy, ability, and achievements.

Problematizing Representation and Constituencies

Another central question emerging from this book concerns the nature and goals of political representation itself. Quotas, and particularly the public debates that they unleash, challenge existing ideas about representation and the types of constituencies that legislators ought to represent. Most notably, the chapters on women's descriptive representation raise questions about who should be a representative. A clear double bind appears, as the same attributes that define legislators' merit, evaluated positively, may also identify politicians as elites or party loyalists, assessed negatively.

The contradictions inherent in defining a qualified candidate stem from the numerous metrics used to measure backgrounds and qualifications: Franceschet and Piscopo, for instance, focus on education and career pathways, while Murray includes legislative productivity. Moreover, as O'Brien notes, different audiences want different outcomes; activists may look to quotas to produce political renewal and greater variation in the attributes of elected officials, while party elites may view loyalty as the only appropriate standard for access to public office.

Charges made against quota women may also call attention to existing problems and tensions within candidate-selection processes. In their chapter on Argentina, Franceschet and Piscopo show that debates over quotas have implied that quota women are the beneficiaries of nepotism, which overlooks the fact that most politicians in Argentina benefit from family connections. In both Argentina and Morocco, perceptions of women's ability to profit politically from kinship ties have become gendered, although a positive development might occur if nepotism can become problematized as a basis for political recruitment. The Belgian case similarly illuminates how quotas politicize the criteria of representativity. In her analysis, Meier finds that female elites are more accepting than male elites of the proposition that biological sex merits representation. Here, quotas fail to politicize questions about men's and women's equality in, and access to, the political sphere.

Related to these debates, several chapters complicate prevailing assumptions regarding constituencies and constituency formation. Larson's chapter on Afghanistan, for example, reveals that although many female MPs report concern with women's issues, they nonetheless prioritize their ethnic and regional identities. Moreover, as Larson notes, there is a gap in Afghanistan between the formal constituency that parliamentarians represent, which is their province, and the more informal constituencies that they feel obliged to serve, namely, their village or district. Because Afghan parliamentarians mobilize voting blocs at these informal levels, female MPs who do focus on women's issues may be speaking only to women from a very specific group.

Political Systems, Context, and Institutions

Another set of themes arising from this volume concerns the question of context. The features of each country's political, institutional, and cultural background play a central role in shaping the effects of quotas on all aspects of women's political representation. The relevant factors that emerge from the case studies can be classified into three broad categories: (1) the degree of democratization and, in some cases, the path a country takes toward democracy; (2) the types of political institutions, including both formal rules and informal norms; and (3) the social and cultural norms associated with gender equality.

Just four of the twelve countries analyzed in the book—Belgium, India, France, and the United Kingdom—have long histories of uninterrupted democracy. The remaining countries have experienced one or many forms of authoritarianism and chaos, including one-party rule, civil war, genocide, or military dictatorship. In some cases, democratic transitions emerged out of domestic processes, but elsewhere, conflicts were resolved through, and democracy assisted by, international actors. In both situations, women's rights often become central to the new order and a key symbol of a country's level of modernization. Consequently, gender quotas are often intricately linked to the process of democratization. In some cases, this confers an automatic legitimacy on the policies, but elsewhere, if democracy is viewed as externally imposed or inherently flawed, then quotas may be perceived as illegitimate. Yet even where quotas are viewed as legitimate, other features of politics may undercut their potential to generate positive effects on women's political representation.

In Uganda, for instance, reserved seats were implemented after a civil war, and the transition to multiparty government has proceeded slowly. The continued dominance of one party has affected the diversity of women elected to the reserved seats. In South Africa, postapartheid politics has also been controlled by an increasingly powerful single party, the ANC, which now uses the quota to stack parliament with professional politicians. This practice has not increased the access and voice of MPs with bases in diverse groups in civil society, including women. In postwar Afghanistan, the rapidly deteriorating security environment means that women who promote gender issues do so at tremendous personal risk, thereby substantially undermining a positive relationship between women's presence and women's substantive representation.

In Rwanda, quotas were also introduced by a hegemonic party in a postconflict system. Women attaining office via this route are clearly beneficiaries of party largesse; as such, they are not perceived to be democratically elected representatives. Rwandans have become accustomed to women's presence and empowerment in the public and private sectors, yet they do not believe that female politicians have made their government any more responsive or any less corrupt. Consequently, quotas have changed citizens' attitudes about women without changing their attitudes about government. Mexico presents another instance where quotas are adopted as part of the democratization process. Unlike in Rwanda, the electoral system has become more competitive, ensuring that female legislators' election is perceived as legitimate. Yet citizens' attitudinal responses to quotas, such as political interest and institutional trust, are inseparable from their dispirited view of politics in general. These findings also hold at the subnational level, where contextual factors other than state-level quotas may explain citizens' lack of engagement and trust.

Beyond the history of democracy, each country's formal institutions and informal norms interact with quotas to shape outcomes in women's representation. A common finding is that quotas rarely disrupt, and may even reinforce, existing recruitment practices. In South Africa, for example, quotas have allowed party elites to increase their control over candidate selection, ensuring the recruitment of party loyalists. In Argentina, Uganda, and Morocco, quotas have been integrated into political systems with deeply entrenched patron-client relations, making attributes such as familial ties, voter mobilization, or benefactor loyalty more salient than gender identity in candidate selection. More than quotas, these factors determine what kinds of women are elected.

Political institutions also have important effects on substantive representation. In Afghanistan, promoting women's policy interests is undermined by the informal rules of the political process. In particular, parliament is not organized into formal political parties but is governed by an overall "culture of political ambiguity," which induces legislators to avoid associating themselves with particular parties, factions, groups, or policy positions, given the risks that such associations might incur. This context undercuts the formation and consolidation of a women's rights agenda. As another example, men continue to dominate the formal and informal power structures of the Brazilian congress, thereby circumscribing the effectiveness of female legislators and reducing the likelihood that any actions they do take on behalf of female constituents will succeed.

The broader social and cultural context, finally, shapes how quotas are received in each country. In Brazil, women's parliamentary behavior appears to reflect deeply held societal norms that designate appropriate spheres of policy expertise for men and women. Female legislators are expected to attend to social issues, which include women's policy issues. However, these dynamics create a double bind for female legislators: their focus on social issues—which involves substantively representing women as a constituency—relegates them to secondary status in congress, where hard policy issues involving the economy, defense, and foreign affairs are those that generate respect and advance careers. This creates potential tensions in that the more women focus on these policy issues, the less able they will be to produce successful legislative outcomes.

Elsewhere, the potential for quotas to empower women is threatened by profound cultural resistance to gender equality. Women may place themselves at risk when they promote women's rights. In Afghanistan in particular, there is a growing and well-organized resistance to "Western" ideas about women's rights and equality. In Rwanda, women outnumber men in parliament but face increased conflict in the home. Cultural expectations about women's primary role as domestic caretakers and subsistence farmers persist, creating more burdens, responsibilities, and conflicts for women who are both elected officials and traditional homemakers. Similarly, in India, exposure to female leaders has caused villagers to update their beliefs about women's ability to lead and made them more willing to vote for women. However, this exposure has not empowered women within the domestic sphere. Existing norms regarding gender roles may thus limit the degree of substantive and symbolic change.

Time and Learning

The case studies further show that the impact of quotas is neither static nor linear. Even the numerical effects of quotas may not be experienced immediately; these may, as in the cases of France and Argentina, take multiple election cycles to be felt. Elsewhere, such as in Belgium, South Africa, and Mexico, the threshold percentages have been increased. In Uganda, because of the stipulation that one seat be reserved for a woman in each district, an increase in the number of districts means an increase in seat reservations and thus the overall percentage of female MPs.

Yet policy gains for female constituents do not necessarily increase with the continued application of gender quotas. Walsh's examination of South Africa shows how quotas' effects vary over electoral terms, even leading to regress rather than progress. In the second postapartheid (and postquota) parliament, shifts in ANC priorities considerably diminished the space to promote gender issues. Female legislators who continued ardently to promote gender issues found themselves increasingly marginalized and even disciplined by party elites. Yet the very existence of the quota—and the party's decision to increase it from 30 percent to 50 percent—insulated party leaders from criticisms that they were not sufficiently attentive to gender equality. Likewise, heightened insecurity in Afghanistan, in combination with the growth of social and religious conservatism, means that, as Larson points out, women face fewer rather than more opportunities to promote a women's rights agenda within parliament. Nonetheless, there is also evidence of gains over time: Childs and Krook's longitudinal study shows that perceptions of a mandate to promote women's interests expanded between 1997 and 2009, while perceptions of negative labels seem to have lessened.

Symbolic representation may be the facet of representation whose results most depend on long-term trends. Citizens may immediately develop positive or negative reactions to the very idea of quotas, as in Belgium and the United Kingdom. Yet deeper attitudinal, cultural, or behavioral shifts may depend on how citizens observe and react to women elected under quotas. For instance, citizen beliefs may be affected by whether voters view quota women as undeserving tokens or meritocratic nominees. Alternatively, citizens may be influenced by the behavior of quota women, such as whether they perpetuate a politics of corruption or generate a politics of renewal. Views on quota women may also be shaped by the performance of the governing regime. In neither Rwanda nor Mexico, for instance, do citizens distinguish between quota policies specifically and government actions generally. The Rwandan case demonstrates, moreover, that quotas may enhance women's empowerment only in the long run. As Burnet finds, women's greater participation in the economy and civil society developed years after the initial quota policy was adopted. Likewise, Beaman, Pande, and Cirone observe greater positive changes in India when seats have been reserved for women more than once. These findings suggest that quotas affect the beliefs of future generations and may not be mature enough for systematic studies of symbolic representation.

INTERACTIVE PROCESSES AMONG FACETS OF REPRESENTATION

The impact of quotas on women's political representation is therefore mediated by other aspects of the political, institutional, and cultural environment. Further, evidence from the chapters in this volume suggests linkages among descriptive, substantive, and symbolic effects. While not explored specifically in the case studies, the effects of quotas on one facet of representation may actually be a result of how the quota affects another aspect. Attention to these connections may help unravel some of the causal processes at work, offering hypotheses to guide future research.

The Effects of Descriptive Representation

The demographic attributes and the political and educational backgrounds of MPs may affect what representatives do and what their presence means for broader social and political change. First, we hypothesize that *descriptive representation affects whether female legislators can successfully undertake substantive representation*. If quotas bring in female parliamentarians who, aside from their sex, remain descriptively similar to male parliamentarians in terms of socioeconomic and professional status, they may be less likely to represent the concerns of ordinary women substantively. If elected women are more similar to women in society than to their male colleagues, they may lack the political capital necessary to act effectively. The South African case illustrates how legislators' descriptive attributes are closely linked to prospects for substantive representation. In the first postapartheid parliament, many of the women elected had links to women's civil society organizations and, as a result, were strong advocates of women's rights. Many of these women were not renominated to the second parliament but instead were replaced by professional politicians who were more concerned with career advancement than with women's policy interests.

Second, we propose that *the descriptive characteristics of female parliamentarians may also determine whether symbolic outcomes are positive or negative*. In these instances, what matters are perceptions about quota women. If such women are perceived as unqualified and undeserving of their seats, public opinion on the suitability of women in leadership positions may actually decrease. Likewise, if women are seen as elite and as unrepresentative of ordinary women, citizens may be skeptical about claims that quotas produce new ways of doing politics. In Morocco, Sater notes, approximately half of citizens polled thought the country had gone too far in promoting women's rights, suggesting that quotas have inspired a backlash. At the same time, Moroccans also expressed growing dissatisfaction with their political class, meaning that women's rights may be increasingly associated with a highly unpopular group of politicians. Finally, in Rwanda, Burnet argues, the governing Rwandan Patriotic Front (RPF) is a highly authoritarian party, and female officials are perceived to be "more of the same"—meaning that they are seen as being as unrepresentative as male officials.

The Effects of Substantive Representation

More innovatively, the chapters in this volume suggest that substantive representation is not the end point of women's representation. We hypothesize that *substantive representation shapes the criteria used to select candidates in future elections, thus reshaping patterns of descriptive representation*. More specifically, if some or many female legislators actively promote women's policy interests, they may be either rewarded or punished by party leaders controlling candidate selection or by voters choosing or rejecting incumbents. In South Africa, the women who were most active on women's issues were not renominated by ANC party elites. In Afghanistan, Larson's conclusions imply that barriers to articulating women's policy concerns may attract, in subsequent electoral rounds, women who have allegiances to other constituent groups.

We further hypothesize that *the legislative behavior of quota women may also determine the attitudinal, behavioral, and cultural changes experienced by the public at large and by women as a specific audience*. In Rwanda, as Burnet's study demonstrates, female officials are perceived to have little effect on policy making; Rwandan citizens thus have no sense of whether or not quotas produce policy changes that benefit women specifically or society generally. Conversely, evidence from India collected by Beaman, Pande, and Cirone suggests that the substantive actions of female politicians may influence symbolic change: when women change and improve upon the provision of public goods, perceptions of politics as a male domain diminish. Finally, while not the focus of the French case study, Murray's finding that quota women are as active in their legislative duties as their nonquota counterparts implies a greater demonstration of women's legislative competence. This productivity may erode resistance to women's inclusion and improve their future electoral prospects.

The Effects of Symbolic Representation

Turning to the third aspect of representation, we hypothesize that *the meanings given to women's political presence as a result of quota policies determine the descriptive characteristics of subsequent female candidates.* On the one hand, the use of quotas to elect more women may provide positive role models for prospective female candidates. The data from India show that voters exposed to female leaders under quotas may support female candidates more generally; such shifts may persuade a more diverse group of women to come forward who might not otherwise consider running. On the other hand, the Mexican case suggests that disenchantment with the political system and decreases in both men's and women's political engagement may discourage women from running at all. While Zetterberg's statistical results cannot link the decline in political interest to quota policies, the trend nonetheless suggests that fewer women will enter the nomination pool, which may negatively affect diversity in the demographic and political profiles of MPs.

Finally, we hypothesize that *symbolic representation may also influence the likelihood that MPs undertake the substantive representation of women.* As the British case study reveals, negative stereotyping of all female Labour MPs as quota women can make some women hesitant about focusing too much on women's policy interests. Further, if quotas are viewed as a means for political patronage, as they are in many of the cases studied in this volume, there may be few expectations—and thus little pressure—from civil society groups that female MPs will or should represent women as a group. Taken together, these hypotheses anticipate how trends in relation to one facet of representation may influence the other aspects, thus shaping the broader effects of quotas on women's social, economic, and political status.

CONCLUSIONS AND DIRECTIONS FOR FUTURE RESEARCH

Gender quotas are still a relatively new reform worldwide, with most policies having appeared in the last fifteen years. Seeking to understand the origins and immediate effects of these measures, initial scholarly attention sought to explain patterns in quota design, adoption, and implementation. Yet, as suggested in quota debates, quotas are often expected to have a much broader impact, shaping dynamics of candidate recruitment, policy making, public opinion, and mass political engagement.

The case studies in this volume provide a more comprehensive picture of what quota reforms can and do achieve in terms of their descriptive, substantive, and symbolic effects. Taken together, they point to important tensions and trade-offs that are likely to endure, indicating not only that the impact of quotas is often mixed but also that certain debates are unlikely to be resolved. For instance, disagreements about how to assess political qualifications abound: some associate measures of merit with the typical qualifications of male politicians, while others emphasize that female legislators must better resemble female citizens rather than mirror the existing political class. Differences across these two metrics mean that scholars—along with activists and politicians—are likely to disagree about quota impact.

In addition to further exploring these tensions, the next task for future research will be twofold. First, scholars ought to draw on comparative insights to connect patterns of quota impact to variations in the contexts—both spatial and temporal—in which they are introduced and which therefore mediate their effects on different facets of representation. Second, researchers must refine and test hypotheses about the interactions among types of representation. The case studies in this book offer some initial insights in both regards, yet research that systematically explores these possibilities is needed. Research designs might build on the data and conclusions from the studies in this book, shedding further light on a variety of dynamics that have long been naturalized. The chapters here reveal how such an investigation presents opportunities to rethink the backgrounds and qualifications necessary to hold office, explore how such characteristics shape actions at different stages of the policy-making process, and assess the implications of these actions for how citizens relate to the political process—and to policy makers themselves.

Contributors

Lori Beaman is Assistant Professor of Economics at Northwestern University. She received her Ph.D. from Yale University in 2007. In 2007–2008, she was a Robert Wood Johnson Scholar in Health Policy Research at the University of California, Berkeley. Her fields of interest are labor and development economics. Her research has looked at the role of social networks in providing job information to refugees resettled in the United States and the impact of female political leadership on gender bias in rural India. Her research has been published in the *Quarterly Journal of Economics*, the *Review of Economic Studies*, and the *Journal of Development Economics*, among other venues.

Jennie Burnet is Assistant Professor of Anthropology at the University of Louisville. Her research interests include gender, ethnicity, race, war, genocide, and reconciliation in postconflict societies, and her geographic specializations are Rwanda, Burundi, and the African Great Lakes region. Her recent publications include an article on gender balance and the meanings of women in governance in postgenocide Rwanda (*African Affairs*, 2008) and an article on truth, reconciliation, and revenge in Rwanda (*Journal of Genocide Studies and Prevention*, 2008), both drawing on field research carried out in Rwanda between 1997 and 2007. Her book, *Genocide Lives in Us: Women, Memory, and Silence in Post-Genocide Rwanda* (University of Wisconsin Press, forthcoming in summer 2012), examines the role of women in the aftermath of the 1994 genocide in Rwanda, focusing on the consequences of ethnic classification and the politics of memory and reconciliation in postgenocide Rwanda.

Sarah Childs is Professor of Politics and Gender at the University of Bristol (United Kingdom). Her research centers on the relationships among sex, gender, and politics and is concerned, both theoretically and empirically, with questions of women's descriptive, substantive, and symbolic representation. She has written extensively on women's political representation in the United Kingdom since 1997, especially on the feminization of British political parties, particularly under New Labour, women's political recruitment to the House of Commons, and the substantive representation of women ("acting for" women). She is the author of *New Labour's Women MPs: Women Representing Women* (Routledge, 2004) and *Women and British Party Politics* (Routledge, 2008) and the coeditor with Mona Lena Krook of *Women, Gender, and Politics: A Reader* (Oxford University Press, 2010). Her latest book, *Sex, Gender, and the Conservative Party: From Iron Lady to Kitten Heels*, coauthored with Paul Webb, was published in fall 2011.

Alexandra Cirone is a Ph.D. student in Political Science at Columbia University. Her focus includes comparative politics and quantitative methods, with a regional interest in western Europe. Before beginning her graduate work, she was the research manager at the Center for International Development at the Harvard Kennedy School, working for Rohini Pande and Asim Ijaz Khwaja.

Drude Dahlerup is Professor of Political Science at Stockholm University (Sweden). Her main research interests include women in politics, gender quotas worldwide, social movements, and feminist theory. She is the editor of *Women, Quotas, and Politics* (Routledge, 2006) and the author of articles on quotas appearing in numerous edited volumes and journals such as *Representation, Policy and Politics, Politics & Gender*, and the *International Feminist Journal of Politics*. She is the leader of a research team associated with several quota projects (http://www.statsvet.su.se/wip) and coeditor of a report on the implementation of gender quotas in the European Parliament, and she has been an international consultant on gender quotas in Cambodia, Sierra Leone, and Tunisia.

Susan Franceschet is Associate Professor of Political Science at the University of Calgary (Canada), where she has taught since 2006. Her research focuses on the impact of women in politics on public policy, gender quotas in comparative perspective, and women's substantive representation. She is the author of *Women and Politics in Chile* (Lynne Rienner, 2005) and has published numerous articles on gender and politics in Latin America in such journals as *Comparative Political Studies, Latin American Research Review,* and the *Journal of Legislative Studies*. Together with Jennifer M. Piscopo, she published "Gender Quotas and Women's Substantive Representation: Lessons from Argentina" in *Politics & Gender* (2008). She is currently conducting a research project on the impact of women in executive office, funded by the Canadian Social Science and Humanities Research Council.

Mona Lena Krook is Assistant Professor of Political Science and Women, Gender, and Sexuality Studies at Washington University in St. Louis. In 2008–2009, she was a fellow at the Radcliffe Institute of Advanced Study at Harvard University and a nonresidential fellow in the Women and Public Policy Program at the Harvard Kennedy School. She was recently granted a five-year Faculty Early Career Development (CAREER) Award from the National Science Foundation to study the comparative impact of electoral gender quotas. She is the author of *Quotas for Women in Politics: Gender and Candidate Selection Reform Worldwide* (Oxford University Press, 2009), which develops a general framework for analyzing the adoption and implementation of gender quotas around the globe. She is also coeditor with Sarah Childs of *Women, Gender, and Politics: A Reader* (Oxford University Press, 2010) and the author of articles in the *British Journal of Political Science, Comparative Politics,* the *European Journal of Political Research, Perspectives on Politics, Political Research Quarterly,* and *Politics & Gender,* among others.

Anna Larson is a research fellow and Ph.D. candidate at the Post-War Reconstruction and Development Unit (PRDU) at York University (United Kingdom), where she focuses on democratization processes in Afghanistan. Between 2006 and 2010, she was a researcher with the gender and governance teams at the Kabul-based Afghanistan Research and Evaluation Unit (AREU), and she has been working in Afghanistan on governance and gender issues since 2004. Her main areas of research focus while at AREU included women's presence in parliament, gender mainstreaming in the Afghan administration, political party development, Afghan perceptions of democratization, and elections, on which she has published numerous articles and policy papers. Recent publications on women's parliamentary presence include "Women's Political Presence: A Path to Promoting Gender Interests?" in *Land of the Unconquerable: Lives of Contemporary Afghan Women* (University of California Press, 2011).

Petra Meier is Associate Professor of Political Science at the University of Antwerp (Belgium). Her major areas of research are theories on democracy and representation, the normative foundations of electoral systems and electoral system design, feminist approaches to public policies, and Belgian politics. She is coeditor with Emanuela Lombardo and Mieke Verloo of *The Discursive Politics of Gender Equality: Stretching, Bending and Policymaking* (Routledge, 2009) and has written a number of recent articles on gender quotas published in the *Journal of Women, Politics, and Policy* (coauthored with Emanuela Lombardo, 2010), the *International Feminist Journal of Politics* (2008), and the *Swiss Political Science Review* (coauthored with Dries Verlet, 2008) and a chapter on Belgium in *Women and Legislative Representation: Electoral Systems, Political Parties, and Sex Quotas* (edited by Manon Tremblay, Palgrave, 2008).

Luis Felipe Miguel is Associate Professor at the Institute of Political Science at the University of Brasilia (Brazil). He has published widely on topics related to media and politics, theories of democracy, and gender and politics. He is the author of numerous articles on gender quotas in Brazil, including pieces in the *Revista Brasileira de Ciências Sociais* (2000), the *Revista Estudos Feministas* (2006), and the *Bulletin of Latin American Research* (2008). His 2001 book, *Caleidoscópio Convexo* (coauthored with Flávia Biroli), is about gender, media, and politics in Brazil.

Rainbow Murray is Senior Lecturer in Politics at Queen Mary, University of London. Her primary research interests lie in gender and politics, candidate selection, and French politics. She has written extensively on the implementation of the parity law in French legislative elections in such journals as *Political Research Quarterly, Party Politics, Parliamentary Affairs,* and *Politics & Gender.* She is also the author of *Parties, Gender Quotas, and Candidate Selection in France* (Palgrave, 2010) and editor of *Cracking the Highest Glass Ceiling: A Global Comparison of Women's Campaigns for Executive Office* (Praeger, 2010). She is the convener of an international research network on Women in French Politics and the convener of the Women and Politics Specialist Group of the Political Studies Association. She coedits the *Political Data Yearbook,* part of the *European Journal of Political Research.*

Diana Z. O'Brien is a Ph.D. candidate in Political Science at Washington University in St. Louis. Her primary interests are comparative politics and quantitative methodology, and she is also pursuing a graduate certificate in Women, Gender, and Sexuality Studies. Her research focuses on the relationship between political institutions and women's descriptive and substantive representation. She has coauthored two articles with Mona Lena Krook on gender quotas, including a paper on the adoption of quotas in postconflict Afghanistan and Iraq (*International Feminist Journal of Politics*, 2010) and a study of the origins and design of quotas for women and minorities around the globe (*Comparative Politics*, 2010).

Rohini Pande is Mohammed Kamal Professor of Public Policy at the Harvard Kennedy School. Her research focuses on the economic analysis of the politics and consequences of different forms of redistribution, principally in developing countries. Before joining the Kennedy School, she was Associate Professor of Economics at Yale University, and she has also taught at MIT and Columbia. A Rhodes Scholar, she is the recipient of several National Science Foundation and other research grants. She holds a Ph.D. and an M.Sc. in Economics from the London School of Economics, an M.A. in Philosophy, Politics, and Economics from Oxford, and a B.A. in Economics from St. Stephens College, Delhi University. Her research has been published in the *Quarterly Journal of Economics, American Economics Review*, the *Journal of Development Economics*, and the *Journal of the European Economics Association*, among other venues.

Jennifer M. Piscopo is Assistant Professor of Public Policy at Salem College. Her research on women and politics in Latin America has appeared in *Politics & Gender, Parliamentary Affairs,* and several edited volumes. Her dissertation, *Do Women Represent Women: Gender and Policy in Argentina and Mexico,* examined how female legislators set agendas for women's rights, achieve changes to gender policy regimes, and oversee the implementation of these reforms. She received her M.Phil. in Latin American Studies from the University of Cambridge, where she was a Gates Cambridge Scholar, and her Ph.D. from the University of California, San Diego.

James N. Sater is Associate Professor of Political Science at the American University of Sharjah (United Arab Emirates). Previously, he was Assistant Professor of Middle East and North African Politics at Al Akhawayn University (Morocco). He has worked on state and civil society relations in the Maghreb, women's rights movements and parliamentarians, political parties, public opinion, and the process of democratization. He is the author of *Civil Society and Political Change in Morocco* (Routledge, 2007) and has contributed articles to *Democratization*, the *Journal of North African Studies*, and *Mediterranean Politics*. He recently published his second book, *Morocco: Challenges to Tradition and Modernity* (Routledge, 2010).

Denise Walsh is Associate Professor of Politics and Studies in Women and Gender at the University of Virginia. Her research interests include deliberative theory, democratization, multiculturalism, and gender and politics in southern Africa. Her doctoral dissertation, *Just Debate: Culture and Gender Justice in the New South Africa* (2006), received the Best Dissertation Prize from the Women in Politics Section of the American Political Science Association in 2007. Her book, *Women's Rights in Democratizing States: Just Debate and Gender Justice in the Public Sphere* (Cambridge University Press, 2011), analyzes outcomes on women's rights in Poland, Chile, and South Africa, and argues that improving the quality of democracy is crucial for advancing gender justice. She is currently working on her second book, *Culture versus Women's Rights? The Contradictions of Intersectionality Policies in Liberal Democracies*, which investigates state responses to competing claims for women's rights and cultural rights in Canada, South Africa, and India.

Pär Zetterberg is Researcher in the Department of Government at Uppsala University (Sweden). His doctoral dissertation, *Engineering Equality? Assessing the Multiple Impacts of Electoral Gender Quotas* (2009), focused on the long-term consequences of gender quotas and their possibilities to serve as a tool to disrupt gender inequalities in politics, with an empirical focus in Latin America and particularly Mexico. He has written on the impact of quotas on female representatives' legislative autonomy (*Parliamentary Affairs*, 2008) and on female citizens' political empowerment (*Political Research Quarterly*, 2009). He is also interested in research on political inequalities in society more broadly and the challenges to political integration of traditionally excluded groups (such as women, youth, immigrants, and indigenous peoples).

Index

CPSIA information can be obtained at www.ICGtesting.com
Printed in the USA
BVOW06s2247070916

461102BV00003B/9/P